Marketing Your Library

Marketing Your Library

Tips and Tools That Work

Edited by Carol Smallwood,
Vera Gubnitskaia *and* Kerol Harrod

Foreword by Michael Germano

McFarland & Company, Inc., Publishers
Jefferson, North Carolina, and London

SELECTED RECENT MCFARLAND WORKS FROM CAROL SMALLWOOD AND OTHERS

Mentoring in Librarianship: Essays on Working with Adults and Students to Further the Profession, edited by Carol Smallwood and Rebecca Tolley-Stokes (2012), *Women on Poetry: Writing, Revising, Publishing and Teaching*, edited by Carol Smallwood, Colleen S. Harris and Cynthia Brackett-Vincent (2012), *Thinking Outside the Book: Essays for Innovative Librarians*, edited by Carol Smallwood (2008), *Helpful Hints for the School Library: Ideas for Organization, Time Management and Bulletin Boards, with a Resource Guide*, by Carol Smallwood (1993).

ISBN 978-0-7864-6543-9

softcover : acid free paper ∞

LIBRARY OF CONGRESS CATALOGUING DATA ARE AVAILABLE

British Library cataloguing data are available

Cover photograph by Lane V. Erickson

Front cover design by Bernadette Skok (bskok@ptd.net)

Manufactured in the United States of America

McFarland & Company, Inc., Publishers
Box 611, Jefferson, North Carolina 28640
www.mcfarlandpub.com

To Carolyn Harrod,
the family of Vera Gubnitskaia,
and the contributors.

Table of Contents

Foreword

Michael Germano

As a former information industry marketing and sales professional who is currently employed as a business librarian and professor of marketing, I am continually amazed and gratified to see the willingness and outright enthusiasm with which librarians attack the task of marketing. The interest in library marketing is all the more fascinating when one considers that library marketers are oftentimes operating on intuition alone. Few librarians have prior professional experience marketing products or services. Moreover, only a fraction of librarians who market are exclusively assigned that responsibility within their organization. Given the current economic climate, librarians have begun to recognize the critical importance of marketing as a means of self-preservation, largely accepting that the future of libraries requires marketing in order to increase library use and perceptions of worth.

In my view, as an observer and practitioner, library marketing needs to reach a higher level of sophistication if it wishes to successfully support the marketing needs of libraries in the twenty-first century. Library market planning and strategy should be premised upon thorough environmental and competitive scans that understand users' alternatives and why they may or may not choose them. It should also be based upon solid market research that allows library marketers to understand library patrons, current as well as potential ones, and their specific needs. When library marketers connect patron needs to the benefits of having those needs met through the library's offerings, value is created as opposed to mere familiarity or awareness.

During my time in the information industry, I learned what happened when I assumed what was important to a customer as opposed to researching and discovering what customers benefited from or considered valuable. A more sophisticated form of library marketing, as represented by this volume, will no doubt result in library marketing that increases patron engagement and provides a heightened perception of the library's ability to meet unique user needs. The end result is marketing that not only raises awareness, but solidly confirms the importance of library programs and services to patrons.

Preface

Marketing Your Library is a collection intended for public, academic, special, school librarians, LIS faculty, Friends of the Library, and board members looking for successful examples of marketing when so much is changing in the profession: brand management, campaigns, community outreach, techniques, social media, and other tools. It provides guidance on planning as well as execution. It is for beginners as well as old hands — solo librarians and those part of a large staff. The anthology includes chapters centered on practical results by librarians making hard choices to provide the best service.

Marketing is crucial to librarians, no matter what type of library you work at or what position you hold. You may have had helpful marketing classes, read books on it, attended workshops and webinars filled with well-designed organization charts, but the editors hope these chapters will provide important practical and valuable insight on marketing techniques that have been tested. The essays begin with coverage of the fundamentals and end with specific events and implementations, with coverage of everything in between.

Contributions were sought from practicing public, school, academic, and special librarians from different areas in the United States. The 25 chapters were written by at least one librarian or co-authored by two or three. The editors sought concise, how-to case studies based on successful and innovative marketing. The chapters are arranged in seven parts: Fundamentals; Strategy; Finding Resources; Getting Recognized; Media Matters; Using Community Partnerships; and Event Planning and Implementation.

The 39 contributors share their backgrounds in a section at the end of the book with their name, library of employment, city/state location, employment title, where they got their degrees, awards, publications, and career highlights. Michael Germano, library faculty member at California State University, Los Angeles, dedicated to the College of Business and Economics, notes in the Foreword: "A more sophisticated form of library marketing, as represented by this volume, will no doubt result in library marketing that increases patron engagement and provides a heightened perception of the library's ability to meet unique user needs." The editors hope *Marketing Your Library* will prove a practical help to librarians. The index is a detailed aid that should help you quickly locate exactly what you need.

It was a privilege working with the contributors willing to share their experiences with fellow librarians. These dedicated and creative professionals have presented many effective accounts of library marketing, informing us of what really works in these challenging times. — The Editors

PART I

Fundamentals

1

The Art of Personal Selling

Techniques for Library Marketing

WAYNE E. FINLEY

One of the basic principles of business tells us that it takes fewer resources to retain existing customers than it does to attract new ones. So, what can librarians do to keep existing patrons, especially if there are few resources to spend on new programs or services? The answer: personal selling. By employing sales techniques such as up-selling, cross-selling, and closing, library staff can "sell" existing patrons on becoming more active users, and get patrons interested in new library programming, services, and collections.

Why Personal Selling?

A library's promotional mix consists of four core components: advertising, sales promotions, public relations, and personal selling. Of all these elements, personal selling is, perhaps, the most important. And without library employees playing the role of the sales staff, it simply cannot get done.

The reason that personal selling is so important, especially in a library setting, is that it allows for direct interaction with the customer. By contrast, advertising, sales promotions, and public relations are usually geared towards large audiences (television commercials or magazine advertising, for example) and simply give information to the customer. In a personal selling interaction, the salesperson has first-hand opportunities to assess the needs of customers, receive feedback, and then connect customers with the product or service that best meets their needs.

The Library Sales Force

Some people throughout the library community may be uneasy at the thought of librarians or library employees as salespeople, but whether or not it's called "sales," the practice is already happening in libraries everywhere. Take the case of a fictional patron, a college student who is using the library for the first time (Patron A). While the patron may think that he is on a simple trip to the library to get a book, his trip might helpfully be seen as a business transaction with multiple opportunities for personal selling by the library staff (a.k.a. the sales staff). The first opportunity to promote the library is a greeting from staff members. Often in retail, it's the reception of the customer by sales staff that can set the tone for the entire transaction. A simple "hello" from a person at a help desk or a librarian who is passing by can make a great impression on the customer. In this case, the library is trying to "sell" the organization as a welcoming place that the patron will want to visit again and again.

Another opportunity for selling presents itself at the reference desk. If patrons are unfamiliar with the library catalog or the layout of the library itself, the reference desk will be their natural starting point. Again, customer service is key: the reference librarian needs to use the reference interview to match the customer with the correct product. In retail, it's the role of the salesperson to interpret the needs of customers, both spoken and unspoken, and match them with the correct products from the company's product line. While the difference with most library transactions is the omission of a monetary exchange, the principle that governs the successful interaction is the same. If the salesperson is unsuccessful in meeting the needs of the customer, the likelihood of a completed transaction diminishes, especially if the customer is unfamiliar with the product. The same is true with librarians dealing with patrons at the reference desk. Consider the following exchange:

PATRON A: Hi! I'm looking for a book on Italy.

REFERENCE LIBRARIAN: I'd be happy to help you with that. (Notices the patron is wearing a college t-shirt and carrying a backpack). Are you working on a research report? (Begins an interview).

PATRON A: No. Actually, I'm planning to study abroad next semester, and I'd like to learn a little more about the culture.

REFERENCE LIBRARIAN: Do you know where you'll be staying? (Continues the interview, trying to narrow down the patron's specific needs).

PATRON A: I'm staying in Rome, but would like to travel in Florence and Venice.

REFERENCE LIBRARIAN: I think a good place to start, then, might be looking at some of our travel guides and travel DVDs. Does this sound good? (Offers a product suggestion based upon the patron's needs and follows up with verification.)

Once the reference librarian has found the right item for the customer, the actual transaction has to take place. It's now up to the library page to help deliver the product, and the circulation librarian to close the deal. If the customer is having trouble finding the book on the shelf or is unfamiliar with the layout of the stacks, it's likely he will turn to people in the library who look like they work there; thus, a page is a likely salesperson, especially since pages are often "on the floor" (much like salespeople at a retail store). When the page correctly matches the customer with the items (in this case, the aforementioned travel books and DVDs), the role of salesperson now falls to the circulation attendant, whose job is more than just checking out the book. Here, the salesperson has many opportunities to "sell" the customer on all the other services, programs, and collections the library has, and must "seal the deal." In this case, the circulation attendant might suggest the following:

PATRON A: Hello. I'd like to borrow these books and DVDs.

CIRCULATION ATTENDANT: I see you're interested in travel in Italy. We also have a collection of Italian phrase books.

PATRON A: No, thanks. I'll be studying the language when I travel there this summer.

In this example, Patron A isn't interested in what the circulation attendant is attempting to "sell." But at the very least, the library staff hopes that the patron leaves the library with what he intended and is satisfied with the outcome and level of service. In the perfect library transaction (similar to the perfect business transaction), the library staff has exceeded the customer's expectations, and the customer leaves the library happy, having consumed more library products than he or she originally intended.

Sales Techniques

It will take individual efforts as well as library-wide collaboration to reach the optimal level of "sales" in the library. Unfortunately, both library education and literature give little insight into the application of sales techniques in library settings. To understand how to best apply these techniques to everyday situations, librarians can turn to the sales profession for guidance.

Personal selling is, unsurprisingly, quite personal. In most situations, selling happens in a one-on-one setting between the sales representative and the customer. This prospect may seem intimidating to some, but by understanding the processes and techniques that go along with effective sales, librarians and other library workers can capitalize on the insights of the sales profession.

1. Finding Customers

It's hard to sell products without customers, and it is just as hard to promote library products and services without patrons. In the sales industry, the process of finding new customers is called "prospecting," and it can be done in many ways. For example, a salesperson could ask friends or clients for referrals. A company could spend thousands of dollars on lists of potential customers or analyze purchasing patterns and demographics in order to figure out who might buy their products. These forms of prospecting aren't very well suited for library settings, primarily because of cost. Another form of prospecting, the "cold call," however, can be highly effective for librarians. Salespeople perform cold calls when they approach potential customers for the first time, usually by telephone, e-mail, or in person. This should sound familiar to anyone who works on the front lines of a library.

The best example of a potential cold call in a library is the "lost" patron — someone who is not sure what is available in the library and is hesitant to ask for assistance. If a member of the library staff sees a new patron in need of help, approaching that patron is essentially a cold call. All it takes to engage the patron is a simple phrase such as "Can I help you?" or "Do you need help finding something?" From there, the librarian can begin the selling process, and a great way to start is by using a pitch.

2. The Pitch

One of the essential components to a sales interaction is the pitch. A pitch, which can be either prepared or impromptu, is a speech given to a customer by a salesperson that is intended to motivate the customer to take action. Pitches are commonplace in the sales industry. The best example that correlates to the library world comes from restaurants.

When a server sees a customer sit down at a table in a restaurant, there is little question that the person is there to dine and is a perspective customer, unlike other shopping situations such as jewelry stores and car dealerships where people may only be interested in browsing. Yet, despite knowing that the customer is already likely to purchase a dinner, the server in a good restaurant will deliver a pitch about the night's specials. But why, when all of the information is on the menu, would the server take the time to give a speech about the food? In addition to making the experience more enjoyable for the diner, the server uses the pitch to clarify any questions about products and give additional information. The server doesn't assume that the customer has full product knowledge or has read the entire menu. By giving the pitch, the server makes sure that the diner can make the best decision and is matched to the item that best suits his or her preferences. This practice increases the level of satisfaction and the likelihood that the diner will return. Librarians and library staff function in a similar way to the server.

When patrons come to the library, it's safe to assume that they are there to check out a product or utilize a service. But a librarian, much like the server in the restaurant, is aware that most patrons don't always know exactly what they are looking for, or where to find it if they do. That's where the pitch comes into play.

The pitch is especially important when trying to sell patrons on library programs or services. By delivering a pre-arranged pitch, librarians can make sure they convey all the essential facts in an efficient manner. Here's an example of a pitch for a summer reading program:

> Have you heard about our summer reading kick-off program? On Monday, June 6th, at 6:30 P.M., the library will host the kick-off program where patrons have the opportunity to register for all of our summer reading events. During the kick-off program, we'll have drawings for great prizes, including an iPad, food, beverages, live jazz music for the adults, and a carnival for kids. The event is free and open to the community. Would you like a flyer with additional information?

Pitches like the one presented above can be intimidating for some, but again, the sales industry has a solution for this: the script. Consider the restaurant example. It's safe to assume that the server was working from a memorized script or selected talking points. Having a script makes it easier to ensure that the main points are covered, and it promotes consistency between transactions and customers. This is why if the diner were to return to the same restaurant the next evening and had a different server, a similar, if not identical, pitch would be heard. Creating and memorizing scripts for different types of library offerings will promote efficient and consistent customer service.

The final key to successful pitches is practice. By practicing the pitch and rehearsing the script, the librarian will give a more fluid and effective delivery without having to read from a piece of paper, thus making sure that the correct information is passed on to the patron. Plus, solid sales pitches demonstrate strong product knowledge, another essential component to any sales regimen. What's more, if the pitches are uniform, library staff can easily detect what aspects of the pitch generate more positive responses from patrons. This uniformity makes it easier to adjust the information included in the pitch, thereby increasing its effectiveness.

3. Product Knowledge

Ask almost anyone about the best experiences they've had with salespeople and two words will usually come into play: friendly and knowledgeable. Conversely, ask someone about their worst sales interactions and they will inevitably say that the salespeople were rude or didn't know what they were talking about. The value of being a friendly librarian or salesperson is self-explanatory. The value of being knowledgeable about library services and programs, on the other hand, can be easily overlooked by library staff.

To properly match a customer with the right product, the salesperson needs to know what products are available. Becoming knowledgeable about the library's offerings can be done in a number of ways, including:

- Regularly examining the library's calendar of events and website
- Keeping up to date with new collections
- Taking note when items and services are discontinued
- Talking with colleagues in other departments
- Asking patrons which items they like/dislike

By regularly keeping up to date with library products and services, library staff will also have opportunities to adjust their pitches to the specific needs of different patrons.

4. Know the Customer

In order to actively promote relevant library services, librarians must strive to learn more about their patrons. Programming directors need to have a good understanding of the library's community to know what programs will be successful. Collection managers need to know the wants and needs of patrons in order to build strong collections that circulate regularly and have information readily available for users. This type of general customer knowledge is developed over time and is quite valuable. To effectively sell to patrons, however, librarians need to know how to "read" them and ask good questions.

Effective reference librarians already know the value of learning more about patrons through the reference interview process. The same goes for salespeople. By conversing with a client, the salesperson takes information about the customer (likes, dislikes, price range, etc.) and begins matching those needs with relevant products and services.

Perfect examples of situations where the library staff can learn more about the customer occur every day at the circulation desk. Imagine that a woman in her late 20s comes to the circulation desk carrying a stack of children's books and videos. Other than gender, age, and the items the patron is checking out, the circulation attendant knows nothing about her. A good salesperson would use this opportunity to find out more about the customer in an effort to sell more products and services. All it takes is asking a few non-prying questions. Let's look at the interaction between a circulation attendant and another fictional patron. This time, Patron B is a mother of two who just moved to town and is new to the library.

PATRON B: Hello. I'd like to check out these items, but I don't have a library card.
CIRCULATION ATTENDANT: Hi! I can help you with that. We'll just have to get you registered. Do you live in the library district?
PATRON B: Yes, my family and I moved here last week.

Once the circulation attendant learns more about the patron, then the process of up-selling and cross-selling can begin.

5. Up-selling, Cross-selling, and Objections

Up-selling and cross-selling are two sales techniques that all librarians need to have in their sales repertoire. Though somewhat similar, the two forms of selling are essential components to a complete sales regimen. Up-selling is the term used for convincing a customer to buy a greater quantity of a certain product or to buy products of a greater value. When the salesperson convinces the customer to buy complimentary items, that is cross-selling. Below are some commercial examples of cross-selling and up-selling in comparison to their library counterparts.

- Up-selling

  COMMERCIAL: A couple sets out to buy a laptop computer for $500, but the salesperson convinces them to buy an upgraded version for $750 and an additional desktop computer.

  LIBRARY: A patron comes to the library to check out a single book, but checks out several after being made aware of their availability by the librarian.

- Cross-selling

  COMMERCIAL: A customer purchases a computer and is convinced by the salesperson to purchase additional software and an extended warranty.

  LIBRARY: A patron comes to the circulation desk to check out a book and is convinced by the circulation attendant to sign up for a library program.

Cross-selling and up-selling are easy in library settings since patrons aren't being asked to spend money. Instead of trying to earn a greater sales commission, librarians are trying to increase the satisfaction of their patrons, not to mention their circulation statistics and program attendance. Because of the lack of pressure in these library sales situations, it takes little effort to up-sell or cross-sell, as long as the librarian correctly matches complementary products to the needs of the patron.

Continuing the example of Patron B will demonstrate the up-sell in action.

PATRON B: Yes, my family and I moved here last week.

CIRCULATION ATTENDANT: I can register you for a library card. Would anyone else in your family like to sign up? By signing up, they have access to all library materials and get priority registration to all library programming.

PATRON B: Yes, that would be great. I'd like to sign up my two boys for library cards.

By interacting with the patron and explaining the benefits of registration, the circulation attendant was able to conduct the up-sell and increase the number of new card registrations from one to three.

- Objections

Sometimes during an attempt to cross-sell or up-sell, the salesperson may encounter objections. Objections come in many forms and can include anything from prices being prohibitively high to a problem with the color of a given product. In a commercial sales setting, the salesperson will either try to assuage the customer's objections or offer substitute products. The role of the librarian when dealing with objections is somewhat different. Rather than pressuring patrons, the librarian should simply offer additional information to try and meet their specific needs.

6. Closing and Following Up

It's important not to overlook closing a sales transaction. In commercial situations, closing a sale happens when the customer commits to making a purchase. A close can come in the form of a signed contract, the actual purchase of a product, or a down payment. Library staff can also close by making sure patrons can check out their materials or perhaps signing them up for a program or service. At the very least, library staff can close a transaction by asking if there is anything else they can do for the patron.

After the sale has closed, there is one more action that the library staff must take. In commercial sales that lend themselves to relationships between the salesperson and the customer (usually high-price transactions such as car or appliance sales), the salesperson will follow up on the transaction to see whether the customer is satisfied or needs additional goods. The follow-up can come in the form of a phone call, a thank-you letter, or an e-mail. Granted, most libraries don't have the human resources to contact each patron after each transaction. However, librarians can build relationships with patrons and follow up in other ways. In a public library setting, a circulation librarian who recommends the latest best-selling novel can ask the patron how he liked the book the next time they interact. In an academic setting, a reference librarian who helped an undergraduate student find articles for her research paper can ask the student if her research is going well when passing her in the stacks. By following-up with patrons, librarians can demonstrate their interest in providing assistance, as well as build relationships that will lead to trust and future transactions.

Sales Training

Although individual librarians can effectively employ sales techniques on their own, library-wide cooperation and administrative support can help yield even greater results, especially when it comes to practice. Many university marketing programs and corporate training programs use sales simulations as a way to train future salespeople. During these sales simulations, participants take turns role-playing the parts of salesperson and customer, while training staff observe and later critique the interaction. During these simulations, participants get to practice the skills mentioned earlier, including delivering pitches, dealing with objections, cross-selling, up-selling, and closing. Not only does this type of training increase the effectiveness of personal selling techniques, it also can promote teamwork.

Library administrators who support personal selling should set aside time for library employees to participate in sales simulations. Ideally, the staff would receive a significant amount of time to practice during in-service periods. However, efficient practice during staff meetings is also beneficial. Though potentially time consuming, administrators will find that these simulations can be highly effective.

Sales Incentives

In the business world, companies rely on sales incentives (sales commissions, bonuses, reward programs, etc.) as a way to motivate their sales force to sell more goods and services. Library administrators can offer similar incentives to their staff in the form of individual and team rewards as a way to promote the use of personal selling techniques in the library.

For example, the staff member who signed up the most patrons for programs during the month could receive a monetary prize or individual recognition by the administration. Volume-based incentives are not the only type; staff members may also receive awards for qualitative factors such as the quality of customer service and patron satisfaction. Administrators can use direct observation or patron surveys to assess individual accomplishments. As a way to promote teamwork and camaraderie among library employees, group incentives are highly effective. One advantage of group awards over individual awards is that it encourages co-workers to assist one another in improving their sales techniques.

Conclusion

The personal selling methods mentioned above shouldn't seem foreign for those who work in libraries, especially since they already practice many of these interactions and techniques every day. However, by being aware of these techniques and what they can do, library staff can apply them for the increased benefit of their patrons.

2

Brand Management Strategies
for Information Services

Christine A. Olson

Introduction

Before you begin reading this chapter, I ask that you gather examples of all the printed materials your library produces. Go to your website and print out the home page along with pages from your blog or other web presence. Now lay all the examples out on a large table. What visual impression do you get? What stands out? If your library has a logo, how does it look? Note the headlines or the top areas of the materials. Consider the vocabulary and the message statements. How do you characterize the communication style? Is it friendly? Cold? Chatty? Terse?

This exercise, whatever the outcome, provides insights into the verbal and visual impact your information service is making, and the imprints being left on the memories of everyone who encounters it. Even if you don't actively manage your brand — or you didn't think you had one — the images and words used by your library combine to make an impression: the essence of branding. This chapter reviews a set of critical strategies for creating and maintaining a brand.

The Basics of Branding and Brand Memory

Many people think that branding focuses on visuals, and that a nifty logo design is all that's needed to successfully brand an organization. It's true that logos, colors, and words allow people to make quick associations with a certain brand, but visuals function mainly as placeholders and recall cues for memories and perceptions. Your brand represents your library, what it stands for, and all its services and products.

A brand, through its messages and countless interactions with people, makes a promise. It sets up expectations through promises either expressed or implied. Once a person has experienced the brand by interacting with it, brand memories are shaped representing the perceptions of whether or not expectations were met. Recalling good memories about library experiences helps people to select your services over other options. Likewise, if bad experiences or unsatisfactory results are associated with your brand, people will seek alternative services that either performed better or promise to do so.

It's easy to see how a brand goes far beyond being only a logo, name, and tagline (which I'll discuss later). A brand is in perpetual motion and has a synergy of its own. Your goal is to manage your brand and all that goes into making it produce desired results.

Brand Audit

Before developing or refining your library's brand strategy, it will be helpful to know what people think of your brand right now and all the different ways people interact with it. Conducting a brand audit is a good first step because it examines the brand from the perspective of the information service customer. Even if you haven't implemented a branding strategy in the past, an audit can provide insights into how your unmanaged brand is perceived by members of the customer group you are targeting.

A quick brand audit captures perceptions and memories for four important brand components:

1. Brand promise: Uncover what people think your brand stands for and what they expect from your brand.
2. Visual images: Identify all the ways your brand is visually represented across all different surfaces and mediums.
3. Messages: Reveal how the messages you send are interpreted.
4. Awareness: Learn what people remember and think about your brand. What cues are used to remember the brand and what features do people use to rank your brand in comparison to competing brands?

Gathering this information is best done through short, personal interviews. Focus groups should be avoided for a quick brand audit because group dynamics can distort insights into perceptions and influence memories. Written questionnaires may not yield usable results unless the audit questions are asked immediately after an interaction.

Basically you are seeking to:

- Uncover the positive and negative associations people have with your brand
- Determine the perceived value of the brand by different groups of people
- Discover how much loyalty there is to the brand and how it stacks up to competitors

The level of effort that you put into the brand audit is your decision. Some libraries will want to conduct a full set of research activities while others will aim to gather quick insights. Regardless of the methodology or level of effort, you are sure to learn about some perceptions and memories that are surprising, and that's the point.

Brand Touchpoints

You and your staff can get started on the brand audit by conducting an exhaustive review of your library's brand touchpoints. Touchpoints are every instance where your brand interacts with, or "touches," a person. Every time a person encounters your brand, that place, situation, interface, experience, or other encounter is a "touchpoint." If you did the materials review exercise outlined in the introduction of this chapter, then you have already begun identifying and assessing some of your brand's touchpoints.

Ultimately, your brand is defined by everyone who has contact with your information service. Because every interaction with your library is a touchpoint, touchpoint experiences impact how your brand is perceived and remembered. One negative experience at one touchpoint can influence how your overall brand is perceived.

Every information service has a different set of touchpoints, but here are some touchpoint categories to get you started. Notice that staff members are included as touchpoints. The interactions with receptionists, book shelvers, volunteers, reference staff, and others are important to evaluate in the mix of brand touchpoints.

- Electronic (website, iPhone apps, e-mail alerts, blogs, Facebook pages, podcasts)
- Signage (internal and external, award plaques and certificates, bulletin boards, book trucks)
- Promotion (event announcements, contests, flyers, posters, brochures)
- Stationery (badges, letterhead/envelopes, invitations, business cards)
- Materials (book plates, catalogs, guides, training, membership/borrowing cards, advertising items)
- Communications (newsletters, fundraising, staff announcements, templates, annual reports)
- Forms (service requests, ILL, job announcements, membership)
- Products (packaging, presentation)
- Physical place (event venues, reading areas, shelving, floor mats)
- People (volunteers, reference, shelvers, Friends of the Library, board members, greeters, voicemail messages)

Brand Mission and Vision

Many people, when developing a brand from scratch or transforming an existing one, start with the visual elements of logo and brand colors. Jumping to these components is premature without having finalized mission and vision statements. The decisions made during the process of developing these statements guide both visual and verbal communications for your brand. Be sure to begin your brand strategy efforts with defining the mission and vision for the brand. The visual brand elements come later.

Simply stated, the mission statement for your brand should clearly and succinctly articulate what you do, for whom, and its core uniqueness. Here's an example of a mission statement from Starbucks. It's prefaced with this statement: "The Starbucks mission statement is more than words on a piece of paper — it's the philosophy that guides how we do business every day." This is an insight into their brand and how they keep their brand on track. The Starbucks Mission Statement is: "To inspire and nurture the human spirit — one person, one cup, and one neighborhood at a time."

While the mission statement addresses your core business, your brand's vision statement should be aligned with the future, portraying what your brand will be in two, three or five years. Here's an example of a vision statement taken from the global mining company called Vale: "To be the largest mining company in the world and to surpass the established standards of excellence in research, development, project implementation and business operations." The mission and vision statements should answer the basic questions people typically ask of a brand:

- Who are you?
- What are you?
- What about you?
- What about you and me?

Developing these statements takes patience and considerable thought. Brainstorming sessions should identify the greatest possible number of ideas, opinions, and insights. All of the vocabulary, concepts, decisions, and discussions that surface during the development of the mission and vision statements will be useful later for crafting the brand tagline and brand promise statements. The same words and thoughts will also contribute to messages to be delivered through your brand's touchpoints.

Brand Promise and Brand Tagline

With your mission and vision finalized, you can move on to two more important pieces of your brand strategy: the brand promise and the tagline. Each of these components plays a role in answering the basic questions people ask of a brand noted in the preceding section.

1. Brand Promise

Ultimately, the brand is held accountable by people for their experience with brand touchpoints. To set expectations, the brand makes a promise about what people can expect from the brand. For the environmental preservation group The Nature Conservancy, "Protecting nature, for people today and future generations" is their brand promise. It's their pledge to help you preserve the plants, animals, and natural communities that represent the diversity of life for the benefit of all people. The promise identifies what The Nature Conservancy brand represents. The statement is short and reflects the core feature of the brand, which helps to differentiate it from other environmental groups.

Composing your library's brand promise requires that you thoroughly understand your brand and what it stands for in order to express its promise. What is the unique promise that you make to people? To help you begin, start your statement with "At [your library], the customer can always expect..." or "We promise to deliver...."

2. Brand Tagline

Developing the brand tagline follows on the heels of the brand promise. Where the promise can be a statement, the tagline is fewer than seven words. There is some confusion about the difference between a tagline and a slogan, and sometimes the two words are used interchangeably. However, there is a difference. A tagline is an enduring, short line used to reinforce the brand's memorability. A slogan is a short-lived, promotion campaign catch phrase. Taglines don't change very often, whereas slogans live only while a promotion campaign is in progress. For example, "Touching Lives, Improving Life" is the tagline for P&G (Procter & Gamble). Whereas "Have You Tried This Yet?" is the slogan for an advertising campaign encouraging shoppers to try P&G's most innovative products.

A tagline is normally present in the brand logo design with the tagline words giving verbal meaning to the brand name and the visual design. The tagline begins the process of establishing desirable word associations for the brand in the memories and perceptions created during every brand touchpoint. Some taglines are descriptive or functional, while others inspire. Having a tagline that connects on an emotional level can help people put their trust in a brand. As long as the brand touchpoint experiences consistently earn that trust, people will be loyal to your brand and become brand ambassadors.

Brand Logo

After thinking about your brand from various 360 degree perspectives, and having finalized its mission, vision, promise, and tagline, you are now ready for the brand's visual representation. All the words and statements identified during the preceding work provide direction to the graphic designer in a document called a Design Brief. The brief specifies what the visual brand image should reflect and not include, and provides guidance to the designer about creating a visual image for the brand and the supporting visual brand system. (The brand resource center for NHS, the National Health Service (UK), noted at the end of this chapter includes an outline for the contents of a Design Brief.)

A logo typically consists of of two elements: a symbol and the brand name spelled out in a particular typeface. Sometimes a brand logo relies only on the typeface and brand name. These brand design treatments are called logotypes, and there is no graphic symbol associated with the brand.

Working with the designer, evaluating logo designs, and selecting one to represent your brand is a process to be done by two or three individuals. It's very difficult for a large group of people to reach a consensus about a design because everyone has different visual tastes and reactions to color and shapes. It is rare for a logo to be liked by everyone. One evaluation test is to close your eyes and try to see the basic shape and color of the design. Too many details will make a design difficult to see in your mind's eye. The best way to evaluate logo designs is to establish objective evaluation criteria, such as:

- Memorability
- Ease of recognition
- Looks good large and small
- Uniqueness
- Ability to project the same image across mediums (paper, digital, signage, silk-screen, etc.)
- Looks good in one-color applications and full color
- Is not trendy
- Allows for future minor changes as design styles evolve

- Is not ugly or suggestive of an undesirable image
- Doesn't attempt to literally represent the library's mission or vision

Color plays a very important role in distinguishing your brand from competing brands and establishing its presence. Color is such a strong visual brand element that the original logo design should be done as black and white or grayscale so that you see the design without the influence of color. Once you select the design, different color combinations can be applied for your selection.

Brand Guidelines

Looking back at the materials gathering exercise in the introduction of this chapter, it should be evident that consistency is a key consideration for setting up touchpoint experiences. A style guide spells out how to present the brand so the brand's visual image and verbal messages can be applied consistently across the organization, making sure the end result is a coordinated, single, strong brand image being delivered through all communication channels.

Brand style guides can be short five-page documents, a comprehensive series of materials, or a series of pages in the communications section of your library's website. The scope of the guidelines depends on how much consistency you want to establish for the brand and how many people are involved in creating and managing brand touchpoints. The development of a style guide is normally a collaborative effort with the designer taking responsibility for the visual brand standards and the communications manager being responsible for the verbal messaging guidelines. The contents of a style guide can include:

- An introduction to the brand and what it represents
- Name
- The logo
- Logo image with and without tagline
- Logo colors
- Applications on different paper-based materials (letterhead, flyers, newsletters, etc)
- Digital media (blogs, electronic signature blocks, slides)
- Forms
- Promotional items (pens, mugs, t-shirts)
- Exhibits
- Website
- Signage
- Packaging
- Tagline
- Mission, vision, and promise statements
- Guidelines for social media writing

Other guidelines can be included for specific brand touchpoints such as voicemail messages, business cards, packaging, inventory control, speciality advertising vendors, and clip art and stock photography sources.

Brand Launch and Stewardship

Rolling out your new or revamped brand requires a detailed plan of events, logistics, schedule, and budget. While a soft launch can be done that introduces the brand as communications activities arise, your best approach will be to set a date when all touchpoints will reflect the new brand. On the plus side, soft launches lower the intensity of brand launch activities and spread costs and resource allocations over an extended period of time. However, such a launch usually loses its punch and in the beginning can actually add to the confusion of your brand image and verbal messages.

If possible, launch your brand as a coordinated, one-time event. This is a time when you can garner visibility and awareness for your library and its services, so be sure to allow yourself enough time to get everything in order. Two pieces of advice:

- Create your best schedule and then add 20 percent more time to it.
- Minimize surprises with the understanding that the unexpected will happen, especially if it involves the weather, technology, animals, or human nature.

Regardless of how you launch the brand, be sure to roll it out first to your staff. It's critical that you engage your organization with the brand from the beginning to ensure that all touchpoints will present the brand consistently from day one. The staff rollout may include role-playing, elevator speech practice, style guide review, launch schedule, and other activities to allow the staff to become comfortable with the changes and to embrace the brand. Make the meetings fun and engaging so everyone is excited to present the brand at all the touchpoints that have been identified.

With your brand ready to be launched, now is the time to select the brand steward. This is the person or team responsible for keeping the brand flame alive. Usually someone in the communications area assumes this role, and it's best to select someone who has brand management experience or has been involved in the development of your brand and who understands the goals of the brand management strategies. Some brand stewards are a little too enthusiastic and become "logo cops." Instead, brand stewards need to nurture the complete brand system and monitor all the brand touchpoints. They should constantly monitor the progress of the brand's presence and memorability (internally and externally), developing and deploying additional brand tools as needed.

Nurturing the brand experience, also known as "keeping the brand," requires the brand steward to make sure brand management strategies are integrated into all marketing and communications activities of your library. This includes the mechanics of brand management, such as the brand identity guidelines, product design, and communicating in a single voice. Some organizations require that all materials be submitted to the communications group for brand review before being produced. Other organizations have a process in place where the communications group prepares all visual and written materials for the entire organization. Still other organizations use extensive template file libraries and ready-to-use artwork to manage the presentation of their brand.

Another important responsibility of the brand steward is ensuring that your library and staff are "living the brand," especially its stated or implied ethics and values. Your brand steward should constantly engage the entire library in brand-building and awareness exercises to keep the brand promise, mission, and vision alive and relevant. These activities can increase brand loyalty among staff members, resulting in higher-quality products and services, and solid, positive touchpoint interactions with your library users.

Brand Loyalty

Branding has always played an important role in an organization's communications mix, but it's never been so critical as in today's world of social media communications channels. In the past, organizations had time to react to negative brand experiences and reduce the impact such experiences had on brand perceptions and, ultimately, brand loyalty. Today, time is of the essence. One negative experience posted across social media channels can spell disaster for an organization and its brand. A grievance of this nature needs to be addressed quickly and properly. On the other hand, social media channels can be the brand's ally when positive touchpoint experiences go "viral" across communication streams.

Building and maintaining loyalty is a primary goal of a library brand management strategy because it fosters usage. People loyal to a brand are its best customers and advocates. Brand loyalty influences usage decisions when people are faced with making a choice. Brand loyalty is at the crux of preference statements in which people say they "prefer brand x over brand y." They have made a commitment to the brand regardless of competitor offerings, features, price, or other factors.

When faced with the decision to use your library or another similar service, what will people decide? What action will they take? If your brand has earned their loyalty by consistently delivering on its promise and value, chances are they will select your library service.

Your Brand Management Strategy

Branding permeates all aspects of a marketing and communications program, and obviously is not an activity to be done one week and forgotten the next. If your library has a strategic plan, then a section of it should be devoted to brand management.

Keep in mind that a strong brand is not built overnight, and a commitment is necessary to see it through over the course of years. Resist the temptation to limit your branding strategies to only visuals, and make sure that you and your staff can easily articulate the brand promise and deliver it. Frequently check that your branding efforts are:

- Coordinated across your library organization
- Consistent through all communications channels, both visual and verbal
- Comprehensive to maximize the exposure of the brand and leverage its impact
- Clear so that brand messages are easy to understand and the brand promise is realized
- Constant without a break so there's never a lapse at any touchpoint

Creating or transforming a brand for a library, a person, a product, or service requires carefully planned work, time, and energy. As you read chapters in this book about marketing methods and review other marketing resources, look for opportunities to bring your brand to life, and never underestimate the power of what a well-managed brand can do for your library.

Additional Resources

There are a great many resources on the Internet which address branding issues. Here are several websites that can provide additional reading and background resources for a brand management strategy.

- *Marketing Profs.* http://www.marketingprofs.com

Devoted to marketing and communications topics, this subscriber-based resource also offers free articles and tools to website visitors.

- *BrandChannel.* http://www.brandchannel.com

This resource is an active, online exchange of branding ideas, tips, and insights. Its tagline is "always branding. always on."

- *Ries' Pieces.* http://ries.typepad.com

This blog is written by Laura Ries, daughter of Al Ries, and co-author with him on a number of books about branding, including *The 22 Immutable Laws of Branding* (1998). Her blog is entertaining and delivers insights and ideas about all aspects of branding.

- *NHS Brand Guidelines.* http://www.nhsidentity.nhs.uk

The brand resource center for NHS, the National Health Service, is a goldmine of examples. The site includes their brand guidelines, tools, and resources, and is one of the most comprehensive brand communications resources available for browsing. The NHS brand system is complex, and you may not need all the components it includes, but reviewing the materials can provide a good understanding of what goes into the development of a brand system, augmenting what has been covered in this chapter. An outline for a Design Brief can be found at: http://www.nhsidentity.nhs.uk/tools-and-resources/design-styles-and-initiatives/putting-together-a-design-brief

3

Developing and Launching a Successful Library Messaging Campaign

CHRISTINA STOLL

We are surrounded by messages every day. In our homes, at our jobs, and often many places in between. From billboard signs, TV commercials, and radio ads to whatever might pop up on mobile devices and the Internet, messages are used to advertise a new restaurant, promote political agendas, or sell the newest "thing a ma-jig."

Libraries also use messaging to promote their services and programming. Some do it quite well, while others may still struggle with where to even start. What makes one form of messaging more successful than another? Why do some messaging campaigns fail while others thrive?

Below is the three-phase process I've developed after implementing several library messaging campaigns. It should be used as a guide with the understanding that there will be variations with each type of messaging project you undertake. Even at the same library, developing messages for the teen department is going to be different than your preschool audience.

Phase 1

- Identify the Goal of Your Message and Your Desired Outcome or Expectations
  What is the purpose of your message? What do you hope to achieve, change, start or stop?
  What would the success of your particular messaging campaign look and feel like?
  What is your project's timeline, budget, and resources?
- Do Your Homework
  Gather all of the facts and information about your message at the start.
  Investigate what's been done already, what was successful, and what failed.
  Identify your biggest challenges and where your quick wins are going to be.
- Involve Invested Parties

Whom do you need on your side to promote your message (or at least not block it)?

Consider co-workers, community members, and even competitors.

- Identify Your Audience and Their Communication Tools

Look to your messaging goals and expected outcomes; do you have a new audience you want to target or an existing group you're looking to impact in some way?

Once your audience is identified, capture how they receive and share information (e.g., newspaper, social media, or e-mail).

Phase 2

- Develop Your Message(s)

Start with a primary message and then add sub-messages as needed.

- Match Your Message to Your Audience

Using the same facts, modify your messages if you have multiple audiences.

Be sure to match the right message to the right audience and the right communication method.

- Using Paid Versus Free Messaging Tools

Based on your project's budget, determine if you can pay for messaging methods (like a paid ad in a local newspaper) or if a free tool (like a no-cost ad in the same newspaper's social media) would work just as well.

- Launch Your Message

Using your project's timeline and the scheduling deadlines of your communication methods, identify which message has to go out first through which means.

- Be Consistent

Develop a publishing schedule for each message (a spreadsheet works great) that identifies the communication method used, format, deadlines, contact information, and any additional notes.

This schedule becomes a great tracking source and measurement tool. Include a section for recording any feedback you get with each message.

Phase 3

- Capture Your Messages

Using your messaging scheduler as a tracking tool, follow up by recording the date and location of where you see or hear each message.

If possible, capture each message for your own records. This can be an online copy or a printed version that can be scanned and saved electronically.

- Evaluate and Measure the Impact of Your Message

Informal measurement should be happening throughout your project. Count the number of messages launched, the different formats, number and size of audiences (new and existing), as well as the communication method used for each message.

A more formal evaluation of the project should be conducted at the end (or for longer projects, at various points along the way). Evaluation can be as simple as answering the questions you set up as part of your campaign's original goals and expectations.

Combine the measurement you've collected throughout with any narrative feedback and the sampling messages you've captured to create an Outcomes Report. This report can be used for presenting the project to administration or library boards, and it makes a great historical document or reference for future messaging projects.

Library Messaging Campaign Scenarios

The following four examples are from my own library career, intended to provide the practical application of my process in different library settings with varying types of messages and audiences.

Message Example #1: Advocating for Certified School Media Specialists

As a former Library Services Consultant for the Metropolitan Library System (MLS), now merged into Reaching Across Illinois Library System (RAILS), one of my roles was to serve as advocate for local school libraries. School librarians would often contact the system for assistance in being "their voice" when library positions were threatened.

During my time with MLS, I developed a lengthy amount of research material on the impact of a school library on the health of its school. I also researched what having a certified school media specialist meant to student learning. I used information from various sources, such as the *Illinois Study: How Powerful Libraries Make Powerful Learners* (ISLMA 2003), in the development of the campaign messages. Doing my homework and getting the correct facts were crucial to successfully getting the message to my two audiences: school library staff and school administrators (principals, superintendents, and school board members).

I developed the first message as a means of providing the school library staff with the tools they needed to develop their own messages. They were then able to target both their local administration as well as create messages to gain support from parents and students (Stoll 2010). I armed the library staff with information on the professional benefits of having a school media certification and included the process of obtaining the certification, including schooling options, funding sources, and how to request support from their school district.

Using the same facts, my second message was targeted at school administrators. This became helpful in situations where either the library staff felt they could not speak up for themselves or in cases where the library had already been closed and there were no staff.

Spreading these messages was conducted in the following manner:

- Creating one-page informational flyers that were mailed and e-mailed to all MLS school library staff and administrators and posted to the MLS website.
- Phone call and in-person meetings were conducted with both library staff and administrators within school districts where a pending threat to the library staff positions was known. All school library personnel and administrative staff involved were pro-

vided with an additional packet of information around solutions from training to funding sources, each designed for their unique situation.

• When a school library position was up for elimination, library staff were provided additional talking points for board presentations. Working with MLS's Executive Director, a personalized letter of support was sent directly to all school board members and administration.

When library staff had the information and resources to speak up for their positions, when school administrators were provided with facts about the impact of having a certified school media specialist in their school, and when parents and students were educated about the value of having a certified librarian, the result was that school library positions were saved.

A message can only be as successful as the facts and data behind your message. By doing your homework before you even start to develop your message, you strengthen the success of your message and your messaging campaign.

Message Example #2: Revitalizing Library Association Membership

For my next messaging scenario, some background information is needed. As a board member of the Special Library Association's Illinois Chapter (SLA IL), 2011–2012, my role was to oversee all external communication, including the chapter's website, social media, public relations, and outreach committees.

The local special library community was hit hard by the economy starting in 2009. As a result, membership involvement declined. An opportunity at the end of 2010 came before the newly elected board to be one of the first chapters to develop a new website using SLA's nationally branded theme. This and the fact that the SLA Annual Conference was coming to Chicago in 2012 provided the Illinois Chapter a huge opportunity to revitalize its membership.

Our chapter's Board President at the time, Lorene Kennard, owner of Walnut Avenue Research, developed our "One Thing" message as part of her presidency. Lorene's reasoning behind the theme was simple: "I honestly feel that everyone can do one thing for the chapter. We are our chapter. We are SLA. The organization is what we make it."

Given that my role involved a considerable amount of the chapter's communication, I assisted with spreading the Chapter's "One Thing" message by including it in places where members were already focused:

• Lorene's quarterly presidential letters to the chapter, which were posted to our website and promoted though e-mail, RSS feeds, and the chapter's social media tools.
• Using the phrase in member newsletter articles when promoting member involvement.
• Mentioning the phrase ("One Thing") in other chapter communications as a stand-alone message.
• Using the phrase at meetings.
• At the chapter holiday party, taking place towards the end of the year, Lorene plans on asking attendees to add their "One Thing" to their name badges, and then use this as part of the program.

This particular message is a great example of setting realistic goals to ensure success at the end. The outcome of this message, while slow at first, did finally start to have an impact around the first quarter of the year when member involvement picked up. Here are some of the ways members stepped up:

- Several new member writers have contributed to the chapter's online newsletter, the *Informant*, and several new members are serving in committee roles for the first time.
- 39 members have volunteered to work on the local SLA IL 2012 Conference Committee.
- A library school student member from Dominican University's Graduate School of Library and Information Science program offered to process the chapter's archives, which are housed at the school.
- The SLA Student Group from the University of Illinois at Urbana-Champaign participated in a presentation on the benefits of being an SLA member, resulting in a new partnership between the chapter and the student group.

Setting a goal for your message at the start of your campaign and establishing how you will measure that impact helps to determine how successful your message campaign ultimately was. If you can't measure your message's impact, good or bad, you've wasted a lot of time, energy, and possibly financial resources as well. Set your message up to be successful at the start with realistic goals and a plan for validating your message's outcome.

Message Example #3: Re-branding a Public Library's Image

As Assistant Director of the Carol Stream Public Library from December 2005 to August 2006, I oversaw the library's re-branding efforts through internal staff marketing changes and external messaging throughout the community. The project also saw the design of a new logo through a community-wide contest.

I knew that the success of any message I developed would depend on getting buy-in from its most valuable audience: the library staff. An internal marketing team was established, and I was the administration representative. One staff member from each of the library's four departments (adult services, circulation, technical services, and youth services) met with me once a month. Together, we developed the library's new internal branding concepts and implementation plan.

Team members not only served as voices for their departments, but they were also my project champions and informal messengers. At each meeting, they shared project ideas and feedback they had received. Getting vital feedback and gaining support along the way from your audience and those individuals who are going to help or hinder your message is important.

The team's collaboration brought about a consensus on many of the messaging elements that had been put together separately by each department. One example was in the selection of the library's new marketing color scheme. The team believed it was important that each department should have its own individual feel. As a result, adult services used a more primary color pallet and youth services went with a pastel version of our branded colors.

The marketing team also served as informal educators on the new branding. Not only did they train the staff in their departments, they also served as a contact people within their departments that staff could approach if they had questions or concerns about the project. This allowed the library staff to become part of the message and the re-branding of the library.

We highlighted Library Worker's Day during National Library Week as a "thank you" to the staff and as a messaging technique to re-image the library. Staff were presented with flowers and breakfast on the morning of the celebration. Also, a banner, press release, and a library staff book display were used to promote the work of the staff to the community.

With the staff on board with the library's new image, the second part of this messaging campaign was directed towards its other audience: the community. Following my practice of locating the communication streams already in place, I used the following methods to spread our new library image:

- Internal branding changes that impacted the library's signage and use of flyers throughout all departments; re-designing the library's lobby with a freestanding billboard.
- Implementation of a community-wide logo contest to identify a new logo image (the final logo design was developed by our newsletter's graphic artist using the winning submission).
- Developing ongoing press releases, which were submitted to:
    Local newspapers, schools, religious organizations, and the newsletters of several community groups.
    Cable access channels.
- Connecting with the local high school newsletter, inviting student reporters to write original library stories.
- Inviting local reporters and photographers to all library events.
- Partnering with the local park district to share event flyers at each of our locations, exchanging event information for each of our newsletters, and posting our event information on their outdoor sign.
- Attending the local Chamber of Commerce and Rotary Club meetings and events with the library director.
- Hosting a library table at community events and school meetings to promote programming and library card sign-ups.

One of the elements that I love most about this messaging campaign is that it provides an example of how you can do messaging with any size budget. I've coined this project my "library re-branding on a construction paper budget." The breakdown of paid versus free resources used for this project were:

- All communication methods used above to push out the library's new image were free, minus library staff time and paper.
- The lobby redesign cost was the purchase of a new billboard and paper for flyers.
- Attending community events included staff time and promotional flyers.
- The library's newsletter costs didn't change.
- The staff celebration costs were for four-dozen carnation boutonnieres, coffee cake, and juice.

• The logo redesign contest fees equated to paying our newsletter graphic artist, a gift card for the winning logo design, the rental of a snow cone maker, plus a couple bags of ice. The party to unveil the new logo had already been budgeted as part of the library's summer reading program.

Two of the outcomes of this messaging campaign included the library being selected as "Chicago's 101 Best & Brightest Companies to Work For" by the National Association for Business Resources (NABR 2006), and the Logo Reveal Summer Bash holding one of the library's highest attendance records.

For me, the greatest reward of this project was something that one of the library staff shared with me towards the end of the project. This staff member had not been in favor of the library branding from the start, but she let me know that my process for involving the staff and informing them along the way changed her mind to a more positive outlook on the marketing effort.

A message can sell a new product or service, but if your message can change a person's thinking, then that is one of the best outcomes you can ask for. For a successful messaging campaign, identify your key allies and your potential challengers and invite them to your table before you even start developing your message.

Message Example #4: Promoting Library Programming

During my time at MLS (see Message Example #1), I was also a member of its continuing education (CE) team. The team developed around 200 face-to-face and online workshops annually for library professionals. As part of our CE development process, we launched a member survey about the program itself. One piece of feedback we received was that members were unsure of how to be informed of our workshop offerings. As a result, we developed a successful model for promoting library programming that could easily be scaled to fit any library size, type, or audience.

The goal of our messaging campaign was to first inform our audience, the CE members, how they could find out about our upcoming learning events. Over time, we used these same methods to simply promote the events themselves. By making our message "You asked to be informed about our CE offerings, and here is how," we kept it simple and realistic. Members caught on quickly, which is why we were then able to transition the original messaging campaign to a promotion of our CE offerings.

This messaging project included several other steps from my three-phase process, such as being consistent with the messaging as well as adding messages to the communication streams already being used by your audience. MLS had a very large audience, serving around 1,500 academic, public, school, and special libraries, all with varying staff sizes. We needed our message to reach as many members as possible without adding a huge amount of additional work for the system staff. Identifying how our members already received and shared information became an important aspect; once we had our messages developed, the work involved with pushing the messages out was almost done.

Our communication methods for promoting both how to hear about our workshops and eventually the workshops themselves included:

- Developing a one-page flyer that listed the ways a member could find out about our CE offerings. This was distributed via our van delivery system to libraries and placed with the other workshop flyers at our office locations, in classrooms, and posted online.
- Messaging was added to our online newsletter in a dedicated section of each issue that also listed our upcoming workshops.
- E-mail messages went out through a dedicated CE mailing list that members could subscribe to. It provided information about upcoming workshops, registration changes, and cancellations.
- Staff made announcements at workshops and other key meetings.
- Messaging was added to our printed six-month CE Calendar, directing members back to our CE website and the CE mailing list.

Over time, we added targeted workshop offerings though e-mails to selected networking groups and in flyers distributed at their meetings. Typically, this was for groups that had either requested a specific programming topic or the subject matter was of interest to them. This technique aided in filling in any remaining gaps where members only wanted to hear about workshops pertaining to them.

By setting a realistic goal, identifying our very large audience's preferred communication means, and being consistent with our messages in a variety of ways, our messaging effect went beyond just the campaign. Members not only learned where to locate workshop information, but this knowledge then impacted the success of our programming along the way.

Conclusion — Now Go Have Fun with Your Messages

It is my belief that each of the messaging campaign examples presented was successful due to following these fundamental elements of my process:

- Doing Your Homework
- Keeping Expectations Real
- Involving Your Key Contributors In the Process
- Developing Your Message Around Your Target Audience
- Avoiding Time Wasters by Re-using Already Established Communication Means
- Setting up Attainable Measurements

One of my core professional beliefs and practices is to "work smarter, not harder." By designing and sharing my messaging campaign process, I hope I've provided other library professionals with a framework that they can easily set up for their own messaging projects, thus leaving more time for the fun part of marketing — being creative.

Works Cited

ISLMA Illinois School Library Media Association. 2003. "Illinois Study" http://www.islma.org/Illinois Study.htm (accessed May 27, 2011).

NABR National Association for Business Resources. 2006. "Chicago's 101 Best and Brightest Companies to Work For" http://www.101bestandbrightest.com/regions/chicago (accessed May 27, 2011).

Stoll, Christina. 2010. "It's up to You to Save Your Library When Faced with Budget Cuts." *ISLMAnews*, Spring.

4

Marketing Principles
School Libraries and Beyond

Lesley S. J. Farmer

Overview

What is marketing? How does it differ from public relations or advertising or strategic planning? In his book on strategic public relations planning, Smith (2009) asserted that public relations focuses on long-term interaction between an organization and its publics, while marketing is a management function that focuses on more immediate products and services that respond to consumer wants and needs; the core is economic exchange. The American Marketing Association defined marketing as "an organizational function and a set of processes for creating, communicating, and delivering value to customers and for managing customer relationships in ways that benefit the organization and its stakeholder" (Wood 2010, 2). Public relations' core principles are values and relationships. Marketing planning is a four-part structured process (Smith 2009), which is explained below.

Why do school libraries need marketing? At this point in time, the school community "public" has so many information choices that they may be unaware of potentially well-matched options. Especially as the role of the school library is sometimes unclear, school librarians need to define their value. In so doing, they should examine their potential clientele market, their publics. In addition, as the local school site, education in general, and these publics change, the school library media program needs to respond in a timely manner in order to stay relevant. Marketing provides a systematic process for identifying and delivering optimal products and services. This process also results in improving the school library media program as a whole and increasing its value.

Step 1: Marketing Research for School Libraries

Before librarians can market the school library, they need to conduct market research: gathering and analyzing data about the school library media program, its publics, the school organization, and the current set of circumstances facing it.

Publics / Markets

In order for school library media programs to add value to their publics, school librarians first need to identify their publics: their market. The primary public, which is internal, is the school community, which may be subdivided into students, teachers, support specialists (e.g., nurses, reading coaches), support staff, administrators, and parents. These subdivisions can be further segmented: kindergartners, science teachers, club advisors, and so on. Secondary publics can include schools in the same or neighboring districts, local libraries and librarians, and the local community at large (including daycare centers, postsecondary institutions, recreation centers, local agencies, bookstores, media outlets, and other businesses). Intervening publics, those entities that can help send a message to another public, should also be identified; typical members of that public include administrators, parents, other librarians, and newspapers. It should be noted that in today's digital society, anyone using social media can assume that role, including students. According to public relations experts Guth and Marsh (2012), for each public or market segment school librarians need to know:

- How each influences the school library media program's ability to achieve its goals
- What is its opinion of the school library media program
- What its stake or value is relative to the school library media program
- Who are its opinion leaders and decision makers
- What are its demographics
- What are its psychographics (e.g., their political leanings, religion, attitudes, values)

SWOT

Next, school librarians need to identify what they can offer in terms of products and services: the internal environment. They also need to analyze the external environment to understand the issues that impact their publics. The foundation for market and customer analysis is a SWOT analysis (strength, weakness, opportunity, threat). In school libraries, strengths and weaknesses may arise from personnel, boards, support groups, facilities, money, collections, services, technology, customer database, open hours, etc. External issues might be local demographics, competition, technology, politics, governments at different levels, public and private agencies, economic environment, legal environment, etc.

A SWOT analysis can be based on the total school library media program, or it can focus on one aspect of the program. Since one of the functions of the school library is instruction, a focused SWOT analysis might identify:

- Current library-related curriculum that is provided in the school library and offered by competitors such as classroom teachers, public libraries, and online information providers
- Existing and potential instructors and instructional designers in the school library and elsewhere
- Existing and potential resources, including learning aids, in the school library and elsewhere
- Existing and potential learners and learning needs, in the school library and elsewhere

School librarians do well to align efforts with school-wide priorities. In that respect, SWOT analysis can help clarify a compelling situation in terms of the role a particular school library media program can play. For instance, students might be performing poorly on standardized tests (certainly a significant concern for administrators). Alternatively, a growing incidence of cyberbullying might be negatively impacting the school. A SWOT analysis might uncover the following factors for the second situation:

- Strengths: rich digital collection that supports the curriculum, class set of Internet-connected computers, access throughout the day, flexible scheduling, tech-savvy library staff, filtering software used, acceptable use policy in place
- Weaknesses: no library lessons on cyberbullying, no mention of cyberbullying or digital safety beyond acceptable use policy on library website
- Opportunities: e-rate compliance requires instruction on digital safety, administrators and teachers don't know how to deal with cyberbullying (school librarian can serve as an expert)
- Threats: no place in the curriculum for digital safety instruction, administrators and parents want to cut off access to all social media, technicians don't want to deal with intranets or social media

Once school librarians know what they can offer (or have the capacity to provide), they can determine which market to target. If librarians try to reach everyone, that approach is called mass marketing, and tries to find an issue or value that is the common denominator for everyone. Alternatively, librarians can focus on a few key market segments to provide more specific services or approaches. In general, school librarians tend to segment markets (that is, potential users) by age or type of use: e.g., parents who want to volunteer in the library, reluctant readers, techies, manga fans. Typically, an organization has resources or services that are underused/undervalued that they want to push. Perhaps they see a target user market potential that has ignored them. In general, librarians should try to go to the biggest bang for the buck: the best return for their efforts. For instance, a likely niche is entering users: new students and employees. Referring to the SWOT example above, school librarians might target health classes.

At this point, librarians can gather more specific data that can inform their marketing decisions. A needs assessment is an effective way to find out about the current knowledge, capabilities, interests, and values of each school community segment. Through a school-wide survey, the librarian may find out that no one understands cyberbullying or how to deal with it. On the other hand, the librarian may discover that 97 percent of students use social media, and 36 percent have been involved in cyberbullying. The librarian should also assess the learning context; how might cyberbullying fit into the curriculum? How might the school schedule fit in cyberbullying instruction?

Step 2: School Library Market Strategy

At the marketing strategy stage, school librarians establish their goals and objectives, formulate their action plan, and develop their message. The above SWOT analysis reveals a great opportunity for librarians to provide new value to the school library media program. The overarching goal could be a reduction in student cyberbullying, with the media program playing a key role in reaching that goal. The specific objective would follow: to instruct the school community about cyberbullying and how to deal with it.

The action plan incorporates a "marketing mix," which refers to the marketing tools of product, placement (channel), pricing, and promotion (some marketers add the tool of people): the four or five Ps. These tools aid in developing an effective marketing strategy.

Products are more than boxes; they can be goods, services, places, ideas, organizations, and people. Wood noted: "When planning services, marketers must focus on delivering benefits through the appropriate combination of activities, people, facilities, and information" (2010, 82). Product development, such as cyberbullying instructional design, needs to go through development processes to ensure its success (italics refer to cyberbullying-specific implications):

1. Determine the curriculum content: *cyberbullying definitions, characteristics, factors contributing to cyberbullying, its prevalence and consequences, ways to deal with it. School librarians can research existing cyberbullying curriculum (see http://k12digital citizenship.wikispaces.com for a list).*
2. Determine the context of the curriculum: *health education, civics education, language arts.*
3. Identify resources: *content-specific resources such as learning objects and Internet tutorials (see http://k12digitalcitizenship.wikispaces.com for a list); production-centric resources such as wikis and podcasting tools; task-specific resources such as WebQuests.*
4. Determine the time frame: *one-period/one-shot learning presentation, one-week unit, monthly single-period activities.*
5. Determine who will teach: *librarian, computer teacher, librarian and classroom teacher.*
6. Determine where the instruction will occur: *school library, classroom, computer lab, online, via web conference, at home.*
7. Determine how students will be grouped for instruction: *individually, small groups, class as a whole, mix of the above depending on the part of the learning activity.*
8. Develop ways to differentiate and scaffold learning: *working in pairs, extension activities, choice of projects or resources.*
9. Determine and implement assessment instrument: *authentic performance, podcast product, quiz.*

What makes a good product/service? Performance, features, reliability, durability, esthetics, and perceived quality all need to be considered.

Branding distinguishes the product and builds connotations that lead to valuing and loyalty. For example, the American Library Association's (ALA) @yourlibrary campaign created memorable branding and helped libraries around the world by providing an easily recognizable brand that libraries could adopt and leverage at the local level. All of the marketing communication should have a consistent look and tone that reinforces the message, such as ALA did. In general, posters and flyers should have one message and one graphic; supporting documents can have more detail. The digital citizenship logo used in the wiki mentioned above has been branded by the California School Library Association, for example (http://www.csla.net).

Pricing strategy may seem irrelevant for school libraries, but school library media programs do cost. Organizations need to show good return on investment to their corporate/institutional body. Certainly, instructional design and delivery cost time and labor. Publicizing the instruction, say with printed flyers and posters, can run up a bill. Library portal development and digital resource costs can be significant. Depending on the setting of the instruction, computer lab and demonstration equipment can be sizeable. If librarians spend considerable time designing and publicizing a cyberbullying workshop, and pay for a lab aide to help run the session, a low return on investment will result if only a handful of students attend.

The third part of the marketing mix is "place": how, when, where to make the media program's products/services available to the target market. To do that well requires knowing how that target market accesses goods/services, the external environment (including competitors) as well as the product itself and its life cycle. What value accrues along the way from its inception to its delivery? What is the flow — the logistics? For example, the tendency is to deliver cyberbullying instruction in the school library, but librarians could conduct a web conference to be shown in the classroom. Increasingly, library instruction is done in the form of self-paced online tutorials so that learners can access the information anywhere at their convenience, which was done for the digital citizenship professional development modules (see http://ecitizenship.csla.net/). Such online methods might be particularly appropriate to engage parents.

Step 3: School Library Marketing Tactics

At the tactical point, school librarians select the tactics to communicate their marketing message and implement their strategic plan.

The fourth P, Promotion, calls upon the advertising "front line" and public relations tools as well as other techniques. Note that communication will change over the life cycle of the marketing initiative. Using the cyberbullying instructional marketing example, the research-stage needs assessment can serve as a promotional opportunity, leveraging surveys and interviews as ways to inform publics of potential curriculum. On the other hand, at the point of delivery, other formats such as websites and flyers are more appropriate.

The communication arena has really changed lately because of Web 2.0. For instance, viral marketing, which happens as people pass along marketing messages, has become an effective approach because of interactive telecommunications channels. The trend is to co-opt/enlist the help of the target market to identify the desired product as well as to communicate about it. School librarians should be aware that they are sharing control of the message and communication channel, so they should be prepared: are they happy with what people Twitter about the school library media programs? Potentially, electronic word-of-mouth may be the most effective advertisement of media programs.

Another aspect of public relations is relationship marketing, which refers to establishing and maintaining long-term relationships beyond a single marketing initiative: having loyal "customers." This approach aligns well with media programs and reinforces the concept of lifelong learning. The underlying idea is that the library staff is interested in its clientele and addresses their needs in a timely and professional manner. Shaik (2009) stated that three levels of relational marketing exist:

- Level one: price incentive (most school libraries offer free borrowing and services)
- Level two: social bonding (well evident when publics say "OUR" school library)
- Level three: developing customized programs to meet user needs (effective service and instruction should provide this option)

The bottom-line benefit of marketing is impact, and of course, marketing is only as effective as the product or service that is being sold. Instructional design planning, as noted earlier, requires high-quality decision-making and implementation. Additionally, to ensure that goals are reached, support must be present in the form of learner support and internal marketing (getting the school community on board). The learner focus and support can be confusing: think of wanting happy readers — school librarians need to provide them with good service (e.g., readers' advisory, good reading material in stock) to attain the goal. Those conditions apply to cyberbullying instruction in that prepared instructors, accessible materials, and good technical support must be provided. Support is also needed for the marketing aspect of the effort: clearance to conduct needs assessments, available communication channels, opportunities to inform the school community and train library staff.

Step 4: School Library Marketing Evaluation

The best marketing plan is the one that sells, that gets optimum results. Did the marketing plan work? School librarians should assess their marketing plan's effectiveness all along the way and make adjustments accordingly. Indeed, the type of assessment measures/instruments should be determined from the start. The "metrics" concept is often used; it refers to numerical measures of specific performance-related activities and outcomes that can be applied to marketing evaluation. The most obvious result is student learning, which can apply to their work, be it academic or in their daily life. For example, instruction on database use might result in a teacher discovering a seminal paper that facilitates reading comprehension for English learners.

Focusing on assessing the marketing performance, school librarians should examine the marketing strategy, operation, and relations with the target market. An effective approach to assessment is a systems approach where each input and output factor is identified. The following critical questions can guide librarian's assessment of marketing efforts at benchmark points: when researching, when strategizing, when implementing, and when reflecting/debriefing (Wood 2010, 140):

- Does the goal focus on the publics' needs and interests?
- Does the marketing mix reflect the results of the market research?
- Do the library staff understand the marketing plan, and have the skills and resources to implement it?
- How do the library staff manage the marketing mix?
- How are marketing problems analyzed and addressed?
- Do the library staff achieve the intended program and marketing goals?

- Do the library staff have good relationships with their publics?
- How are publics' comments and priorities gathered, analyzed, and incorporated into marketing plans?
- How do publics perceive the school library's marketing goal, and have those perceptions changed over time?

Conclusions

Marketing provides a systematic way for school librarians to both satisfy their publics and improve their school library media programs. To that end, school library marketing encompasses both internal practices and collaboration with several publics. As resources and information-processing experts, school librarians are uniquely positioned to document, communicate about, and assess marketing efforts. Concurrently, assessing each marketing step to make sure that planning and implementation is done effectively, the bottom line being a value-added, improved school library media program.

Works Cited

Guth, David W., and Charles Marsh. 2012. *Public Relations: A Values-Driven Approach.* 5th ed. Boston: Allyn & Bacon.

Shaik, Najmuddin. 2009. "Marketing Strategies for Distance Learning Programs: A Theoretical Framework." In Ugur Demiray and Necip Serdar Sever (Eds.), *The Challenges for Marketing Distance Education in Online Environments*: 125–171. Turkey: Anadolu University.

Smith, Ronald. 2009. *Strategic Planning for Public Relations.* 3rd ed. New York: Routledge.

Wood, Marion. 2010. *The Marketing Plan Handbook.* 4th ed. Upper Saddle River, NJ: Prentice Hall.

5

Marketing Public Libraries

An International Perspective

DEBORAH LINES ANDERSEN *and*
DAVID F. ANDERSEN

Comparing Marketing Approaches in Other Nations

Public libraries outside of the United States respond to a variety of users in ways that can be quite similar, or quite different, from those seen in the U.S. Since one never knows where the perfect strategy for a public library might surface, this chapter focuses on marketing approaches that have been used in other nations. In particular, and based upon the experiences of the authors, this chapter explores marketing strategies that have been used in Glasgow, Scotland; Montréal, Canada; and Puebla, México. To round out this international discussion, the fourth public library case is that of Albany, New York, a city that has successfully gone through a transformation in public library chartering, funding, citizen support, and facilities development in the last several years. The chapter ends with a comparative roundup of marketing strategies that hold promise for increasing library support, attendance, programs, funding, and users.

Glasgow, Scotland

Glasgow, Scotland, is a city of approximately 750,000 people in 68 square miles. It maintains 33 public libraries as well as a central research center, the Mitchell Library. Although the major language of the country is English, there are sections of the city where Chinese, Hindi, Urdu, or Punjabi are predominant. It is a major commercial hub for the country and attracts individuals from a wide variety of countries. The challenges for the city reside in meeting the needs of a varied population, in an urban center that has limited parking but a well-developed public transportation system. Funding is provided by the city to an overarching department of cultural affairs, and public libraries are on the same city budget line item and compete for funds with parks, public swimming pools, museums, and city athletic facilities.

To meet the wide variety of needs that urban centers face, the city has focused on specific ways to brand its libraries. Much of this branding has to do with capitalizing on the co-location of the libraries with other public facilities. Other marketing makes use of the city's rich cultural heritage, its effort to provide computing facilities in every public library, its emphasis on children and education, the strength of the public transportation system, and the number of libraries in the city — making each branch library a true community library.

• **Partnering with Public Facilities**: Given that the same commission pays for libraries and other cultural services, the libraries of Glasgow have partnered with these services in a variety of ways, both physical and informational. Pollok and Springburn Libraries reside in the same buildings as their respective indoor community swimming pools. Pollok, in particular, uses this juxtaposition to promote health, athletics, and fitness in its collection and in the posters on its walls. A large glass window in the library looks out over the swimming facility as a constant reminder of this pairing of library and recreation. Springburn Library does not have a librarian in the library. Instead, upon entering the building, citizens have a receptionist who will direct them to the library, computing facility, fitness center, and gymnasiums located throughout the building.

• **Promoting Cultural Heritage**: Public libraries in Glasgow also use partnering to promote cultural heritage. Many libraries share space with city museums or display collections of historic photos and/or artifacts within their facilities. Additionally, many of the libraries sell maps and pamphlets about the history of the area or famous individuals who have lived there. Not only can citizens read about their community, but they also can help support the library through purchase of these materials. Libraries also sell pens, paper, notebooks, and a variety of items for library use. Additionally, libraries are proud of their physical spaces, many of which were funded by Andrew Carnegie in the early 1900s. The stained glass windows and ceilings, dark natural wood, signage (even if no longer apropos), attractive wooden library tables, and shelving have been preserved as a reminder of the beginnings of these libraries. Stepping into many of them is physically like stepping into the past, but with the modern conveniences of library catalogs and computing.

• **Focusing on Children and Young Adults**: Glasgow libraries have prominent and large children's areas, much as one might see in the United States. There are areas for toddlers and young children. Libraries will have all the children's chairs, tables, and stacks in one color, making age designations obvious for all, but especially for the library patron who cannot yet read signs. Young adult spaces are always distinct from the children, defined by couches, coffee tables, extra pillows, signs for teen materials, and walls that divide them from the rest of the library. Color coding for teens, although not uniform throughout the city, is nonetheless clearly done.

• **Leveraging Public Transportation Services**: It is possible, in most cases, to move from one public library to the next in Glasgow with just one bus ride. Public libraries focus on this geographic proximity by prominently displaying literature about programs and exhibits in other branch libraries. Postcards advertising a children's art exhibit might be found on library tables in many neighboring libraries. Libraries also maintain highly visible kiosks of bus schedules as well as other cultural events taking place in the city.

• **Stressing Computing**: Glasgow undertook a massive campaign to install public computers in every one of its libraries, with the last, Langside, receiving its computers in spring 2003. Not only were computers installed in libraries, but a major, multi-organizational effort was made to educate citizens about computing. Public displays promoted computing not just for employment or education, but also for pursuit of personal interests or hobbies, and for developing self-confidence. This last goal underlines these libraries' interest in lifelong learning and attracting individuals to the library for everyday, personal goals and pursuits.

• **Creating Distinct Community Libraries:** By focusing on lifelong learning, Glasgow public libraries have added distinct features to their spaces that might be at odds with what classically trained librarians expect. Libraries throw out their newspapers at the end of the day. (Mitchell Library maintains back issues.) There are soda machines in the main reading rooms. Furniture often consists of couches and sofas, with very few or no tables and straight-backed chairs to be seen. Individuals can buy coffee and sandwiches at the Stirling Library, taking their purchases into the stacks to select a book and read it while snacking. Multiple sections of the Stirling Library have shelving around the edges of the space with sofas, coffee tables, and an individual desk with a helpful information professional. Located in the center of the city, in the first public library building, Stirling also has an extensive set of computers for quick access to Internet and e-mail, national and international magazines and newspapers, an extensive music collection, and self checkout to speed up the visits of citizens and business persons alike who take their lunch hour to visit the library (Andersen 2004).

Montréal, Canada

Montréal is an island city with an interesting past. In 2006, it had 1,621,000 citizens living in an area of 1,644 square miles. At one time it was a very small city, with many other towns surrounding it on the same island. Over time, these small towns became part of the city proper, some of them not joining until well into the 20th century. But before that, they had their own libraries. Today there are 43 public libraries in this extended Montréal. Funded in part by the communities in which they reside, Montréal libraries have a different funding structure than Glasgow, but again strongly reflect their own regions of the city. An important feature of this city in the province of Québec is its emphasis on the French language. Between 1960 and 1990, a series of "language wars," sometimes actually bursting into violent conflict, led to a wide-scale redefinition of language policies and politics in Québec as well as Montréal. Public signage must be in French first, and collection development is greatly influenced by a population and policy that is francophone. Nonetheless, much of the population speaks English, and there are additional communities where the primary language is Spanish, Greek, or Chinese. Challenges for these libraries are strongly centered on language policy.

• **Balancing Demands for Multiple Languages:** In a city that speaks French as well as English, collection development policy needs to take these, as well as other languages, into account. Libraries for the most part collect in French, but maintain extensive collections of English language novels for adults as well as teens. Amusingly, these are usually noted by signs that say "Romans Anglais"! Non-fiction materials are often interfiled in English and French. Several librarians stated that they needed to pay attention to the demographics of their user base, shifting collections from one library to another as populations moved into the community or shifted from one section of the city to another.

• **Partnering with Educational and Cultural Facilities:** As in Glasgow, libraries in Montréal are often located in the same building as swimming pools, or located on the same piece of land with athletic facilities and schools. The Saint-Michel library is within walking distance of soccer fields and basketball courts, as well as the local public school. Children can and do walk from the school to the library with ease and without crossing any streets.

• **Branding with Distinct Signage:** No matter where one goes in Montréal, the red rosette that identifies a cultural site is large and prominent. This brand goes on museums, archives, libraries, and other cultural centers to identify public places accessible to all citizens. Furthermore, it is not unusual at bus stops to find signage and maps that include library names, addresses, bus routes, and an indication of distance from the current location.

• **Repurposing Existing Buildings:** Some of Montréal's libraries, such as the Westmount and Outremont libraries, were always libraries, built for that purpose. Others have become libraries after starting their lives with other purposes. Many, such as Maisonneuve and Georges-Vanier, were the hôtel de ville (the town hall) when these areas were their own political entities. The Mile End Library was originally the Church of the Ascension, built in 1904, repurposed and refurbished by the city in 1992. Interestingly, the library retains its stained glass windows and other stained glass portraits of saints that give it a distinctly Christian feel. Important for citizen access, these buildings were originally placed in the center of the community to provide access to all. Now repurposed, they continue to be centrally located and near city bus and subway stations.

• **Promoting Children's Literacy:** Among Montréal's 43 libraries, the Hochelaga is unique. It is exclusively a children's and curriculum library for those who work with children, tweens, and young adults. It maintains collections of games, puzzles, and books that range from board books to YA fiction, with spaces for studying as well as story hours. Obviously not possible in a small town or community, the large scale of Montréal makes it possible to devote an entire library and staff to serving this population. For all other libraries of the city, there are extensive children's and young adult sections, usually given equal space as the adult collections, with an emphasis on staff, collections in French and English, and computing facilities.

Puebla, México

Puebla is the name of both this state in México and a city within it. The city is an original colonial city, founded when the Spanish came to México in 1519. It is rich in cultural heritage, colonial and pre-colonial. Although the predominant language today is Spanish, there is also a strong move for children to learn English, and there are over 40 pre-colonial languages spoken throughout the country. The Roman Catholic Church has a strong influence on culture, not only architecturally, with many magnificent structures throughout the region, but also in the everyday lives of the individuals who live there. Pyramids abound in this area, created by pre-colonial Mesoamerican cultures related to the Aztecs and Mayans, reminding one that Spanish influences started only in the 16th century, with rich layers of cultural heritage preceding them.

The population of the state of Puebla, as in much of México, is a mix of individuals with indigenous as well as Spanish heritage. There is a wide range of income levels, and many individuals do not have access or income to purchase personal books or computers. For them, libraries serve as a critical conduit for information. Libraries are funded by individual communities with distinctions made about local versus regional facilities. Those in the state of Puebla, and in particular in the city of Cholula, are housed in historic structures, centrally located near the town plaza, and staffed by individuals who do not have library degrees. Libraries are places for children to study and gain access to books. Although not grand in scale or collections, these libraries meet a critical information need, and their staffs are proud of the facilities they have. The challenge for these libraries is to attract individuals, to keep materials current with limited budgets, and to find funding to meet the needs of citizens.

• **Matching Funding to Election Cycles**: According to a fellow researcher met by the authors on a trip to México, elections are often a time when politicians use public goods to leverage their political positions. This is problematic in that funding may come or go depending upon the political aspirations of incumbents. According to our source, garbage collection was subject to these local political fluctuations until it was made a national funding priority. Libraries in México might be supported when a new party comes to office; they can also atrophy across election cycles.

• **Providing Materials That Citizens Cannot Afford**: In the U.S., we often employ user surveys to establish what our patrons want. Or our patrons vote with their feet, coming to programs or using resources that they like and avoiding others. In Puebla, the librarians and staff were local citizens who knew what was popular, what was new, and what citizens wanted. Their input was critical in distributing scarce resources for the most critical information sources and services. Employees there are the eyes and ears for resource decisions in collection development.

• **Making Do with What Is Available**: In a climate where resources are limited, it is challenging to meet the needs of patrons. The libraries of the cities of Puebla and Cholula used what they had. Some books were donated. Others were provided by the state. Students had encyclopedias that were a few years old, and they used them.

• **Branding with Local Names**: From the point of view of history and support, naming libraries after local, historic figures is an important branding technique. Libraries are often named for important figures, such as the Biblioteca Pública Regional Maestro Vincente T. Mendoza in Cholula (San Pedro municipality). Mendoza was a local folklorist, composer, and artist born in Cholula (1894–1964). Similarly, the public library in Cholula (San Andreas municipality) is the Biblioteca Pública Municipal Quetzacoatl. Quetzacoatl was a major deity of the Aztecs, Toltecs, and other Mesoamerican cultures, and thus another important historic figure for present-day Mexicans.

Albany, New York

The public libraries of the city of Albany, New York, underwent a major campaign to change their funding source. Before 2002, their charter required that they negotiate with the mayor's office each year, hoping for the best budget possible that was 90 percent from the city and 10 percent from other federal and state monies. The hope was that the citizens of Albany (about 100,000 of them in approximately 21.8 square miles) would vote to change the libraries to a public library district that would have its own ability to tax each year. Additionally, the change in charter would mean that citizens might defeat a budget, but the funding for the libraries would never be less than in the previous year. With approximately 30 percent of its citizens being library cardholders, the question was how to market and brand this effort in order to have a positive vote on both the rechartering and the first year's budget — an almost 100 percent increase over that provided by the city in the previous year. The challenge for the library administration, staff, citizen advocates, and the mayor's office was to create a marketing strategy that would work. Additionally, using explicit marketing tactics along with citizen advocacy meetings, the libraries successfully passed a budget referendum in 2007 to build two new branch libraries, repurpose an existing building, and renovate two more.

- **Thinking Through and Implementing Public Relations Options**: The director of the libraries initially stated that he wished to run a survey of citizens in the city to find out how they felt about rechartering. The consultant for the rechartering suggested instead that the survey should be of other libraries that had rechartered. It seemed clear that if 30 percent of the citizens were cardholders, about 30 percent of the voters would be in favor. There was little to be gained by a citizen survey. Thinking through the goals of data collection for marketing efforts is a serious business. Data collection is expensive.

- **Canvassing Others to Find Out What Has Worked**: The consultant canvassed other libraries that had gone through the rechartering process in New York State. The concept was to find out what had worked, what had not worked, and how to leverage citizen and citywide support for this effort.

- **Enlisting the Support of Community Advocates**: Albany has very strong communities with individual personalities. With five branch libraries and a main library, the citizens were eager to support their own communities and get out the vote. Their participation in getting out the vote was critical. In the end, approximately 5,000 individuals went to the polls. Split three to two, the positive vote for the entire city, and for future generations, was decided by less than six percent of the citizenry.

- **Thinking through Timing**: The rechartering vote was timed to coincide with the school budget vote for the year. This was a critical decision. If voters had been upset about the school budget, it is probable that they would have voted "no" for both the schools and the libraries. Since their previous voting patterns and their present sentiments indicated a positive vote, the libraries could ride on this success and have a single citizen turnout.

- **Finding Strong Advocates Willing to Speak for Change**: The director of the libraries, a seasoned administrator who understood how to effect change, went after community members in order to garner support for the libraries. He was looking for individuals who would be willing to run for the office of library trustee — not only creating future strength for the libraries, but also creating much-needed administrative advocacy before the vote (Andersen 2003).

International Marketing Strategies

Thinking through the experiences of these four cities, there is a series of overarching themes that arises about marketing, citizen advocacy, strategy, and public relations for public libraries. The list that follows is a mix of items — some come about only with major campaigns for building new facilities, but others are small, much less costly ways of garnering library use and support.

- **Toss Out Old Notions of Libraries**: Citizens who are used to blogs, texting, and getting information from the Internet are looking for both usual and novel information venues. Attracting individuals could mean meditation gardens, Internet cafes, vending machines in the library, a change of furniture, or teen centers in the library building.
- **Think Living Room As Well as Study Space**: Not everyone comes to the library to study.
- **Focus on Children and Young Adults**: This demographic is the citizen group of the future. Perhaps this might mean focusing on non-voters, who will become voters, when thinking about marketing for the library's strategic plan.
- **Pay Attention to Shifting Demographics**: As seen particularly in Glasgow and Montréal, groups of individuals arrive from their home countries, or move from one section of a city to another, and shift the need for service provision. Staff and language proficiency as well as collections may need to physically move in order to meet these changing needs.
- **Partner with Others**: Glasgow libraries advertise one another's events — music, poetry, or art shows. Albany Public Library has one branch in the same building as a YMCA. Montréal and Glasgow both co-locate their libraries with athletic and cultural facilities.
- **Be Strategic About Funding Sources and Increasing Resources**: Repurposing buildings, partnering with other cultural institutions and other libraries, using local expertise for marketing, and focusing on the best ways to collect citizen input save tax dollars for critical library functions and create community pride and community advocacy for needed projects.
- **Create Community Signage to Identify Public Spaces**: Part of partnering is thinking about the branding of all public venues in a city or town. A prominent, memorable symbol, such as Montréal's red rosette, can enhance the visibility of the library and associate it with other public venues such as art galleries, museums, and senior centers.
- **Take Advantage of Community Groups and Community Pride**: Enlisting citizen groups, and especially segments of the community, can be critical in getting out a vote, or supporting programs and budgets for the library. Albany's campaign for new and renovated libraries included citizen action groups that were populated by library advocates from distinct neighborhoods of the city.
- **Use the Experience of Others to Enhance Marketing Techniques**: Hiring a consultant from a local college or university can create additional vision for marketing campaigns. Other libraries that have untapped expertise and experience of their own are willingly to share if asked.
- **Take Advantage of Untapped Staff Knowledge**: Library staff often are community members. Individuals who shelve books have immense knowledge about user borrowing

patterns. Everyone on the staff, including the custodian and the parking lot attendant, have a lot to say about the library and how to market it, if they are asked.

• **Pay Attention to the Timing of Critical Votes and Activities**: As seen particularly in Albany, it is worth paying attention to the pulse of the community and to other critical events which may affect library programs, library promotion, and library funding opportunities.

• **Repurpose Existing Buildings That Are Centrally Located**: Many cities have examples of buildings that had former lives and are now libraries. These buildings can be used to promote history, and they are often centrally located, providing library venues when land or funding is limited. As seen in México in particular, history provides naming opportunities for libraries and for enhanced civic pride.

• **Promote Culture and History**: Every library and community has a history. Not only can that history promote pride, but it provides an opportunity to create a brand for the library, its environment, and the citizens who live there and can advocate for it.

• **Sell Culture and History**: As seen in Glasgow, there are opportunities to promote history, maps, and other cultural items while raising critical funds for libraries and raising awareness about the library itself.

Marketing is about creating support, about getting individuals to "buy" and invest in the product that the library is selling. Although language, culture, and funding sources may differ across these international examples, they are all in the same business of getting as many people through the doors (actual or virtual) as they can, making their products as visible as possible, and creating a citizenry that is highly vocal in promoting the library.

WORKS CITED

Andersen, Deborah Lines. 2003. "Selling a Public Good: The Case of Rechartering Public Libraries by Referendum in New York State." *Public Library Quarterly* 22: 5–23.

Andersen, Deborah Lines. 2004. "Library as Living Space: How Glasgow, Scotland Defines Its Public Libraries." *JLAMS* (*Journal of the Library Administration and Management Section of the New York Library Association*) 1: 5–11. http://www.nyla.org/associations/13281/files/1304701306_jlamsvln1-2.pdf (accessed July 11, 2011).

PART II

Strategy

6

Growing a Culture
of Marketing

The Smith Library Experience

ROSALIND M. RAM, BECKY LYNN DEMARTINI,
and ZOIA ZERESA ADAM-FALEVAI

Tending a garden requires consistent effort on the part of the gardener. The same can be said about marketing in small libraries. It requires constancy amid change. Marketing needs to continue whether the change deals with little to no funding, new initiatives from management, or the ever-changing nature of information formats. This article will illustrate how the marketing committee of the Joseph F. Smith Library at Brigham Young University-Hawaii (BYUH) created a marketing program and a system for planning and evaluating events.

Small academic libraries generally run on minimal staffing, library resources, and very few or no marketing plans. That was the case in 2006 for the Smith Library. Today, great effort is being put forth by the library to market our resources and services. How did this all come about, especially with the economic downturn in 2008?

Some basic information about our institution and library will help set the stage for our marketing efforts. BYUH is an undergraduate institution whose target area is the Asia-Pacific region. The student body comprises people from over 70 countries. There are four colleges covering fields such as the sciences, business, history, languages, and more. Enrollment is currently at 2,600 with 130 faculty members teaching in 53 programs. The Smith Library has 175,000 print items, 8,600 audiovisual materials, 300 databases, and 350,000 e-materials. University Archives and other special collections are housed in the library. Services include a large information commons, library instruction, interlibrary loans, and academic print reserve and e-reserve.

In 2006, Library Director Douglas Bates added a marketing program to the Smith Library. After reviewing the organization, a cataloging position was exchanged for an outreach librarian position. The new outreach librarian was charged to market, assess marketing activities, and raise funds. Soon, the concept of a marketing committee evolved. Several library staff and faculty members volunteered to serve on the marketing committee. Initial tasks undertaken by the marketing committee included identifying users, defining

49

resources and services, and assessing existing marketing programs. As a result of numerous assessment/evaluation sessions, the marketing committee generated four organizational marketing components. They are:

- Resource/Service to be promoted: what is being marketed?
- Creative/Innovative Idea: how is it being marketed?
- Visibility/Viability: who is being marketed to and why?
- Assessment/Cost: how did it go and how much did it cost?

These four components have since evolved into a marketing model that, when applied, has resulted in successful marketing for our library. When not applied, marketing efforts have been failures or flops. To help illustrate these trends, this article is divided into three sections. The first section on *Events, Activities, and Programs* contains narratives of tried and tested marketing ideas. The next section on *Flops* illustrates marketing ideas that failed. Lastly, *Insights Gained* contains the pearls of wisdom gained by the Smith Library Marketing Committee.

Events, Activities, and Programs

The beauty of a garden is the variety found within. The same is true when marketing a library. Variety is the spice of life. For the last five years, numerous ideas were put into action by the marketing committee. Below are a few examples of some successful marketing efforts and details of what it took to make them work.

1. Reading in Different Languages from Around the World

For the National Library Week theme of 2009, "World Connects @ Your Library," the Smith Library's marketing committee devised an activity called *Reading in Different Languages from Around the World*. With BYUH's large international student body, this activity gave students the opportunity to participate in reading library literature in a foreign language. Language classes were selected from the College of Language, Arts, and Culture. The Samoan, Tongan, Hawaiian, Maori, Japanese, Chinese, French, and Spanish language classes were invited to join in the activity. The students performed in front of an audience made up of peers and library users. Some examples of literature they selected included poetry, short stories, fables, and myths. The students explained their piece in English and then proceeded to perform the piece in a foreign language.

- Many enjoyed listening to a foreign language being read out loud.
- The activity was held in the library lobby at different times of the day. The late afternoon activities were not as well attended as those in the evening.
- The cost was about $100. This included prizes and advertisements.
- This activity required a minimum of two months to plan and prepare due to the number of language classes offered at BYUH and the intense scheduling involved.
- The collaboration between the language classes and the library was a success.
- This is a great idea to repeat in the future.

2. Hidden Treasures @ the Library

The purpose of the *Hidden Treasures @ Your Library* event was to give library patrons an opportunity to learn more about the services and resources in the library in a fun way. To go along with the theme, a pirate map was designed to guide individuals from one area of the library to another. The staff came dressed in pirate costumes. Participants started in the library lobby by collecting gold coins from a treasure chest. They then used the map to go from area to area in the library. Each gold coin had an area name and number printed on it. Each number corresponded to a question about that particular area of the library (e.g. "Circulation #3"). Participants acquired a special token each time they answered a question correctly. Finally, these tokens were exchanged for treats from the treat station.

- The departments that participated were circulation, reference, Pacific Islands Research Room, archives, periodicals, copy center, and media services. Each area had a list of 20 different questions about the services offered and resources available in that area.
- The event was open to the university students, faculty, staff, and even community members.
- The event took about a month to plan, advertise, and prepare. Preparations included the creation of the props such as the treasure chest, gold coins, ocean background, treat station, and area flags. The budget allotted was $500.

3. Edible Books

The Edible Books contest was intended to help advertise the children, young adult, general, and special collections. People were invited to create edible book displays based on a theme, idea, plot and/or cover of the book.

The contest was open to the whole university. The first contest had four entries. Although the entries were few in number, this gave other library users a better idea of what was meant by an edible book. This event caught the attention of one of the Food Services supervisors who then suggested that the library and Food Services collaborate in planning the next Edible Books contest. Food Services offered to provide items/products for the participants to create their edible books. Six months later, another Edible Books contest took place with the following results:

- The BYUH Food Services donated items for the contestants to use. The contest was first displayed and judged at the Food Services Snack Bar and then brought to the library to be displayed the following day.
- Food Services provided the prizes.
- About $200 was used by the library for advertising.
- For the next Edible Books Contest, Food Services plans to invite a pastry chef from a local resort to hold a live demonstration showcasing edible creations.

4. Copyright Awareness Week

The growing concern regarding plagiarism and the illegal downloads of film and music prompted an activity promoting copyright awareness. The library took the initiative to collaborate with different departments in the university that have a stake or interest in copyright compliance, such as the Reading and Writing Center, the Office of Honor, and the BYU-Hawaii Student Association-Student Advisory Council (BYUHSA-SAC). As part of the preparation for the event, each unit tackled a particular aspect of copyright compliance. The library opted to give out information on ways to legally download film and music. The Reading and Writing Center administered a plagiarism quiz. The Office of Honor presented information on academic honesty, and the BYUHSA-SAC held an open-mic forum.

- The purpose of the activity was to educate people on copyright laws.
- Booths were set up at different locations and times throughout the campus over three days.
- Handouts on copyright information, the plagiarism quiz, and video clips were all part of the activities at the booths. Those participating received a copyright cookie — an excellent marketing tool for the event.
- During the open-mic forum, a number of students asked if the copyright activity would be an annual event.
- An estimated 700 people took the plagiarism quiz and received information on copyrights. About 1,000 copyright cookies were given out. The cookies cost about $500. A total of $150 was spent for posters and advertisements for the event.
- It took two months to plan the event.
- In a meeting shortly after the activity, the University Compliance Officer (UCO) informed a group of University personnel that this is exactly what is needed to show due diligence in educating the University's population on copyright issues. The UCO recommended that this be an annual event.

5. Games at the Library

Games are some of the best activities to invite library patrons, particularly students, to participate in library-related events. The participants get to take time off to relax from studies, have fun, and receive prizes. Games offered included:
- *Hopscotch Around the World* by Mary D. Lankford. Various hopscotch games were set up outside and inside the library with rules and instructions.
- *Jeopardy!* @ Your Library. Categories about the Smith Library were incorporated as well as other fun facts.
- *Wheel of Fortune* @ Your Library. The newly elected BYUHSA President and Vice President hosted the game. This was a good opportunity to interact with students and have fun at the same time.
- *Jeopardy!* and *Wheel of Fortune* were fun because they required more participation. They were held in the evenings in the library lobby. *Hopscotch Around the World* was not as successful because it was spread out over a large area and was hard to monitor.
- Overall, the marketing committee values games in the library since they can be designed to promote the library and add some fun to university life.

6. Holokai Library Tutorial

For over 20 years, librarians at Smith Library have taught a bibliographic session for all freshman English courses, introducing students to the library resources available for basic university research. After attending a presentation at the Hawaii Library Association Conference in 2007, campus reference librarians began to design an online tutorial. With help from campus graphic designers and a simple, inexpensive screen-capture program, tutorials were developed and can now be used in any class. This tutorial is named *Holokai*, meaning "the sea voyage" in the Hawaiian language. It follows the story of a team of five canoe paddlers (the school's mascot is a paddler known as Seasider) who help each other along the way with different steps of the research process.

- Working with faculty early on in the process was and continues to be critical. Librarians joined English and other department faculty meetings to explain, promote, and receive feedback on *Holokai*.
- The tutorial was placed prominently on the library's home page. Since 2008, the tutorial has received over 13,000 views, demonstrating its role in the teaching of information literacy.
- The time to create and update the tutorial is the biggest cost.
- The reference librarians value this tool and recognize its part in developing information literacy in library users.

7. Lua Letter Newsletter

The marketing committee decided to publish a library newsletter of sorts called the *Lua Letter* (lua means bathroom in Hawaiian). Yes, it's placed in each bathroom stall in the Smith Library, ready for a captive audience. This is a very inexpensive way to let patrons know of upcoming events and quick facts about the library.

- A minimal amount of the marketing budget was spent to purchase holders for the letters.
- A student designs the letters using PowerPoint or MS Publisher after receiving content from a librarian.
- Around 40 letters have now been published. All are available on the library webpage.
- The campus newspaper, the *Ke Alaka'i*, thought the *Lua Letter* worthy of a story and gave it a very favorable review.

8. Library T-shirts

Don't know what it is about free t-shirts, but they really seem to get people excited. Once a year, the library splurges on t-shirts for each student worker and staff member. An annual t-shirt design contest is held, and the contest is open to any person within the university. Opening it to a wider audience allows for more imaginative, original and professional designs. Student employees often report that their friends ask what they need to do to get a library t-shirt. Naturally, they were led to the library where they participate in library events hoping to get a free t-shirt. It has been really exciting to see students wearing Smith Library t-shirts all around campus and the community.

9. Library Website

The library's home page is an increasingly significant part of the library presence. Evaluating the website with a critical eye requires constant attention to ensure the limited space is used wisely. Recently, a section for marketing library events and resources was created on the home page in a highly visible location. Items added include a calendar of events, advertisements, and announcements. Over time, the library web and marketing teams have learned the following:

- More graphic design skills are needed in web developers.
- Video production skills are key to creating effective marketing videos.
- Collaborating with instructors who specialize in these areas can help identify talent for hire.

Flops

Weeds always seem to spring up in the garden, and without proper tending, can even take over. A gardener is faced with trying all sorts of ways to keep them to a minimum. Likewise, in marketing, not all of the events and activities planned by the marketing committee have turned out smelling like roses. Our experience has been that if an event is a flop, more than likely it is because one or more of our four marketing organizational components was not adhered to.

One activity that comes to mind is *Movies in the Lobby*, which flopped because of the location. There was too much movement in the lobby area to create a movie-watching experience. Some users were annoyed when the volume was turned up because they were studying nearby. Yes, showing the movies did give the library good exposure, but the choice of location created a sore point with users. It fulfilled the criteria of a Creative/Innovative Idea, but had the committee thought this out further and considered the impact on the users near the lobby, the problem could have been avoided. Experience is a hard teacher.

Another example of a marketing idea that flopped was our attempt at offering database workshops. The organizational point that the committee could have spent more time on was Visibility/Viability. It was clear to the committee that it was not enough to simply put out posters, flyers, and e-mail bulletins for upcoming library database workshops. People just do not show up even with reminders. The committee has learned that in order for database workshops to be viable, they have to run in conjunction with a class or an assignment. Coordinating with an instructor ahead of time and conducting the workshop in a classroom setting lends itself to greater viability and higher visibility. In other words, it is best to teach databases when the user has a need, coordinated through a teacher.

Insights Gained

Since 2006, the Smith Library has learned more and more about library users and marketing. Consistently using the model with our four organizational components does make a difference. Assessing marketing activities, establishing a marketing team, standardizing the planning process, being creative with a small budget, and working in concert with other areas of the library and the larger institution are all important in nurturing a successful marketing strategy. Some principles of success we learned:

- Find out the best time to hold events. The gate count is a good tool to help determine this. At the Smith Library, students are more apt to participate in events and activities in the evening and earlier in the week.
- Scheduling is everything. The more coordinated the library activities are in concert with other activities of the larger institution, the better.
- It pays to coordinate with other departments outside the library. To advertise that an event is being "co-sponsored" by other areas shows an effort to bring people and areas together for a great cause. The idea of "many hands making light work" is a very appealing approach with great results.
- Collaboration with other areas allows for sharing the cost of events.
- Assessing events is a must! This process helps determine what to keep doing and what to avoid in the future.
- Ask for help/volunteers from within the library and without. Many people are willing to volunteer their time and talent when approached with a good idea. Simply ask.
- Create a checklist of all the options available at the institution to promote/advertise upcoming activities, events, and programs.
- Assign a person or group of people to facilitate the distribution of marketing materials throughout the institution.
- People are always interested in prizes, food, and giveaways.
- People love "free" stuff.
- Keep management happy by staying within allotted budget.
- Involve users in the planning process. The Smith Library has a student advisory group made up of student workers from different areas.
- Get user involvement in promoting the library. Training students to promote library-related services and resources can be very successful in marketing endeavors. A good example of this is the University Student Orientation. Student representatives from the library established a greater rapport with their peers and are more approachable.
- Use existing services to help the library create professional-looking products. The marketing committee uses the Print Services Department to print posters and the University Photographer or staff members to take photos for the annual READ posters. Both units add professionalism to library marketing materials.

Just like a garden needs constant tending, so does a library marketing program. Sometimes it's a matter of simply jumping in there and not being afraid to learn from a few flops along the way. Use a consistent model while trying new things, minimize expenditures and time spent on projects by involving others, and always remember to have fun as you grow a great marketing program.

7

Establishing the Library in the Cultural Fabric of the Community

Ten Tips for Linking the Library to the World

Barry K. Miller

Historically, the library has been a respected and revered, if not always well-funded, cornerstone of its community. Dictionaries of quotations are filled with tributes to libraries across the centuries, with the author of each quote vying with the others to inspire the reader to support the library and better oneself through the use of it. In the United States in particular, the library has been seen as being as American as baseball and apple pie. It is often described as the heart of the community or the college, the center of learning, the storehouse of knowledge, the cathedral of the mind.

When financial crises occur, however, there is sometimes a tendency to think short-term. When new information containers such e-books gain in popularity, there can be a tendency to think that other, more familiar tools, such as libraries, are less vital. While librarians know that they can enhance what the Internet delivers, and that e-books are just another information container (like books, manuscripts, and videos), others may not. When libraries get overlooked, it can be because some people don't realize that libraries, like individuals, adapt, change, and incorporate new ways with the old.

For those of us in the profession, it is our job to remind these people of our value, demonstrate it, give them context, and make our libraries as essential to them as possible. For us to thrive and not merely survive, it is equally important that they recognize that value.

In 1998, I was hired to help communicate one library's story to the community of which it is a part. The library I joined at The University of North Carolina at Greensboro (UNCG) was a good one, with a solid and deep collection, dedicated and resourceful employees, and a capable and visionary management that had incorporated and pioneered new tools and resources, especially electronic ones. The university and the city of Greensboro were similarly blessed, though the university had once been described affectionately as a "Sleeping Beauty" by one of our university's most illustrious writers, poet and critic

Randall Jarrell (Lowell, Taylor and Warren 1967, 258). My job is to get the word out about the library, and that job is never finished. One of the first things I had to contend with in communicating the library's story was to package it in the context of our campus and community. As a former special librarian in the business world, I had constantly been required to align my corporate library with the mission of the company it served, to link the library to "mission critical" functions. When I came to the academic world, I operated on the same assumption, and I suggest that it also applies for public libraries and school media centers. Much as we'd like it to be, the library is not just "a good thing" in and of itself. It is a reflection of the university or community it serves, and a tool for achieving its purposes.

How does this affect what we do? It means that we do not just advertise new resources or services. It means that we package our publicity around issues that are important to our faculty, administration, students, and community.

When I came to UNCG 12 years ago, I was struck by its mission statement. In addition to teaching and research, our university made service a keystone of its vision. At that time, the mission statement read: "The University ... is a diverse, student-centered research university, linking the Triad and North Carolina to the world through learning, discovery and service." Now the mission reads a bit differently, but the core is much the same: "The University ... will redefine the public research university for the 21st century as an inclusive, collaborative, and responsive institution making a difference in the lives of students and the communities it serves."

Linking to the world? Making a difference? Service? Isn't that what libraries do, too? The library's mission and the university's mission are congruent, if not the same. The University Libraries' mission at UNCG is to "advance and support learning, research and service at The University of North Carolina at Greensboro and throughout the state of North Carolina." Among our goals is to "engage the Piedmont Triad in programs that enhance the life of the university and community and build long-term support for the Libraries."

Thus was established the first guiding principle of our work.

1. Connect to campus priorities and initiatives. Be aware of what is important to your campus, and align the library with those issues whenever you can.
   Some examples:

   - If the university is focused on sustainability, make sure your library is engaged and part of that effort.
   - If the university needs to make sure that students feel it is a warm and inviting place to go to school, make sure the library reflects that goal.
   - If the university needs to create better public awareness of the research activity done there, honor those researchers and promote that research beyond the campus itself.
   - If the university values diversity, participate fully in the embrace of that value, and make sure that your efforts are known. If you can be a leader in that effort, as we have, so much the better.
   - If the campus celebrates its cultural offerings, celebrate how the library promotes those offerings, and offer programming of your own to enhance the experience even more.

Whatever we do, we want to make sure that we are a partner with the faculty and the departments in their efforts, not a competitor for scarce resources. We want our colleagues and administrators to view us as a jewel in their crown.

With these ideas in mind, the rest of the guiding principles followed.

2. Offer a variety of programming to a variety of audiences. The library is one of the few places that can be almost all things to all people. It promotes learning and scholarship in pretty much any field of inquiry.

For example, as a former women's college, we have an excellent collection of women's literature. Therefore, we ran a series focusing on great books by great women and invited the faculty and staff to send us nominations of their favorite books in that category, making the results a feature story in our library magazine. We engaged some of our honors students to conduct public readings from books they particularly cherished that were written by female authors.

When it came time to select the symbolic millionth volume for our collection, we collaborated extensively with faculty to make the selection. After we made it, we engaged theatre faculty to conduct a staged reading of a play based upon the book. We hosted a seminar by education faculty who used special teaching techniques they were pioneering. We invited outside scholars to speak who were doing cutting-edge work with new digital technology to study and understand the work of the author in new ways. We had faculty in two different departments jointly present perspectives on the importance of the book to their disciplines. Each of these efforts gave us the opportunity to promote the library and its millionth volume within the context of our particular university, as well as to offer a way to engage and showcase the talents and work of our faculty and students.

3. Partner strategically and broadly. Choose partners who can help you, and whom you can help, to produce superior products that you couldn't build alone.

From book discussions to lectures and programs, campus partners are part of nearly all of our cultural offerings, and we also invite outside speakers. We go beyond the campus, however, in engaging other partners in planning and publicizing the events, including our local historical museum, an area book festival, and the public library. Recognizing our ability to engage a wide variety of people in our programs, community members with no previous connection to the university have offered us such opportunities as a program featuring Holocaust survivors, which drew an overflow crowd the day after September 11, 2001. We thought that perhaps no one would show up after the tragedies in New York, Washington, and Pennsylvania, but we were mistaken. Then the organizer repeated the program the next night to a capacity crowd in an off-campus facility.

We also partner with faculty and other area universities and organizations on many of our digital projects, including Civil Rights Greensboro, a collection focusing on the history of civil rights in the city where the 1960 sit-ins gained international attention. Another digital project preserves the Race and Slavery Petitions project of a UNCG faculty member that covers nearly 18,000 petitions to state and local courts in fifteen states prior to 1867. The collection is a unique resource for scholars, students, and genealogists. A partnership with the State Library is creating the Literary Map of North Carolina to provide a picture of the state's deep literary heritage and output.

In 2010, our interest in sustainability merged with a touring exhibit we were hosting from ALA about Abraham Lincoln's Journey to Emancipation. How? A documentary filmmaker on our faculty had created a film about sustainability narrated by Senator George McGovern, who also happened to have written a recent book about Lincoln. Working closely with the faculty member, we helped organize and publicize a visit by McGovern to talk not only about sustainability, but also about Abraham Lincoln. The result was a pair of programs that drew large audiences and further cemented the library's role in bringing major speakers to the campus.

4. Be open, and listen to your constituencies. As former IBM CEO Lou Gerstner once told his managers, quoting novelist John le Carré: "a desk is a dangerous place from which to view the world" (Halpern 2011).

A few years ago, a member of the Friends of the UNCG Libraries suggested that we start a book discussion group with discussions led by a member of the faculty. Doing so, she suggested, would give the community a chance to sample the good teaching that takes place here, give an outlet to those who enjoy book discussions, and do something that other book groups in town could not do so easily — have a discussion led by a person very knowledgeable in the field. We have chosen fiction and non-fiction, essays and plays, and for nine years now, we have brought members of the Friends of the UNCG Libraries and members of the community to our Special Collections Reading Room four to six times a year to discuss books that they have read or in which they are interested. Participants in our discussions have told us that of the more than 70 book groups in our area, we are one of the few that has a number of male as well as female attendees. We didn't plan it that way, but it gave us another measure of uniqueness.

Sometimes we have a discussion covering the same book chosen for the all-campus read, so the community can share in that experience. Each time we hold a discussion, we feature a faculty member as the discussion leader. Books are chosen across a variety of disciplines, ranging from nutrition and biology to history and economics. Each year, we are delighted with the books our faculty authors and Friends choose to discuss. We promote this series widely, and have added a number of new members to the Friends of the UNCG Libraries as a result. Several even became board members. Postcards, e-mails, and *Library Columns*, our magazine, alert our Friends to books that they would likely never have encountered and give them an opportunity to read them, whether they participate in the book discussions or not.

One of our most successful projects has been the creation of the Betty H. Carter Women Veterans Historical Project, which documents the experience of women veterans in the American military. The collection, now numbering more than 200 oral history interviews as well as letters, diaries, photographs, and artifacts, has a major web presence that attracts researchers and veterans to our resources. It all began because the University Archivist, Betty Carter, was listening to alumni from the class of 1950 reminisce about the significant role that World War II women veterans played in their educational experience after the war. Betty recognized a need to document that experience, which was being lost, partly because World War II-era veterans are dying, but also because women's stories were often forgotten alongside stories of the combat experiences of male servicemen. Indeed, some of the women veterans themselves had to be convinced of their roles as pioneers, opening up career opportunities for women during the war that continued even after it ended. Women were not just "Rosie the Riveters" on the home front. As our project demonstrates, they often took active roles in the military and "freed a man to fight," as military recruiters put it (Gavin 1957, 16–26).

5. Think creatively. Don't say, "We've never done that," but instead ask, "Why couldn't we do that?"

To promote the Women Veterans Project, Carter and University Librarian Doris Hulbert commissioned a play based on the transcripts of oral history interviews that were interspersed with music from the World War II era. Premiering at our university, "Star-Spangled Girls" has been performed all over the state by the Touring Theatre Ensemble of North Carolina. Each time it is performed, it makes attendees aware of our collection.

Sometimes our role is to make connections. Here's an example where at least four disparate factors came together:

- Our university has an excellent School of Education. For many years, we have produced alumni who serve our state and others as teachers and school media center personnel.
- We attract a number of first-generation college students.
- I happened to be serving on the Board of Directors of a local book festival in a nearby community.
- I personally have a particular interest in children's books and storytelling for all ages.

All of those things came together with our Children's Book Author and Storyteller Series, which is now one of our signature programs. Each September, with the help of our School of Education, we bring a children's book author who is also a storyteller to our community. On a Saturday, that author/storyteller appears under our sponsorship at the local BOOK-MARKS Book Festival, which is attended by 5,000 to 7,000 people. The following Monday, we bring the author/storyteller to our campus for three performances. For the morning performance, we invite 500 elementary school students from area schools to come to the university on a field trip for an hour-long program. We especially like to invite schools that utilize our student teachers.

The day of the event, the children are escorted by their teachers and also our students, particularly our North Carolina Teaching Fellows. Many of these visiting children come from Title I schools, and have never been on a college campus before. Because many of their teachers are our alumni, they are able to point out features of the campus (including the library) to the children during the visit. Because we tend to choose authors who are also prominent storytellers, the children and their teachers really enjoy their visits and send us very nice letters of appreciation for the experience. Often, the children tell us that they want to come back here as college students one day. Attracting future students at a very young age and inspiring them to go to college are nice benefits of the series.

UNC Greensboro students in our kindergarten to sixth grade (K-6) methods classes observe another group of children with the author/storyteller in the afternoon of the visit, and engage the author/storyteller in a Q&A session after the performance. This component of the schedule enables our students to learn how to incorporate storytelling and literature into their classrooms when they begin teaching. We are inspired by the myriad ways our students say they benefit from this experience, ranging from the teaching of diverse cultures to the use of humor in teaching.

The day ends with a public performance, which permits those community members, alumni, students, faculty (and their families) who can't come during the day to attend. Prominent author/storytellers have agreed to participate in our series. They seem to enjoy it and are our allies in finding others from among their colleagues to come in the following years. So far, Jerry and Gloria Pinkney, Carmen Agra Deedy, Willy Claflin, and Tim Tingle have participated in this ongoing series.

When budget concerns last year reduced the resources that some of our campus partners could invest in the Children's Book Author and Storyteller Series, and the library's own resources to devote to it were jeopardized due to a need to spend discretionary dollars for other important purposes, a member of the Friends Board of Directors stepped forward to ensure that the series did not lapse. Why? She saw the library meeting a community need and wanted it to continue, so she and her spouse provided a fund to support it for the next five years. We are most grateful for expressions of support like these.

6. Do things others can't do as well. Most universities have great scholars and teachers. That doesn't necessarily mean that they want to plan or are good at planning things like public programs and communicating about them to interested constituencies.

After the first year, the Dean of our School of Education thanked us for creating the Children's Book Author and Storyteller Series. He said that we had seen an opportunity and acted on it, and he was delighted with the result. We embrace the role of helping promote our university to the communities we serve.

7. Spend at least as much time communicating about programs and finding audiences as you do in conceiving a program in the first place. To contrast with a phrase from one of my favorite films, *Field of Dreams*: if you build it, they won't necessarily come. You have to find the fans and tell them about the game. Only then, if your product is consistently good, will they come and come again.

When I talk with colleagues who conduct library programming, it seems as if they sometimes spend most of their time developing a program and lining up speakers or participants, both of which can take a lot of time and effort. Sometimes lost in the equation is the amount of time and energy spent attracting an audience. Scheduling a program and putting out a sign or a flyer is not usually enough. Competition for the time of patrons and supporters is keen. They, like we, are busy people, with lots of opportunities. Whenever we develop a program, even a small one, we first consider who might come, why, and how we might attract them. Then we try to target our marketing and publicity to make sure that we invite those we think will care most about the program. When we hosted Native American storyteller Tim Tingle, for example, we got in touch with Native American groups on campus and in the community and issued special invitations that were enthusiastically accepted. They became partners in our publicity. When we hosted the Abraham Lincoln exhibit, we invited the North Carolina Civil War Round Table and the History Club to be involved with us, and they volunteered to support us with funds to bring speakers we would not otherwise have been able to bring.

8. Communicate continuously and in diverse ways. With or without money, there is no single way to get the word out. It has to be done clearly and usually concisely, but the medium for communication can be anything from word-of-mouth to printed matter to multimedia. Also, understand what is newsworthy and what isn't. Always ask, "Who is going to care about this?"

I maintain a publicity checklist to remind me of the different vehicles we have to communicate, and we prepare a publicity plan for nearly every major undertaking. We don't spend a lot of money. We don't often use paid advertising, but depending on the program and the potential audience, we employ such tools as campus newsletters and newspapers, alumni e-mails, the library magazine, web pages, blogs, podcasts, and social media to communicate about the library and its offerings and programs. Often Friends Board members with media contacts help us place stories that we couldn't get on our own. We call, we write, we ask partners on and off campus to help us spread the word, and in so doing we educate them about what the library has to offer. Rarely do we find them unable to work with us, and never have they been unwilling.

9. Understand your brand and protect it. Ask yourself: "If we do this, how does it affect how people perceive the library? Does it enhance both the library and the university?"

Telling the library's story only works if the product you are describing is a good one. Our University Libraries work hard to assess our value and enhance our customer service. We employ tools such as LibQual that tell us our constituencies generally think we are meeting and often exceeding their expectations. And each time we evaluate those surveys, we work to improve those areas that receive the lowest levels of satisfaction. Our sophomore and senior surveys show that among the sixteen campuses in our state's university system, our students generally have the highest levels of satisfaction with their library. We aren't the biggest library, or the richest, but we are proud to get high marks for satisfaction among our clientele.

10. If you do it, do it well. Offer high quality experiences that communicate that the library provides a superior product for its patrons, whether they seek resources and services or attend programs.

The university librarian who hired me in 1998 and her successor have had high standards. Recognizing that we can't do everything, they challenge our organization to do what we do as well as we can do it. We have a reputation for high-quality programs and publicity, as well as high-quality library service and resources. Whatever we do, we want it done right, and we want it to reflect well on our university and on our library. If we are to link the university to the community and the world, we know that those links are built one at a time, and that each link builds upon prior experience and success.

Works Cited

Gavin, Lettie. 1957. *American Women in World War I: They Also Served*. Boulder: University Press of Colorado.

Halpern, Tim. 2011. "Louis V. Gerstner Jr. 1942–." *Reference for Business, Encyclopedia of Business,* second edition. www.referenceforbusiness.com/biography/F-L/Gerstner-Louis-V-Jr-1942.html (accessed March 25, 2011).

Lowell, Robert, Peter Taylor, and Robert Penn Warren, eds. 1967. *Randall Jarrell: 1914–1965*. New York: Noonday Press.

8

Community Outreach at the Goddard Space Flight Center Library

Kathleen Monaghan, Ann Marland Dash, *and* Bridget Burns

NASA's Goddard Space Flight Center (GSFC) is a world-recognized center of innovation and discovery. The NASA Goddard Library strives to support the missions and projects of the GSFC by offering services and resources that provide a competitive advantage to the community. In keeping with the guiding principles of the library's vision and mission statements, the overall goal of the marketing and outreach initiative is to ensure that the library is the most valued knowledge resource and partner for targeted audiences at GSFC. Outreach at the NASA Goddard Library refers to the creation and delivery of programs designed to promote awareness of the library by meeting the information needs of the community. The Marketing & Outreach Team is charged with this initiative.

As collections and services offered by the library are delivered directly to the desktop and used remotely, fewer people have a need to come into the physical library. Community outreach programs provide a unique opportunity to enhance the library's image within the Goddard community and offer excellent opportunities for collaboration with community leaders, groups, and organizations that highlight the value library services bring to the GSFC.

As important as outreach is, it works best when it is supported by a marketing strategy. Outreach for the sake of the activity, without clearly defined outcomes or goals, or disparate outreach projects that lack a cohesive message, are not as effective as a series of coordinated outreach activities.

I. Marketing Strategy

To lay the groundwork for future outreach initiatives, the Marketing & Outreach Team identified the following critical marketing criteria:

- Identify the library's key audiences and create profiles of each type of user.
- Define the library's core products and services. Because of their importance to the library's key audiences, the essential products and services should be well-defined focal points on which the Marketing & Outreach Team can concentrate the majority of its efforts.
- Create a consistent brand identity for all marketing materials so that a clear, distinctive image is put forth, allowing all materials to be easily identifiable with the library.

The library supports the entire GSFC community, but usage statistics and other metrics show that certain audiences need and use the library more than others. The Marketing & Outreach Team decided to focus its efforts on the heaviest users with the goal of improving their experience with the library. Key audiences at the NASA Goddard Library fall into three categories of users: scientists, engineers, and management. The goal was to target each group with outreach activities that would be pertinent to its interests. The Marketing & Outreach Team believed that focusing on the people who need the library the most and have the most influence on our long-term viability would help us toward our goal of ensuring the library's continued relevancy to GSFC.

The Library Marketing Plan drafted by the Marketing & Outreach Team guides the goals for outreach activities: to engage with the community about a product or service; to sponsor or participate in community events, raising the library's visibility in the GSFC community; to introduce the library to new GSFC employees; and to interact with customers who do not visit the library building.

These goals ensure that the GSFC community is aware of the products and services available to them through the Goddard Library. Successful implementation of outreach initiatives results in informed customers who will regularly use library products and services to work efficiently and effectively toward the mission and goals of the Goddard Space Flight Center.

II. Outreach Initiatives and Strategies

The Marketing & Outreach Team divides the types of outreach initiatives into several broad categories. Noted below are the types and the communication channels that work most effectively for each.

1. New Product Rollout

A community-wide campaign is utilized for a new product rollout (e.g. database, unified discovery service, etc.) or for a product that has been upgraded or enhanced in some way (e.g. new platform, enhanced search capabilities, etc.). In these cases, all of the available channels are used to get the word out.

2. New Service Pilot

Historically, when rolling out a new service, a proof-of-concept pilot for the service is attempted before embarking on a full-scale launch. In these cases, the focus is on individual outreach and word-of-mouth as a way to obtain feedback and gauge interest in the offering. This is done selectively by targeting specific people or work groups who may benefit most from the new service. The library director is a great resource for potential contacts who might be interested in piloting a new library service. Once the contacts are in place, individual orientations are arranged to present the new service. These contacts can often provide additional contacts who may also be interested in learning about the service.

3. Communication Channels for Online and Digital Promotion

Communication channels are selected by the needs and goals of each campaign. Some of the channels already existed, like a daily community e-mail, and some were developed by the Marketing & Outreach Team through personal contacts and creative thinking. A master list of communication channels was compiled and a template was created to aid in planning outreach campaigns.

4. Print & Digital Communications Pieces

To make the library logo easy for all to use, master templates were created for various types of promotional materials: postcards, posters, table tents, bookmarks, banners, and electronic images for use on websites, screens, and televisions. All digital and print communications pieces are created using these templates to maintain a consistent image. Creating these ahead of time ensures that all digital and print pieces can be quickly and easily recognized as coming from the library.

5. Library Website

In collaboration with the web developer, the Marketing & Outreach Team established two ways to publish content to the library website: a news item feed and a featured resource section. A select group of reference librarians decide together what to publish and when. They also have permissions to add or change content as needed. This content is used to raise awareness for new library content, products, or services, and contains links and invitations for people to comment.

6. Targeted E-mails

Targeted e-mail lists have been constructed in several different ways. Some lists are maintained center-wide, and those addresses are freely available. These are used to target specific organizations or work groups. Other lists have been compiled from e-mail information for library cardholders extracted from the integrated library system and from a daily list of new Goddard employees that the security office provides. Gaining access to the daily list of new employees took some time and patience, including multiple e-mails, several phone calls, and one in-person meeting. However, establishing the relationship with the security office was invaluable in tapping into this hard-to-gather information on new employees.

Instead of text-heavy messages, e-mails to these targeted groups feature tailored, eye-catching images with clickable links to the product and other information. Also, for a new product rollout, staff is asked to include a link to the new product in their e-mail signature blocks.

7. Center Intranet

The GSFC intranet offers a community announcement page as well a daily e-mail news digest delivered to every GSFC employee's e-mail address to post center news and announcements. As the main conduits of center news and the only established means for doing so, these channels are used frequently and extensively. As a result, information can sometimes get buried or lost in the shuffle of multiple announcements. Despite this, they remain the most effective means to reach the entire center population. New products and services are always announced via these channels.

8. Digital Signage on Center

Through observation and by establishing new relationships, the Marketing & Outreach Team has found a few other ways to get out messages about the library's products and services. There are several flat-screen televisions in front of the two Center auditoriums. The person in charge of putting content on those screens was contacted and permission was secured to post images of promotional signage. This connection is now used regularly.

At the Center-sponsored colloquia series, people often arrive early and end up sitting in the auditorium looking at a blank screen before the presenter loads his/her slides. The Marketing & Outreach Team made a request for the audiovisual staff in charge of recording the colloquia to post library promotional imagery on the auditorium screen before the beginning of each colloquia presentation. Both of these visual channels are utilized when promoting a new product.

9. Multimedia

Using Microsoft PowerPoint and TechSmith's Camtasia, the Marketing & Outreach Team creates video commercials to advertise new products. After securing permission and working with the intranet curator's schedule, videos are posted on both the library's website and on the home page of the GSFC intranet site.

10. Social Media

NASA has a closed, internal social network called Yammer. The Marketing & Outreach team monitors the conversations that take place there, participating as appropriate. Information about outreach initiatives is also disseminated through this channel. There is also a Goddard group on LinkedIn. This channel is used to post information, to engage users in conversation, or to ask for feedback about the library.

11. Flyers, Posters, and Table Tents

Most of the Center's buildings allow the hanging of posters and flyers on walls, bulletin boards, and windows. This task is coordinated with the Information Services staff so that the load is dispersed and the center can be canvassed quickly and efficiently. The three Center cafeterias also allow the library to display table tents. Permission is granted in advance via the cafeteria manager. The requests are generally accommodated.

III. Examples of Recent Outreach Initiatives

1. Mobile Librarian Service

As library products and services become more web-based, the physical library does not see as much use as it once did. In an effort to reestablish face-to-face contact with more customers, four days a week reference librarians are assigned to various buildings on the Center campus to serve as "Mobile Librarians."

The following channels are used to advertise the Mobile Librarian service: Center intranet and news bulletins; outdoor signs; news items on the library website; targeted e-mails; flyers, posters, and banners.

This program has increased the library's visibility and exposure in the Goddard community. The reference librarians have established strong relationships with many of the individuals within the buildings they visit. Being in the customer's work environment has also given them insights into customer needs and has informed the products and services the library offers.

Additionally, the Mobile Librarian venue itself is used as a channel to do additional outreach for new products or services by sending the Mobile Librarian out with postcards, signs, or even offering live demonstrations during the Mobile Librarian's shift.

2. Symposia

Special events, targeted at key audiences, help the library engage with the GSFC community. An example of this type of community event was an all-day symposium at Goddard in partnership with the publisher Elsevier.

The program's focus was collaborative research, its present state and future trends: a subject of special interest to GSFC scientists. The event explored trends in scientific collaboration; challenges to scientific collaboration, including disciplinary, regional, international, and social; tools and data sets that support collaboration, such as government guidelines, funding, etc. External speakers, mainly academic experts who publish on this topic, were brought in to share their work and provide guidelines on best practices in scientific collaboration. Goddard scientists and researchers were also identified and invited to present their experiences with scientific collaboration. Including internal speakers resonated with the GSFC community and strengthened the impact of the program.

The event was announced one month before the date and promoted in the following ways: Center intranet and news bulletins; outdoor signs; news items on the library website; targeted e-mails; invitations on internal social media channels; digital signs outside of auditoriums and on intranet homepage; flyers, posters, and banners.

3. GSFC Colloquia Series

Colloquia are offered on Center as a multi-series of lectures that take place regularly throughout the year. The colloquia are attended by a broad swath of the Goddard community, and different colloquia appeal to different groups, such as IT, scientists, engineers, and management. Specific key audiences could be represented at a given talk, making these very attractive venues for targeting various constituencies. Providing streaming access and DVD recordings of colloquia presentations for our customers has helped the library cultivate partnerships with the colloquia chairs and offer a highly valued service to the GSFC community.

Over time, we have forged partnerships not only with the colloquia chairs, who allow us to distribute literature before and after the event, and speak before the colloquia begin, but also with the audiovisual staff recording the event. Through these relationships, we have worked out an agreement where, on request, large digital promotional images are displayed on the screen in the auditorium before each event begins.

4. New Hires Outreach

Reaching out to new hires introduces new members of the GSFC community to the library's products and services. One avenue for this involves a partnership with the GSFC Human Resources Department. It distributes library promotional literature to new hires during the formal GSFC orientations. Additionally, the daily e-mail list of new hires is used to contact those people with a digital brochure. Finally, information packets that outline key products and services are stocked at the library information desk. New hires receive these when they come to get a library card or to tour the library.

IV. Evaluation

1. Customer feedback

Always striving to do an outstanding job for every customer helps create a strong relationship with users. The feedback we receive from customers bears this out. Further, it can manifest itself in positive word-of-mouth exposure and advocacy, which is the most compelling advertisement for library products and services.

Two ongoing services are in-depth searching and customized instruction. The following are some examples of feedback received by satisfied customers.

A program manager contacted the library because he needed a bibliography compiled for a NASA GSFC project, SeaWifs, that had spanned more than 20 years. He was extremely pleased with the output delivered: "Many organizations say that, but I have met precious few who actually DO it. You folks are a pleasant exception."

A senior technical writer requested an instructional session on locating and citing data sets and articles for himself and his summer intern staff. A customized instructional handout with highlights and tips for obtaining productive search results was produced, and an instructional session was conducted. The senior technical writer was impressed with the quality of the presentation. He followed up with a request for a series of additional customized instructional sessions. He sent the following feedback:

"You went beyond the call of duty, and by doing so, you made a difference in the success of this major research project ... I look forward to working with you in the future — perhaps in training summer interns next year."

These are just two examples of how providing excellent customer service with each and every customer can demonstrate the library's value to the organization and bolster the library's reputation.

2. Using Feedback to Re-Tool Outreach

We gauge reactions to our promotional efforts and then change or retool our efforts based on the feedback we receive from the community. Usually, people are asked to give us feedback either via a form on the library website or on the back of promotional postcards. We keep in mind our goals for the rollout and continue with outreach efforts until we've reached those goals.

Here is an example of how we retooled one product rollout.

The NASA Goddard Library Search (GLS), the library's brand name for the Serials Solution product Summon, was purchased for a one-year trial. As an expensive resource, strong usage for it among our users would be required to justify its ongoing cost. After the initial rollout, feedback was received via a web-based survey, e-mail, and in-person comments. However, the volume of feedback needed in order to make a decision about continuing this resource had not been achieved.

The initial GLS project plan had always included concerted, ongoing promotional efforts. After evaluating the initial reaction to GLS, it was determined that the following steps should be implemented to help increase visibility and awareness for the product:

The original design was a simple search box similar to Google. Changes to marketing/design elements included:

- Updating the slogans on the promotional pieces to emphasize that GLS is a new product
- Adding the actual feedback survey on the flip side of the promotional postcards along with a link to the online feedback form
- Identifying the product by name on the library website, adding the tagline "Try the NEW NASA Goddard Library Search," and adding "Find books, journals, eBooks, and more" to the search box itself in light gray letters that disappear as soon as text is entered

Finally, in order to strengthen the visual connection between the print pieces and the digital search box on the website, the "Search Library" button on the website was changed to match the image on all of the print promotional materials.

For ongoing, Center-wide, in-person outreach, an information table was staffed outside of upcoming colloquia presentations to offer information and live demonstrations of GLS for people before and after the colloquia events. Promotional visits were also made to Center cafeterias and at Mobile Librarian venues.

Highlights of comments received after retooling outreach:

- "It's awesome. I've used it. Can I have a postcard for a friend?"
- "...gave a favorable review of Summon. He said it's easier to search than multiple databases, and he has found what he wanted so far."
- "Tried that new Internet search (Summon). It's really good. Somebody's doing something right."
- Spoke to two people from two different generations who had tried the new tool: "I

use it every day," and "Worked well for my search. All the documents I needed came up in the search. Very pleased with it."

While the second wave of promotional efforts increased awareness, additional tactics were implemented with the specific purpose of getting more people to fill out the feedback form.

- Creating a new ad specifically seeking GLS feedback
- E-mailing digital postcards with a link to the online survey
- Announcing GLS via social media (e.g. Yammer, OpenGoddard Group on LinkedIn)
- Projecting a GLS announcement on large screen before each colloquium
- Showing a video commercial prior to colloquia presentations

In the end, over 50 feedback forms were submitted. Anecdotal feedback was also gathered in the Mobile Librarian log, in-person at Center events, and via social media. At the holiday party, someone from the IT Department told us that the Improving Center Communications Team she is on met and discussed how they could be more proactive "like the library." They said that our NASA Goddard Library Search promotional campaign inspired them to start similar marketing strategies. She said they discussed how the "library just gets out there and gets the word out!"

V. Conclusion

Outreach furthers the goals of a marketing plan and overall strategic plan for the library and ensures the viability and relevance of the library for the future. To demonstrate effectiveness, it is imperative to obtain meaningful feedback and measurements that can be shared with the library administration, the library steering committee, and the library's Program Evaluation Board. To this end, metrics are compiled and analyzed. In addition, anecdotal feedback provided via web forms, e-mail, and thank-you notes is also recorded. All of the feedback by our customers is captured in a shared folder on the library's intranet. Library staff understands the value of these stories and knows to forward them on to the managers who curate them. This story bank is invaluable when preparing reports and presentations.

A good deal of time is spent highlighting services in outreach campaigns because in recent library history, the focus has been on providing content directly to users' desktops. In effect, by making resources so seamlessly accessible, customers don't realize the library's role in delivering it.

When planning outreach, start with the background work of creating a marketing strategy, and let the rationale for your outreach activities be the goals you set out in your marketing strategy.

PART III
Finding Resources

9

Low Cost/No Cost, High Reward

Successful Programming in a Difficult Economy

Paul S. Edwards

Across the nation, public libraries have become familiar targets when cutbacks are proposed to municipal budgets and/or public service expenditures. In an age where access to information is no farther away than our fingertips, the relevance of public libraries and the necessity for bearing their cost is readily questioned. Therefore, as public library professionals, we must shepherd our libraries into the twenty-first century with a renewed sense of creativity and flexibility. It is incumbent upon today's library professionals to ensure that public libraries continue to evolve and to develop new strategies in order to survive. This chapter will discuss how one library, the Grove Hall Branch of the Boston Public Library system, has employed a unique strategy of "low cost/no cost" programming to optimize and expand its service to its community.

Striving to establish and develop partnerships and collaborative relationships is part of the daily mission at the Grove Hall Library. Conversations with stakeholders in the community, organizations in the area, and with representatives of institutional bodies are driven by an effort to demonstrate how the library can meet their needs and further their mission. Therefore, it is important to approach everyone as potential partners in programming. Always be optimistic and open minded, because you never know how a casual contact in the community may benefit your library.

Clearly, opportunities can drop out of the sky. It is, however, important to nurture and explore options on your own, with your staff, your library users, and with potential collaborators and partners. A transparent level of communication, a frank exchange of ideas, and sharing goals with potential partners will serve everyone well. Just as in any relationship, a level of trust and familiarity will go a long way toward producing positive outcomes.

The Grove Hall Branch Library has utilized a dynamic approach to programming that minimizes costs and expands program offerings to its diverse community. In the following pages, three programs conducted at the Grove Hall Branch Library will be dis-

73

cussed. Each example will show how the program was developed and how it led to the creation of other programs and invaluable connections in the community. Finally, a brief checklist of strategies and techniques for successful marketing and programming will be provided.

Adult Education and Professional Development Opportunities Open House

The Adult Education and Professional Development Opportunities Open House at the Grove Hall Library is a prime example of how a program concept can drop out of the sky and into your lap. One day a representative from a major online university came to the library to speak with staff about conducting a reach-out session at the library. It would have been easy to turn aside the offer, as public libraries typically do not allow for-profit companies to promote their businesses in the library. In an effort to be transparent, we shared this concern with the representative. We listened, however, and considered how a relationship with this organization might be developed.

Soon after our initial conversation, we were invited to visit a reach-out session that the university was hosting at a local senior housing development. In the meantime, we brainstormed and thought about how this particular relationship could benefit the library's users, particularly since a significant number of our users are non-traditional students.

According to a study conducted by Karen Antell (2004, 230), a large percentage of non-traditional students are inclined to use their local public library instead of their college library. Our experience at Grove Hall supports Antell's argument, as every day a number of non-traditional college students visit the library to study and do research. Furthermore, with an ever-present need to address the concerns of non-traditional students, job seekers, and those wishing to develop and expand their vocational skill sets, we realized that we could be on the right path to a meaningful program opportunity.

We therefore approached the university and explained to them that we could host a program, but that their role in the program would need to be as a contributor, not as the sole presenter. Couched in an "open house" format, they could have a presence at the function alongside other organizations. In addition, we requested that they contribute refreshments to the event, which they agreed to do. Our open-minded and honest approach to the university's representative brought about a productive collaboration with the library.

In the days following our discussion with the university, we approached several local colleges, nonprofit adult education organizations, and a variety of community resource concerns. By the time the Adult Education and Professional Development Open House occurred, we had nine organizations involved in the program, representing a vast array of services and opportunities that our library users could learn about and access. We also had a fine offering of refreshments for all to enjoy. In the end, the total cost to the library was less than $15.

This event has continued to provide dividends both to the Grove Hall library and its users, long after the initial event. For example, one of the organizations that participated in the open house is a local nonprofit computer training organization known as the Timothy Smith Network (TSN). Since our initial event, the TSN has used our library on several occasions to reach out to local residents to publicize their menu of programs. Hosting these informational sessions has raised the profile of our library in the community, resulted in an increase in first-time visitors, and has helped us and the TSN accomplish our missions.

We have also collaborated with other organizations in this way to disseminate information about their programs and services. Boston University is a large private university located in the city of Boston that offers several scholarships to city residents and parents of Boston Public School students. After learning about our open house, a representative from Boston University called the Grove Hall Library to see if we could work with them to publicize their scholarship offerings. Since all the scholarships are targeted to patrons in our service area, a relationship with Boston University made a lot of sense for our community and for the university. Subsequently, a handful of informational sessions were planned and conducted. As a result, a new relationship with a community stakeholder was established, and our library's users became better informed about educational resources in their community.

Local Resources: Stumbling into a Program Where You Least Expect to Find One

Reaching out to your community can open doors and opportunities that may surprise you and benefit your library. The University of Massachusetts-Boston is a major public and commuter-oriented institution. The campus is located just a few miles from the Grove Hall Library. As mentioned earlier, we serve a large number of non-traditional students, and our library has maintained an ongoing dialogue with various departments at the university.

One department at the university is named for William Joiner, a former Grove Hall neighborhood resident. Joiner was a writer and a Vietnam War veteran. Initially, we approached the William Joiner Center for the Study of War and Social Consequences in order to explore the possibility of obtaining an exhibit to commemorate Veterans Day. A representative at the center offered to loan us a collection of photographs of the only African-American Women's Army Corps (WAC) unit in World War II to be stationed overseas in Europe during the war.

The 6888th Central Postal Directory WAC Battalion photo exhibit became a powerful and popular feature at Grove Hall. Visitors to the library often comment about the photos and express their gratitude to us for providing this extraordinary educational and historically significant exhibit. All of this was made possible by reaching out to and visiting a relatively small department at a large university. If our relationship with the Joiner Center had only yielded the 6888th WAC Battalion exhibit, it would be considered a success. Yet we were in for an unexpected and pleasant surprise.

During the initial visit with the Joiner Center's director, he mentioned several events and activities that were in development that might offer collaborative opportunities for the Joiner Center and our library. He mentioned how the Joiner Center had recently established an award known as the Grace Paley Visiting Writer Award. In 2010, the recipient was a renowned poet/writer from New York City, Aracelis Girmay.

Shortly after providing the photo exhibit, the Joiner Center notified us that Aracelis

Girmay wanted to visit the Grove Hall Library. It was an offer that we happily accepted. Parenthetically, this opportunity was in fact the result of follow-up calls and maintaining a line of dialogue with the Joiner Center. Opportunities such as this can dissipate unless you are diligent in maintaining the relationships you have built.

Aracelis Girmay's visit to the library was a resounding success. Girmay read poetry and conducted a writer's workshop for a group of students from a nearby middle school. The Joiner Center's association with the library allowed the Center to fulfill its mission of offering educational programming to the community. At the same time, our library's users benefited mightily from Aracelis Girmay's program, and a simple query about a Veterans Day exhibit led to a program that enriched the lives of 40 middle school students in our neighborhood.

Colleges are fertile ground for library programming endeavors. In many cases, local colleges are committed to providing community service programming to civic groups, schools, and public libraries. The Grove Hall Library is fortunate to be located in a city with many institutions of higher education. Networking with local colleges and universities can lead to unexpected program opportunities, and with today's technology, the range and scope of collaborative efforts can bridge distances and geographic challenges (Edwards 2008, 38–42). If your library is located near a college or university, or if your community is served by a college's distance learning program, do not hesitate to view these institutions as potential programming partners.

Both of the programs offered by the Joiner Center came to the library free of charge. Our profile at the university was enhanced as a result of the programs, and this new relationship has led to discussions about program ideas with other departments at the university. In one instance, we are developing program concepts with one of the university's departments that will lead to a writing workshop for our young adults. We are also developing outreach/program opportunities with another department that will serve the higher educational pursuits of non-traditional students and seniors. This brand of program development can take time, and often feels slow and cumbersome. Do not be discouraged. Patience and persistence will pay off and demonstrate to your stakeholders that the library is a reliable resource in the community.

Often, your library will be the first organization to contact a given organization or university department. They may have no idea what library programming looks like, or the benefits that they will realize in partnering with your library. Take time to explore programming ideas that will be mutually beneficial for you and your would-be partner.

Transform Your Library with Art

In April 2009, the Grove Hall Library moved into a new facility. Soon after moving, we realized that our new building was wonderful and spacious; however, it really needed something extra to enliven the atmosphere. As such, we asked to be put in touch with alumni or current students at several local colleges who might be interested in exhibiting their work.

We encountered a few dead ends at first, but the concept eventually took hold with one school and with some individual artists. In the end, the effort proved to be wildly successful. Once word began to spread, it only took a few days for e-mails and phone calls so start trickling in from artists as far away as New Hampshire, Texas, Michigan, and Connecticut, as well as just across town. One of the artists is an American who is currently living in Japan. We quickly learned that there are a number of outstanding artists who are ready, willing, and happy to exhibit their work. Offering artists an opportunity to exhibit helps them professionally and helps to build their resume. It can also transform the look and feel of your library (Davis 2001, 3–8).

Within a matter of weeks, we had our first exhibit up and running. We soon had an exhibition schedule, lining up art exhibits through the next eight months. In the meantime, other artists approached us to inquire about arranging a timeframe for them to show as well.

Our exhibits have featured paintings, photography, sculptures, and even interactive furniture, plinths, and creative lighting devices that our young adults used while reading and hanging out in the library. These exhibits create a dynamic atmosphere in our library space, and an opportunity for the library to attract art fans who might otherwise not come to the library. One of our artists, for instance, shipped his pieces in from Michigan, and several others were happy to travel hundreds of miles round-trip to bring their work to the library.

Surprising and intriguing developments have arisen as a result of this endeavor. For example, we are currently discussing program concepts with artists who have expressed an interest in working with local youth on art projects.

At times, even your library's environment can inspire creativity. While discussing exhibit options with one photographer, she was impressed by the number of young people who were visiting the library. She suggested that we explore and develop an "interactive exhibit" that our local youth could create. Moreover, she expressed interest in working with our library's young adults, offering advice on mediums of their choosing in order to build an exhibit for the library. Working with talented people may yield creative concepts that will serve your library well.

A few of our exhibitors have even donated pieces for permanent display at the library. This gesture of kindness and generosity further illustrates the positive energy and feelings that can be generated by this brand of programming.

Finally, hosting art exhibits generates free publicity. Local newspapers, online publications, and alumni reports have mentioned our art exhibits. Professional artists and their associated communities also promote their exhibits. All of this serves the library's effort to be visible in the community and beyond. Advertising art exhibits will also liven up your Facebook page and bulletin board displays. Given the fact that this programming effort has come at no cost to the library, we could not be more pleased with the results.

Low Cost/No Cost Strategies and Approaches

Today's front-line library professionals have a lot on their plates. We are all tasked with stretching our resources in dramatic fashion, sometimes just to meet our basic needs. The workplace challenges that we face are not unique to libraries; organizations in every community are also trying to stretch their budgets. Sometimes they need libraries for assistance with outreach and marketing. Therefore, good old-fashioned networking in your neighborhood, discussing the issues that impact your neighborhood with local stakeholders, or just visiting the shops and businesses surrounding your facility are ways to promote your library and to discover program opportunities. The resources of public libraries are marketable commodities, a fact that may be overlooked by people and organizations in your community unless you identify and present those opportunities to them.

At the Grove Hall Library, for example, we have a local human services agency that uses the library as a meeting place for one-on-one sessions with their clients. One day, after discussing the challenges that seniors and their caregivers face in finding services for loved ones facing dementia-related disorders, we found common ground with this organization.

Soon a program was developed that involved our library hosting a representative from a social service agency who provided information for caregivers. In this case, the representative answered questions, listened to people's concerns, and assisted in connecting them to local service options and care providers in the area. Unfortunately, this particular event was not well attended. Keep in mind that robust attendance is not the only indicator of successful programming: those who did attend this event gathered information that will serve them and their loved ones well.

It is critical to remember some basic rules when it comes to developing low cost/no cost programs at your library:

1. Be proactive and always be alert for opportunities to promote your library.
2. Emphasize the three most marketable commodities of the library: your facility, your resources, and your mission.
3. Be open-minded when working with stakeholders.
4. Whenever possible, create opportunities to speak to people about their needs and how your library can work with them to further their organization's mission. Remember, the organizations operating in your neighborhood more than likely reflect the needs of that specific neighborhood.
5. Finally, be sure to follow through with stakeholders. These days, with hectic schedules and ever-increasing workloads, it is easy to lose track of your community connections. Drop a line, drop in, but do not drop off of the radar.

Conclusion

Today's public libraries face a myriad of challenges and obstacles. Maintaining relevance in a culture of ever-evolving technology and shrinking budgets puts stress on public libraries and their ability to provide robust programming for their users. Thus, it is critical to be agile and innovative in order to thrive in today's challenging environment.

In the final analysis, there is no absolute science to providing low cost/no cost programming. Getting to know your library's stakeholders, networking in your area, and talking to people about your library and its gifts are the lynchpins to success. Strategies and approaches will vary depending on the personality of your library and its staff. Also, not every effort or concept will succeed or work the way you planned it on paper, but do not get discouraged. Once you enjoy a few successes, the energy and momentum will energize you and your library.

WORKS CITED

Antell, Karen. 2004. "Why do College Students Use Public Libraries? A Phenomenological Study." *Reference and User Services Quarterly* 43: 227–236.

Davis, Kathy. 2001. "Murals in Mississippi Libraries: Bringing Communities and Art Together." *Mississippi Libraries* 65 (1): 3–8.

Edwards, Paul S. 2008. "Library Service in the Lower Mississippi Delta Region: Issues and Opportunities." *Rural Libraries* 28 (2): 37–51.

10

Marketing Small
and Rural Public Libraries

MICHELLE A. MCINTYRE *and* MELINDA TANNER

Small and rural libraries really are a community's best-kept secret. Excellent services and resources often go unnoticed because libraries tend to market to their users and not their communities. Marketing to the entire community leads to long-term development opportunities as well as sustainability. It's time for libraries to tell their secret, and tell it to everyone.

Some small or rural libraries understandably feel they do not possess the skills, time, or funds to market and advertise. Partnerships between public libraries and businesses are somewhat unusual in rural areas. However, building mutually beneficial business partnerships will assist in the library's efforts to market and advertise. A public library can be successful at building business partnerships if they connect with as many individuals and businesses throughout the community as possible. These partnerships can result in free advertising and sponsorship for events and services, which in turn can lead to more connections and sponsors. Even simple gestures like sending thank-you notes can end up being as effective as formal advertisement. Tools such as these, as well as other low-cost ideas, allow public libraries to successfully market and advertise at minimal to no costs.

Marketing and Connecting

What does marketing mean in the twenty-first century? Marketing equals connecting! Connect your library to your community. The worst thing you can do is no marketing at all. Although it may seem overwhelming, especially if you are the only staff member of a small community library, marketing is not as hard as you think.

What are you trying to accomplish with marketing? Think of marketing as identifying customers and potential customers, giving them what they need or want, and creating repeat customers. The initial goal is to keep them coming back, but the ultimate goal is for them to tell others about how well your library has met their needs. Word of mouth is still a tried-and-true way to get the word out, but do not rely on it as the only way.

Work your community. Out of sight does mean out of mind. Even in a small town, there are people who will say, "I didn't know the library did that!" or worse yet, "We have a library?" If your library exists in a vacuum, then that may indeed be the case: out of sight, out of mind. In a small community, the library is most often the only game in town. Do not just sit back and wait for people to walk through your doors. Be where you are least expected. Know what is happening in your community, and make the library a part of it. Even the smallest of communities have a ballpark; serve lemonade after a ballgame. That is the last place people will expect to see the "library lady." Have a few tricks up your sleeve. Inform the community's organizations if they ever need a speaker that you would be happy to oblige.

Keep ready-to-go program ideas on hand, and take advantage of an opportunity that presents itself. Everyone knows that a quiet library one minute can be overflowing with kids the next. Have a card file of ideas ready to go for "drop in" programs. This is an opportunity to conduct a spontaneous story time. The kids will have a memorable experience at the library and the overwhelmed grandmother who brought them in will be your biggest fan and not hesitate to tell others about the library.

Connect with your community's school district. Establish a professional relationship with the schools' librarians and reading specialists. Believe it or not, there are actually school districts out there that consider their community's public library as an "extension" of the district. They value the library as a vital resource and location for their students both after school and in the summer.

Some of the most overlooked marketing tools are the people around you, the original "social network." This includes groups you assist, groups that meet in the library, local businesses you have helped with land maps or historical research, or a local attorney searching old newspapers. Everyone who walks into your library is a potential spokesperson, good or bad. Make sure it is good — consistently! People also include your staff (if you are fortunate enough to have any) and library volunteers (including board members). Collect data on your board members. Find out where they go to church, what their interests or hobbies are, what clubs and organizations they belong to, where they work, and any special talents. Board members are your advocates and can market your library to people and in places you may never have imagined. The same is true for library staff or volunteers. Know their likes, dislikes, connections, interests, and hobbies. A quirky pastime may turn into a wonderful marketing opportunity for your library. A staff member who happens to be a part of the local Polar Bear Club is one example. Build a marketing campaign around that club's annual plunge. You just never know until you try!

Staff members at small libraries are also the original "Amazon"— they know who is visiting and how often. They know visitors by name and what and how much they are reading. They can anticipate and recommend what authors or genres users might want to read next and in what format. Polite, attentive staff members are the key to happy customers. Happy customers are repeat customers, and will spread the word about the library. Keep doing what you do best!

Other people you should not ignore — community "celebrities." Find them and connect with them. Use members of your community for programming: mayor, sheriff, firefighter, doctor, dentist, etc. Branch out into the greater community. Find a member of the National Guard, a farmer, a coal miner, a beautician, or a quilter. What about famous ex-residents? With the Internet, the world has indeed become smaller. If they still have a connection to the community, find it and connect with them. Invite them into the library during their next visit to read, tell a story, or talk about growing up in the community. While they may donate time or money to your library, they could also lead to bigger sponsors.

Preparation for Sponsorship Meetings

Small and rural public libraries rarely employ development officers. Directors, staff, and board members fall into the category of those having to make "the ask." Approaching a business for sponsorship is not as easy as saying "are you willing to support the public library with a donation?" Businesses and corporations want to know what they are getting in return for their donation. Knowing how to approach a sponsor or corporation for an annual donation or gift will secure financial returns for the library.

One of the easiest ways to identify potential sponsors is by picking up the local newspaper. Read every headline and article that may have the slightest possibility of impacting your library. Pay particular attention to the business pages, Chamber of Commerce notes, and inserts advertising vendor fairs. Another excellent place to gather information about potential sponsors is Chamber of Commerce websites, which often have a section about members and their contact information. When looking at these sources, take note of businesses in your service area or businesses you personally patronize. Ask board members and volunteers to do the same. Building connections can make it easier when approaching potential sponsors or donors.

Once your list of potential sponsors is compiled and connections are made, it is time to start planning. When planning for your meeting, do your homework. Study the business. Learn its owners and mission statement. Ask yourself how the business can benefit from a public library partner. Research the types of organizations the business has sponsored and supported in the past. Pay attention to where and at what level they have provided sponsorship. Determine if the business has a policy concerning sponsorships of nonprofits. Some larger corporations have their own foundations or already sponsor a national nonprofit.

You are now ready to make an appointment. Locate an individual with connections to your library and the business you wish to approach. Allow that person to make the initial contact and schedule an appointment. The representative and library staff member should go to the appointment together. You will be given a limited amount of time to present the library's case. Be prepared and confident when making "the ask." Provide a brief introduction about the library and its services. Identify why the library needs their support and be prepared to discuss different categories and levels of sponsorships. Provide examples of how the public library has invested in the community. Mention other nonprofits similar to yours that they have sponsored in the past. It is your job to provide the potential sponsor with information they need to make a decision. Explain why their investment is crucial to the success of the public library. Also, present them with a Sponsorship Information Packet, which would include the following:

- Information about the library, including contact information
- A document outlining sponsorship levels

- An outline of recognition for their sponsorship
- Deadline for monetary sponsorship for programs, events, or prizes

There can be potential drawbacks to sponsorships. Be cautious if the sponsor asks the library to do something that is not possible. Never agree to something the library cannot produce; politely explain why and suggest alternatives. Secure monetary sponsorships prior to the event. Never rely on the promise that the money is coming. In some cases, it never does. Normally, you will not encounter problems with corporate sponsorships. But if you do, be prepared to say no, thank them for their time, and walk away.

Fundraisers, Friendraisers, and Signature Events

Fundraisers, friendraisers, and signature events can produce positive results for a public library. Fundraisers are just that: a way to raise money. Friendraisers are less about raising money and more about raising awareness of the public library's needs. Annual signature events are used to build relationships and goodwill in the community with the possibility of raising substantial funding. When these events are planned well, they are fun for attendees and yield benefits for the public library.

Planning is key to any successful event. Fundraisers and friendraisers can take weeks or months to plan. A signature event can take several months to a year. Each event has some basic planning and questions to consider:

- Why are you having the event? To raise funds or raise awareness?
- What kind of event are you having? Is it a small or large gathering? Is it open to the public or are there tickets/invitations?
- Where and when will it take place? Library or off site?
- How many volunteers will be needed?
- Does the event require permits, licenses, or insurance?

Problems may occur during the event. Try to anticipate potential problems and have a well-thought-out backup plan in place. It is imperative that your guests do not know if anything goes wrong. If possible, take discussions about the problem to another area in the facility. This will allow you to openly discuss a quick remedy. Always remember it may be a distressing situation to you, but if your guests never learn of the problem, their evening will not have been impacted.

Events can be costly. For a public library, spending money to raise money is not something we are typically comfortable doing. Paying for the necessities of an event always presents a challenge. However, with innovative thinking and planning, costs can be minimized. These events lend themselves easily to sponsorship. Businesses are willing to donate items in return for recognition, free advertising, and the added opportunity to be seen as a library supporter.

A public library facility is not always the appropriate place to host an event. It may lack space, parking, or functionality. Renting a venue can be a learning experience. Be prepared to be surprised at the items you will need to rent and the cost for each. Ask for any venue rules and regulations and a price list. Be sure to have a signed contract listing all details.

Some things to consider when planning an event of this nature are:

- Venue
- Media advertising: television, radio, print
- Printing of tickets, brochures, and invitations
- Technology and sound system
- Tables and chairs
- Table linens and settings
- Food and beverages
- Centerpieces
- Entertainment
- Door prizes
- Gifts for emcee and special guests

Other considerations include sponsor recognition, signage, and nametags. Sponsors should have business cards attached to donated items. Include corporate sponsors in any advertising or signage. Recognize table sponsors with tent cards bearing their corporate logo. Include a list of event sponsors on signage welcoming guests. Library board members, staff, and committee members should wear nametags noting their position in the organization and be seated among the guests so they can answer questions concerning the event and the library. Throughout the night, announce sponsors by name and thank them for their contributions. Announce a general thank you to everyone at the end, and, if possible, say how much funding has been contributed. Post signage on the doors at the end of the event that thanks attendees for supporting the public library. Always remember: you can never say "thank you" enough.

Preparation is the most important aspect of any successful fundraising venture. Using these methods will help increase not only funding, but committed partners who, over time, will become more invested in the library. Hard work in the beginning stages will pay long-term rewards in the end.

Formal Advertising

Radio, television, and billboard ads are used to draw the public's attention. Ad representatives from media outlets are willing to meet with any potential customer. Be upfront when calling to make an appointment with ad representatives. Tell them you are from a library and would like to discuss any advertising services available to nonprofit organizations.

In preparation for the meeting, know your budget limitations. Be prepared to provide representatives with any information that is to be in the ad. It is also important to have a general idea how you want the ad to look or sound. When meeting with ad representatives, it is always good to discuss the following:

- Nonprofit pricing package
- How long the ad will run
- Costs of production and graphic design
- Which type of media to use to reach target audience: television/radio, newspaper/magazine, or others, such as billboards

- For television and radio, discuss the time of day your ad will run and its length in seconds or minutes
- For newspaper or magazine ads, know the size of the ad, inside or back page, color or black and white
- For billboards, know the size and location, lighted or non-lighted

Even if the library does not have an advertising budget, there are a variety of ways you can advertise. Some media outlets offer a small percentage of free advertising to non-profits. The free price tag is often dependent on the type of organization, nature of the event, and who you know. Determine if the company has a policy concerning free advertising. If the ad representatives do not know, kindly ask them to inquire with their company. Remember it never hurts to ask.

If you wish to have a billboard ad at low cost, get in your car and take a drive through your service area. Take note of billboards that are outdated or blank. Record the current advertisement, location of the billboard, and note the company listed as the contact for advertising. Contact the advertising firm and discuss your interest in placing a billboard ad. Tell them the location of the billboard, and mention you noticed it was outdated or blank. They may consider giving you a reduced or free ad to have an updated, appealing space that may bring some new attention to the billboard's location.

Sponsorships are another approach to free advertising. Often, media outlets are excited to provide their clients with the opportunity to support a local library. Discuss with your ad representative the possibility of having the library ad paid for by a sponsor. Some media outlets may offer special pricing for sponsored ads. Be prepared to present a list of potential sponsors. Start with businesses or individuals with which the library already has an established relationship: board member and patron business owners, and businesses you patronize professionally or personally. There is a greater chance of success by starting with businesses that already have a vested interest in the library.

In return for paying for the ad, the sponsor has the opportunity to include their tagline and logo. Commonly used tag lines include: brought to you by —, this ad sponsored by —, and proud supporter of your public library. The sponsor may not require anything in return for their support. However, the library could be asked to have their business cards on hand for patrons, pass out coupons, or post flyers. It is a good idea to have policies in place addressing these requests prior to accepting a sponsorship. Sponsorships are a win-win for both parties. The library obtains the attention they are seeking and the sponsor feels they have supported a community service.

Thank You and Acknowledgments

It is imperative for public libraries to keep themselves in the minds of their supporters. One way to do this is by thanking and acknowledging the people and businesses that have made an impact. Sometimes small gestures can set into motion a chain of events that provides a flood of support. A handwritten note, acknowledgment, or return support can make a difference in the success of your library.

Often we forget how important it is to take a minute and say "thank you." Every day, people feel overlooked for doing what they are asked to do, or for volunteering their service, time, or money. This is the time for the all-important thank-you note, which serves as an acknowledgment of how much you appreciate what has been done for the library. Handwritten thank-you notes and acknowledgments go a long way in establishing relationships, strengthening partnerships, or keeping in touch with business partners and colleagues. If you are unsure about sending a thank-you, ask yourself—would I take the time to thank them in person? If the answer is yes, take the time and follow up with a handwritten note. Send thank-you notes to:

- Colleagues who met with you to discuss an issue affecting your library
- Someone who made a special effort for your library
- Persons or businesses that made an important contribution to your event
- Facilities that offered you meeting space
- People attending to the details to make a library event successful

Train yourself to be on the lookout for information about your colleagues and business partners. Make a mental or handwritten note when you learn of the accomplishments of colleagues and business partners. Send them congratulatory notes. By sending a congratulatory note, you are recognizing the accomplishment and also showing the person or business you have an interest in their venture. Learn about accomplishments in:

- Local newspapers
- Newsletters of local organizations
- School district newsletters
- Chamber of Commerce websites

Also acknowledge any accomplishments of the library and its staff in local publications. This serves a dual purpose: not only are the staff members' achievements being highlighted and appreciated, but the public is made aware of the latest news at the library.

Public libraries interested in building lasting relationships need to take the time to support and recognize their business partners. Patronize businesses that sponsor events. If a local restaurant sponsors the coffee and dessert at a library event, hold a volunteer appreciation event at their business. Volunteer at events sponsored by your business partners. Library personnel can help with set up, staff sign-in tables, or man the punch bowl. Offer to staff information tables at vendor fairs for your business partners. Tell attendees about the commitment the business has made to the public library.

Thinking Thrifty

Do you have a brand? If not, get one! Even a library mascot works as a brand. Keep an open mind to branding opportunities. Something as simple as a flamingo may open new opportunities for getting the word out about your library. Not every brand is as fun as a flamingo, but branding is a way to create energy in and around your community. Sometimes you luck into a brand, such as a library located in an old train station. Create a noticeable brand and put it on everything: letterhead, bookmarks, book bags, stickers, etc.

You do not need to purchase expensive software or technology in order to market. Take advantage of cheap or free resources, such as Tech Soup (www.techsoup.org). Utilize social media. Facebook and YouTube are ways to market your services to a tech-savvy audience. You no longer need to be a "techie" to maintain a webpage. Anyone can learn to post events and pictures to a website. Keep an online presence at all times. There is a new generation that knows no other form of communication. It is how you reach them. Do not think you have to know every social medium; pick one and master it. Get a library kid to show you how. And, whatever you do, do not forget to capture it in pictures! Take pictures at every event, of an ordinary day at the library, or of new items or displays. Nothing tells the library's story better. Pictures are a great way to market the library's services. Pictures put a face to the services.

Borrow ideas that have worked for others. The Internet is a great resource for "visiting" other libraries and organizations without leaving your chair. Visit library websites, other nonprofits, and even corporate giants. Ideas can be adapted for the smaller community. When you are in other towns, visit libraries: pick up flyers and brochures, and talk to the librarians. Marketing is hot these days. Read books by gurus in the field. Pay attention to what successful groups/organizations are doing to market their services/products.

Marketing your library cannot be done with a standard formula, such as "do this, then that." What works in one community will not necessarily work in another. Also be careful in assuming that certain ideas will not work. Ideas that did not work 20 years ago may be just what you need today. Be open-minded and flexible. Learn to recognize opportunities to market the library, and do not be afraid to use a current trend as a catalyst for marketing. Remember, it all boils down to making connections and showing appreciation. Oh, and thank you!

Marketing Our Library
Through Charitable Causes

ANNA ERCOLI SCHNITZER

In these days of flattened budgets and heightened expectations, when libraries seek to provide patrons with media in both old and new formats, librarians are always looking for novel, inexpensive ways to market themselves. In striving for an original, even unique method of making itself a visible presence in the community, the University of Michigan's Taubman Health Sciences Library (HSL), formerly known as Taubman Medical Library, began taking an active role in charitable causes. Although specific metrics in this type of broad-based enterprise are difficult to obtain, we believe that we have received sufficient informal acknowledgments to reveal that through our efforts we have developed a positive image for the library both inside and outside of our university.

Approximately five years ago, our library was fortunate enough to be the recipient of an administrative change of vision, a much more expansive and far-reaching one than had been in place previously, and one that allowed us to pursue a number of unusual and previously unaccustomed activities for an academic library. We believe that over time, in a low-key, almost-subliminal way, our library's name has become closely associated with a large number of charitable causes, thus presenting a positive image to our community.

Below is a list of some possible charitable efforts that your library can be involved with, some examples of how we accomplished the particular activities that we ourselves undertook, and results that we have observed along the way.

Establish Relationships with Community Organizations Already Involved in Charity Work

Eyeglass Recycling for the Lions Club

One major charitable opportunity came into play for us when we began to collaborate on a continuous basis with the Ann Arbor Host Lions Club, a well-established local organization of some 100 members (www.annarborlions.org).

A formal process was put into place whereby one of our librarians would post regular notices in "The Hospital Bulletin" asking hospital employees to send old spectacles to the librarian by campus mail. There is also an occasional message published in "The Library Newsletter." In addition, a box provided by the Lions Club was placed in the library foyer for eyeglasses to be deposited by walk-in patrons. Recently, the coordinator of the internal hospital website offered to feature the announcement on the health system intranet as well.

In 2009, the Ann Arbor Host Lions Club proudly announced that it had collected 100,000 pairs of glasses from the local area. Seventeen large packing boxes full of those spectacles came through the Taubman Health Sciences Library, which is continuing to be a collection point for eyeglasses. In recent months, used hearing aids are also being collected.

The librarian who helped with the collection process and the library director were invited to attend an annual celebratory luncheon hosted by the Lions Club where the members showed their gratitude for the library's assistance. In addition, the librarian was invited to a luncheon/meeting where the keynote speaker described the biannual distribution of eyeglasses abroad.

In addition to contributing to humanitarian values, we believe that our library's participation in this intense recycling effort helps market our library internally to the contributors of the eyeglasses and to anyone who takes part in this effort. Any time a potential patron sees the library's name in a request for recycled eyeglasses or any time someone sends in an old pair or two, there will be a positive association with our library. For example, a coordinator in the University Hospital's Division of Gastroenterology in the Department of Internal Medicine wrote: "*Thank you for organizing such a great cause here at the U! I'm always happy to donate to things like this, and even more happy to find a home for something I cannot use.*"

While many opticians' and ophthalmologists' offices and other venues also collect and recycle eyeglasses, we at Taubman Health Sciences Library are happy to do our part and, in the process, lend our library's name to this worthwhile project. Recycling eyeglasses was our library's first and, so far, longest-lasting exercise in marketing itself via charitable efforts.

Another very positive aspect of the charitable activities we engage in is that the publicity we use is free. In addition to the notices that we place in our internal university publications, we take the opportunity to use online social media such as Facebook and Twitter to communicate with the community in general, which, again, costs the library nothing but a few minutes' time plus just a little extra effort. Our reward is an enhanced public image and another reminder to our patrons that the library is here to serve a variety of patron needs.

Provide Assistance to Non–Mainstream Organizations in Low-Key Ways

Donations for Women's Safe House and Domestic Violence Projects

Our library staff decided that there was a need to show our concern for women in crisis. We put out a call for sample-sized containers of soaps and shampoos like the ones found in hotels. We acquired quite a number of these by sending out our usual notices to our employees and by placing a drop box for these items inside the library front foyer for people who chose to bring them in person.

Cell Phone Recycling

For a period of time, along with requesting eyeglasses, the library asked for cell phones to be donated to the local women's shelter. We did receive quite a number of these, which we proceeded to donate; however, shortly afterwards, we were informed that most of the cell phones could not be used because only the very latest versions would work, and therefore the rest had to be discarded. There were still a few local electronics stores that would accept cell phones to be sent to the Special Olympics, but, again, only the most recent phones were desirable. Consequently, when this discovery was made, we stopped requesting used cell phones and turned to collecting items that would not become obsolete so rapidly. Not everything will work out exactly as you want it to, and this particular project was a learning experience for us in that regard.

Coordinate Your Library's Activities with Established or Ongoing Projects

Book Donations

Several years ago, all of our university libraries were asked by the University Chapter of the Golden Key International Honor Society to assist in gathering used or discarded books for Better World Books (www.betterworldbooks.com). Founded in 2002 by three individuals at the University of Notre Dame, this business prides itself on environmental and social responsibility with a goal of enhancing literacy by taking old books and selling them to help fund literacy projects around the world.

The Better World Books collection was only a one-time event at our library, and it occurred some time ago; however, much more recently we received a message from a dental student at the UM School of Dentistry who was eager to obtain books for children waiting to be seen in the school's pediatric dentistry clinic. We posted a notice in our hospital newsletter and circulated an announcement to our staff about it. In just three days, there were three boxes full of children's picture and storybooks. These were picked up by the dental student and delivered to the pediatric dentistry clinic.

In the past, our library has also served as a collection point for new and gently used books for the Giving Library, which serves young patients at Mott Children's Hospital. The children receive these books at their bedside from volunteers who distribute them Monday through Thursday evenings. The Giving Library provides donors with a wish list of the most popular books, including storyboard books for babies, picture books, popular teen books, sports books, and books in languages other than English.

Gift of Life

Another activity that our library has been involved with for the past year is working with and coordinating the Gift of Life for the University of Michigan libraries as part of the Michigan Organ and Tissue Donation Program. We set up a table in a central area of the reference room, provided some small incentives such as hard candies to attract patrons to the table, and when they approached, inquired whether they were interested in signing up to be a donor of an organ. If patrons agreed, we gave them instructions about how to apply for a special sticker for their driver's license. We also advised out-of-state individuals about how to apply to their own state driver's licensing bureau.

Combining an Environmental and a Charitable Activity

In collaboration with the University of Michigan Procurement Services and Plant Operations, we have an ongoing project called Recycle Write. It is sponsored by an outside company called TerraCycle that takes used and/or useless writing utensils such as pens, pencils, and markers. They refit them for potential reuse and provide $.02 to our University's Mott Children's Hospital for each recycled writing implement. We have a box in the library foyer to hold these items, and every so often one of the librarians reminds the staff to recycle rather than throw away worn-out pens and pencils.

Take Advantage of Opportunities Tied in with Staff Members' Hobbies or Special Interests

Mittens and Scarves for KnitWits

Since members of the library staff probably have a multitude of hobbies or special interests, we thought that we could tap into those as well. One year, as a result of one person's love of knitting, other library staff members (both experienced and novice knitters) spent a number of consecutive lunch hours participating in and assisting KnitWits. This is a group of University of Michigan faculty, staff, students, alumni, and caring friends who create warm wearable goods from donated yarn and fleece for distribution to a wide variety of charitable groups, primarily in the northern United States. Volunteers work with various materials to make around 3,000 warm, wearable items each year. For example, one winter, some 2,535 items were distributed to men, women, and children with HIV/AIDS living in Detroit, Chicago, and New York City; to Hmong and Somali refugee children living in St. Paul, MN; to South Asian women touched by violence and living in New York City; to poverty-stricken families living in rural Appalachian communities; to children on Chippewa and Sioux Reservations in MI and SD; to homeless adults and kids living in Detroit, Atlanta, Baltimore, and Boston; and to at-risk youth living in Detroit, Chicago, and New York City. Our lunch-hour knitters created colorful mittens from donated yarn, and those staff members who found mittens too difficult to make created scarves cut out of donated fleece.

Valentines for Sick Children

Another librarian usually brings in a stack of cute Valentine's Day cards for the children at nearby Mott Children's Hospital. We sign them, and someone volunteers to deliver them to the ChildLife Program at the hospital. This same librarian also regularly creates origami figures out of colorful paper and presents them to the ChildLife Program to be distributed to the hospitalized children to play with. Again, this charitable opportunity came about because of one individual's special interest in pursuing it, but it was taken on as a staff project.

Collecting Jewelry for Kenyan Wheelchairs

Two years ago, because of another staff member's particular interest, we collaborated with Ten Thousand Villages, a store in Ann Arbor that provides fair income to Third World artisans by marketing their handicrafts and telling their stories in North America. The connection was made because one of the library staff is connected with a group involved with disability issues. When she found out about this special project, she alerted the library, and we began to collect costume jewelry from friends and colleagues to be sold at a fair. The proceeds were intended to purchase wheelchairs for disabled artisans in Kenya. By doing our usual advertising to our university colleagues, we accumulated both big and small pieces of jewelry, enough to fill a huge jar, from generous people around the university and the community.

The sale, called "Only Jewelry," was organized by the store, held during the summer at a nearby church (Grace Bible Church on South Maple Road), and all told, brought in nearly $9,000 to be spent for those much-needed wheelchairs in Kenya. Our library's name became better known in the community through this activity. Furthermore, this was an exciting project that we would willingly be associated with the next time the store sponsors it.

Be Alert for World Events That Call for Special, Swift Action

Peru

Occasionally, there is a special call for immediate action. For example, we participated in a last-minute collaborative effort with the University Department of Biological Chemistry and the University Global Reach unit in responding to an unexpected cold front in Peru. We advertised in the usual online media for items. Employees and students responded very quickly, and we filled a very large box and dozens of large bags with donated warm clothes and blankets. The Executive Director of Project Suyana (the group that collected and distributed the donations to Peruvians) contacted us directly to see if we would be willing to put a collection box outside the library. This illustrates that Taubman Library is becoming known both as a reliable team player and a central collection point.

Haiti

Another disaster necessitating prompt action was the earthquake in the country of Haiti. It inspired a campus-wide effort to collect small personal items and clothing for inhabitants who had been heavily impacted by the earthquake. Numerous bags filled with goods were gathered in the library for Haiti. We were confident that these items would reach Haiti because some of our medical students planned to deliver them in person.

Be Aware of Ongoing Local Relief Projects

The Detroit Project

Over a number of years, the library has supported the Detroit Project, a holiday seasonal event that involves collecting warm clothing and nonperishable food for needy groups and individuals in the Detroit area. The organizers provide the library with a barrel to be filled, and we are quite successful at filling it. This is the announcement we send out:

> The Detroit Project, partnering with West Outer Drive United Methodist Church and various UM schools and student groups, is collecting clothes, winter gear, and non-perishable food. A collection box is located just inside the front inner doors of Taubman Medical Library. Collection date is through November 20th. For further information see: www.thedp.org.

Volunteer to Serve as a Drop-Off Point for Other Projects

Neighbor-to-Neighbor Clothing Drive

Every year in late September, the main library of our university sponsors a recycled clothing drive that our more specialized library also takes a role in. We always offer to serve as an additional drop-off point for warm winter clothes and blankets for the homeless and other needy people in the community in preparation for cold weather.

Michigan Harvest Gathering Time

The library has supported Michigan Harvest Gathering Time for the past five or six years. This is a collaborative effort with the University Health Systems, the Michigan Health and Hospital Association, and Palace Sports & Entertainment (home of the Detroit Pistons Basketball Team). It has the goal of stopping hunger and improving the health of Michigan community members. Although this undertaking is carried out on a statewide basis, our library is specifically partnered with the Patient Food and Nutrition Services of the University of Michigan Health System. Cans and packages of non-perishable foods are gathered and held for two weeks, at which time a representative comes to pick them up for distribution to regional food banks. Our local food bank is Food Gatherers, which is an arm of Zingerman's Delicatessen, a well-known local eatery that collects food for the needy all year.

Sponsor-a-Family Holiday Project

Another seasonal goodwill project that the library has been associated with for the past five years is a local one in which staff members volunteer to contribute either gift cards, money, or presents to members of a needy family that has been anonymously assigned to them. This activity is a collaboration with SERVE, a University of Michigan student group, as well as several community organizations. There is a required minimum of $50 to be spent on each individual supported, and our library usually chooses to support a family of five. We are provided by the organizers with a wish list for the holiday season from the family and try to adhere as much as possible to it. Along with toys for the children and household goods and clothes for the family, we have given such practical items as bus tokens, grocery gift cards, and gasoline vouchers. The library staff members have been generous every year since the beginning of our affiliation with Sponsor-a-Family, and there is a wonderful feeling of satisfaction about taking part in this event. We look forward to participating every year.

The Ruth Ellis Center

Another local charitable effort resulted when one of our librarians took an interest in and established a drive for the Ruth Ellis Center in conjunction with the University of Michigan Office of LGBT (Lesbian, Gay, Bisexual, and Transgender Affairs). The Ruth Ellis Center provides short-term and long-term residential safe space and support services for runaway, homeless, and at-risk gay, lesbian, bi-attractional, transgender, and questioning youth in Detroit and Southeastern Michigan. The librarian organized collection points for personal care products in various venues, and our library, being one of them, yielded a large number of items for the Center.

Outreach to the Homeless Shelter

There are frequent, if irregularly scheduled, deliveries throughout the year to the local downtown Delonis Homeless Shelter. Whenever staff members bring in extra, unwanted warm clothing, towels, or perhaps small boxes of tissues, soap, deodorant, or such other practical items, one of the librarians who lives near the shelter walks over and drops these off. These donations, whether big or small, are always gratefully received by the shelter receptionist who then distributes them to the residents.

As a direct result of such outreach efforts, we recently received a very large and costly free-standing magnifying instrument as a gift from the hospital's department of surgery. We plan to place this useful item of adaptive technology in the main reference room for public use. Thus, we believe that now our library can be counted on by a number of collaborative partners, such as the hospital or the homeless shelter, to provide good works in addition to good information. We believe that this positive association assists us in marketing our library as a team player and a resource that can be relied on.

In summary, our philosophy is that by seeking out and consistently participating in such diverse charitable activities, we try, as the saying goes, to do well by doing good. There are no hard metrics that we can view and measure as outcomes; there are no clicks to a website that we can count; all our results are soft ones — human ones. We reach out and become better known to members of the community, both inside and outside the university, in what we consider to be a quiet, yet meaningful manner. Eventually, over time, these other organizations reach out to us in return. They depend on our library to welcome them and serve willingly as a gathering or drop-off point for a variety of items. We also believe that our engaging in such charitable ventures serves to market our library and to encourage users to think of it as a trusted service organization staffed by people who care and who prove it by what they do for others.

Local Heroes Storytime Generates "Marketing Gold" in Community Partnerships

ELISABETH NEWBOLD *and* JUNE ENGEL

Introduction

Along with all libraries during these difficult economic times, San Diego County Library (SDCL) faces new challenges with a shortage of funds. Materials and programming budgets decrease, yet the demand for services still remains. Because of this, branch libraries strive to continue providing quality and educational programming to their communities while promoting such programming through creative low- or no-cost marketing. Librarians everywhere have risen to the challenge; they have learned to be thrifty and creative in their endeavors when developing, maintaining, and promoting quality programs.

As part of their strategic planning, SDCL is focused on three specific county initiatives: public safety, health, and children. The Local Heroes Storytime program addresses all three of these initiatives. Best of all, this successful program can be operated with little or no funding through partnerships with public service providers. As branch managers, we both feel this program is well worth the time and energy we put into it. The payoffs are many, including powerful partnerships and grassroots public relations.

How It Began

The Local Heroes program at San Diego County Library (SDCL) started out simply with a publicity photograph. The picture was of an Imperial Beach Firefighter, Ehren, and a little girl named Lisette at a Library Fire Station Storytime for preschoolers. A few days later, as the photo was being posted to our branch library's Flickr account, it was noted how much the picture resembled an American Library Association's (ALA) READ poster. Discussions followed, with the general staff consensus that the youth of the community would like to see their local public safety personnel featured in posters on the walls of their library. Further conversations saw the construction of a special storytime with opportunities for demonstrations, questions, and discussions with various local service groups. Before our library knew it, we had brainstormed a fun, interactive, monthly program for our children that involved the community and highlighted our library.

From this original model, the program has branched out to include service organizations such as the U.S. Post Office, Coast Guard, Army, EDCO Recycling, the mayor, therapy/service dogs, and many more. As our community's public safety and service organizations are made up of role models and heroes, the title "Local Heroes" (LH) stuck. Other branch libraries in the county picked up the idea. Word of mouth in the neighborhood made this series popular, and we had a marketing program that not only highlighted the heroes and service organizations of our communities, but also developed a new awareness of the library. Our patron counts and circulation statistics went up. In short, our monthly LH series became the hottest ticket in town.

Here is the photograph that got the whole thing started, featuring Imperial Beach firefighter Ehren Kahle and preschooler Lisette Campos.

The Concept

Public safety and service organizations are often taken for granted and often operate in the background until there is a need or crisis. Because most of them are taxpayer-funded organizations, they are interested in marketing their services, just as libraries are. Many of them already have prepared outreach materials/handouts for children and are happy for an opportunity to educate the public. While grade-school children often get class visits, preschoolers don't have many chances to see a paramedic up-close and personal in a non-emergency situation. For that matter, neither do their parents. One of the moms who came to LH Storytime was very happy for the opportunity to ask a paramedic about first aid for snakebites. When they have experiences like this, parents help spread the word about the LH programs to other parents.

Robert Pfohl, Division Chief for the Viejas (CA) Fire Department (also known as "Firefighter Bob" in the LH Storytime program), says it this way: "From my perspective,

I saw the Local Heroes Storytime program provide the fire department with two great opportunities. Not only were we able to connect with the young children and provide fundamental fire safety education, we also were able to demonstrate to everyone involved how their local fire departments work collectively to provide response and service reliability to the entire community."

Having such a role model reading to them is even better than a class visit. Early literacy studies show that the more young children see adults reading, the more likely they will become readers themselves (Albright, Delecki, and Hinkle 2009). Our storytime kids are in awe of the various LHs that come to the library. Sometimes children will dress in appropriate costumes. We've seen little ones walk in wearing princess dresses in August (pageant princess program), firefighter gear in October (National Fire Protection Month), and Santa Clause attire in December (Santa is a popular hero!).

With cameras in hand, we have recorded plenty of memorable LH moments. These photos are valuable marketing tools when shared. We have worked with local newspapers, and they look forward to our articles about LH storytime because of the newsworthy photos. We provide a short article to go along with an appealing picture, making sure to get parents' permission for publication, and the whole town gets a dose of library news. Voilá—free marketing for the library as well as the participating public safety or service organization.

Finding Partners

"In an era when demand for library services is increasing but funding for them is declining, volunteers play an important role in supplementing the high-quality service library staff provide" (ALA 2009). Local Heroes volunteers or partners can be found at many locations within and nearby your city. They pass by the door of your library on a regular basis. Public safety is an obvious choice. Your police, fire, and sheriff's departments are always amenable to meeting with kids and helping to educate them on public safety topics. The kids are also curious about the LHs, as they see them around town and on the news. But, your guests should not be limited to public safety only. Local veterinarians, trash collectors, mail carriers, and your town's city council members are all great resources for this program. There are potential LHs everywhere. You just need to be on the lookout for them.

In some cases, the idea for a program arrives unexpectedly at your library's front door. A few months ago, the Imperial Beach Branch Library had a bomb scare. Our local and county public safety crews came to our aid. Along with our sheriff's department came the San Diego County's Bomb Squad. Happily, the bomb scare turned out to be a hoax. The bomb squad was professional and helpful in keeping us safe and briefed on the situation. While waiting for the "all clear" signal, it suddenly occurred to staff that this team would be a great addition to our LH program. The squad was invited that night to be presenters. A couple of months later, they provided an LH program with stories and a demonstration of their bomb robot, "Little Richie." To this day, it is one of the most popular LH programs the library has generated. If they had not come to our branch that night, we would never have thought of inviting them. Always keep an open mind and an eye for opportunity when planning for this program.

Prepping the Partner

The LH program is first and foremost a partnership between the library and our community. As librarians, we have ventured out to ribbon cuttings, open houses, knocked on doors of sheriff's and police offices, and made many phone calls to initiate LH partnerships. We find that direct interaction with our guests helps to initiate stronger relationships. Our library staff always takes the time to chat with our LH presenters when they come to our building to present a program. We recommend this as it gives the LH participants an opportunity to familiarize themselves with the library and its staff. More importantly, this program becomes more of a collaboration than a duty for them.

The main goal of our Local Heroes presenters is to spend time with the kids promoting outreach and safety values. Captain French of the Imperial Beach (CA) Fire Department states: "I love every chance we get to spend time with the kids and tell them what it is like to be a firefighter and ride on the fire engine. Reading them stories and interacting with them is lots of fun." This philosophy of having fun is shared by all our presenters. Because of this, we want to provide the opportunity for them to create as positive an experience as possible.

As most of these volunteers are not professional presenters or storytellers, it will help your guests be prepared if you provide information before the program. To help facilitate our presenters, we put together a book bag of materials to give to them one week before the event. The book bag contains:

- Eight–10 presenter-themed picture books for the guests to read. They do not need to read them all, but they should be given a good selection to choose from.

Jennifer Santiago, Miss Imperial Beach, and LH storytime friend Ariana Cannon.

- A letter to the presenter providing encouragement and information:
  1. A big thank-you note with a reminder of how children learn valuable reading and educational skills through programs and role models such as the guest LH.
  2. Encouragement for the presenters to bring props representing their department or organization for demonstrations, exhibitions, and hands-on activities.
  3. The basic schedule of the program:
     - Share/read a couple of books.
     - Answer some questions from the audience.
     - Provide a demonstration.
     - Read a few more books.
     - Answer any new questions from the audience.
     - Autograph coloring pages or handout freebies.
  4. The approximate age of children attending.
  5. Statement that this is their program and they can deviate from the outline as they desire.
  6. A big reminder to have FUN! The more fun the reader is having, the more fun it is for the children who are listening.
  7. Contact name and information should they have questions.

The Payoff / Benefits

The Local Heroes Storytime program has created a wonderful marketing experience for SDCL. We like to say that it has become "marketing gold" in our community. This program emphasizes all the good within our neighborhoods. It promotes literacy, outreach, and the library in a fun and educational environment. With the development of this program two years ago, our libraries have experienced a new level of public interest.

The advantages of a successful program are shared between the library and our partners. At the Imperial Beach Branch Library, circulation statistics started to rise significantly. When the LH program was launched in March of 2008, monthly circulation that month was measured at 8,701. By the following March, 2009, this number had risen to 11,072, a 27 percent increase. As the word continued to spread, March 2010 showed a monthly circulation of 15,882, a 43 percent increase from the previous year, with a remarkable overall two-year gain of 83 percent. While not as dramatic, door counts rose an impressive 33 percent during the same two-year period.

The smaller Alpine Branch Library embraced the Local Heroes program in August of 2010. As of this writing, average storytime attendance has doubled, growing from 15 to over 30 within the past year, with some events drawing close to 50 attendees. Each month we see adults coming through our doors for the first time, bringing their children to meet a local hero and learn about his or her job. It's fun for the parents as well, and they tell their friends about it. They often show up with cameras in hand to capture the moment. The children love the program, and our presenters thrive on their adoration.

Positive results from the marketing and outreach opportunities are also being seen by our associates. All of our LH partners are eager to come back because of the many benefits of this series. Chief Clark of the Imperial Beach Fire Department thanked our library for inviting fire fighters to read on several LH occasions. He then added "without you, we would not have as much community involvement as we do!" As our library's statistics have gone up, so have our cooperatives. Everyone who participates in our LH Storytime comes out a winner.

The partnerships that have generated from these storytimes have created stronger bonds between the library and our public safety and service organizations. Through this program, we have gotten to know them, and they in turn have gotten to know us. Now, when we hear an emergency vehicle speeding by, we think of the people who are putting their lives on the line because we have forged personal relationships with them. Between us, there is a strong dedication to serving our communities. The LH program helps to enhance it. This program is not one-sided. We represent the library to them, and we make an effort to attend their open houses, toy drives, etc. Our Local Heroes partners are also able to thrive from our program.

Captain Miller of the San Diego County Sherriff's Department said this about our LH program: "Partnering with the libraries on the Local Heroes program has allowed the community to see law enforcement and firefighters as normal people. There is something about seeing deputy/firefighters in full uniform reading stories to children. In the child's eyes, these people are giants; when in reality, they are just ordinary men and women trying to make a difference in our future." But more importantly, the smiles and more smiles from the kids and their caregivers who attend these programs tell us that this is a win-win program for everyone involved.

New opportunities for community outreach and marketing the library have blossomed in surprising ways, thanks to the LH program. One example: Debbie Stein, Head Teacher over the preschool at Viejas Education Center, on a nearby Indian reservation, began bringing her whole class to the Alpine Branch LH programs. Their curriculum unit on community helpers made it a perfect fit. This new partnership resulted in the librarian being invited to visit their school, read to the children, and talk about the library. Doors were opened in both directions, creating a positive relationship with yet another community organization. From Debbie's perspective: "Bringing the children from our program to the library has been a wonderful experience. The children look forward to picking out new books and sharing them in class. We have especially enjoyed the Local Heroes Storytime, which has sparked many a great conversation as well as dramatic play scenarios. I am grateful as a teacher to have such an exceptional resource available in our community."

Conclusion

By launching, promoting, and enjoying our Local Heroes Storytime program, we have struck it rich in "marketing gold." This program costs next to nothing and has yielded a large return for our respective branches. The payoff is measured in heightened community awareness, increased circulation and program attendance, and strong, positive connections in every direction. Our sponsoring organization, San Diego County, benefits because we are aligned with their primary initiatives. Our neighbors who provide public service and protection reap the marketing benefits of LH right along with us. It strengthens existing bonds within our communities and creates new ones that were not present before. The biggest winners of all are the many children who attend our LH events. They take

Alpine Postmaster Kitty Van Winkle holding LH books in front of the mail truck she brought for the children to explore.

away memories that will inspire them to return to the library again and again to enjoy programs and books. They also gain knowledge about the world around them that is vital to their understanding of how their community functions. And, last but not least, this program is just plain fun for everyone involved!

Appendix: How to Get Started

Now that you know about this idea, how do you get started?

1. Look around your library's community. Who provides everyday services? Here's a list of suggestions to spark your own ideas

- Firefighters (If there is more than one unit in your area, use them all.)
- Postmaster/mail carriers
- Pageant princesses
- Waste/recycle workers
- Law enforcement (There may be several organizations available; use them all.)
- Bomb squad
- Military servicemen/women

- Lifeguards
- Border patrol officers
- Forest service officers
- Bus drivers (school and public)
- School superintendent, principals, cafeteria workers, etc.
- Utilities providers
- Paramedics (they may be a separate organization apart from firefighters)
- Newspaper editors, reporters, photographers
- City council members
- Grocery store manager, cashier, etc.
- Water and wastewater workers
- Construction workers
- Doctors, dentists, veterinarians, physical therapists, etc.

2. Start with one event and try it out — don't get overwhelmed

- Plan at least two months ahead.
- Let your LHs know this is a new program and you are excited about it.
- Get your staff on board early so they can tell customers one-on-one.

3. Make it special and fun for everyone involved — the heroes, the kids, and yourself

- Invite LHs to bring "giveaways" — most of them already have something available.
- Include a craft (i.e. a thank-you poster board for the LH, signed by all the kids).
- Reserve appropriate books ahead of time. Provide books on firefighting for the firefighters to read, etc. Provide additional books on the LH topic for patrons to check out afterward.
- Have your camera charged and ready to take lots of photos.

4. Go overboard with (FREE) publicity — enlist every available outlet, including the LH's organization

- Use your own library's mechanisms that are already in place (Facebook, Twitter, website, e-mails, calendars).
- Make flyers early and get them out beyond the library building, into the community: bulletin boards, laundromats, community/recreation centers, nearby businesses, the LH organization (they will help publicize the event because they do community outreach, too!).
- Send press releases to newspapers, radio, Chamber of Commerce, community websites.
- Announce at regular storytimes in the library.

5. Caveats

- Make sure you have a backup plan — the first priority for LHs is their own job. It is not uncommon for public safety workers to be called to duty during a storytime.

(We have had LHs called out to an emergency just as they arrived to read to the children. Don't let this stop you; cheerfully move ahead with your program and call later to reschedule them.)

- Correspond regularly with LHs beforehand to make sure they have what they need.
- Ask them to arrive early to avoid last-minute panic.
- Provide books ahead of time so they can preview them.
- Don't expect professional storytellers — let them be role models as they are.

6. After the Program

- Send a sincere thank-you note.
- Give them copies of the photos.
- Write an article and send to the paper (with pictures — get permission first!).
- Post photos in the library, on your website, etc. (with permission).
- Use photos in future publicity for this organization.

WORKS CITED

ALA American Library Association. 2009. "ALA Partners in 'United We Serve' Volunteer Effort." *American Libraries* 40 (8/9): 14.

Albright, Meagan, Kevin Delecki, and Sarah Hinkle. 2009. "The Evolution of Early Literacy: A History of Best Practices in Storytimes." *Children & Libraries* 7 (1): 13–18.

PART IV

Getting Recognized

13

Flaunt It If You've Got It!

Karen J. Wanamaker

One of the biggest problems in the field of librarianship is too much modesty and too little flaunting of what we've got. The public persona of being quiet, reserved librarians still seems to prevail. And yet, when librarians gather for conferences, quite another side shows through. We get excited about the latest technology. We revel at best practices. For goodness sake, we can even be found dancing with book carts to loud and pounding rhythms! It's high time to take some of that energy and funnel it into our marketing methods before it's too late.

Libraries of all types are facing major budget cuts. At a conference, someone recently referred to the fact that academic libraries have gone from being the "heart of the campus" to just another cost center. OUCH! That reality hurts. We used to be revered as the gate-keepers for research and information. Now it's a struggle to prove our worth both as a profession and an irreplaceable service to our constituencies. We have to explain to our administrators why we still need a reference desk when we have electronic databases and why we still need a flesh-and-blood librarian when we can get a virtual one via e-mail or text-reference services. We have relied on our historical relevance and reputation for too long—they can't get rid of libraries; we are needed; we provide valuable services. And yet, we're seeing budgets being shredded, libraries being closed, and even academic libraries doing away with the physical books! What IS our value again? And perhaps more importantly, how do we prove it to others?

Fight Numbers with Numbers

When money gets tight, people look to the bottom line. What is the final cost? How much does it take to run your library? What can be cut? So when you have to get down to business with your administration, take along all of the quantitative information you have to support your case. You need to have numbers that show how the money is spent and the value of what you got for those dollars. Most libraries collect at least some statistics, but most probably are not using those statistics to their full potential. My three suggestions: plan out what you will collect, be consistent, and then make active use of the information.

107

A few years back, when our library was undergoing a periodic review on our campus, we ran into a brick wall when we tried to gather five years worth of statistics. Some documents collected statistics for the academic year (September-May), some for the calendar year (January-December), and others the fiscal year (July-June). We weren't just trying to compare apples and oranges — we were trying to make sense of a whole fruit salad! It was abundantly clear that we were not organized in how we were collecting our information. This may not have been as problematic when the budget was plump, but as the budget shrank and more information was being requested by our administration to justify the money that was being spent, it became a chore to pull together information in a timely fashion. Compounding the statistics problem was a general lack of two things: organization and assessment. Both of these are critical components for survival and accreditation.

During the few years since that time, our library has taken great strides towards a system for statistics collection and assessment. We have an actual Assessment Committee now that is creating a thought-out and carefully structured database for statistics. We have looked over what information we can collect, what information we need, and how it will be used. The database is structured so that statistics can be entered monthly. This will allow for any number of combinations of the months (annual, fiscal, etc.) for numerous types of reports or marketing.

Besides using them to justify your needs and wants to your governing bodies, many of these statistics should be shared with your patrons and communities as well. For example, say your library has acquired a new database. This could be interpreted as one new item by your administration and your patrons. However, if you let the numbers work *for* you, you could advertise the new database as offering access to over 3,000 full-text journals or over 30,000 new articles each month, which is a much more powerful message.

Getting Beyond the Numbers

Now that your administrators and patrons have your numbers, they need to know how those numbers live and breathe in your library. It is essential to expand upon just the numbers — to pair the quantitative with the qualitative. Don't just tell them how many were served, tell them who was served; tell them the impact your services had on the patrons; tell them how your services and resources made a difference in the lives of the patrons. To make the numbers come alive, the administrators need to hear about a particular patron who came to the library in tears or ready to scream and left with the research needed and a smile — better yet, they need to hear that from patrons themselves, if possible.

One way to move beyond the numbers is to use your audience in your message. Of course librarians and staff and directors think that the libraries are valuable. Of course we think we should get funded to support our services and resources and our patrons. But when our patrons speak out about our value, it compounds the impact of that message. Here are some examples of what I mean in relation to academic libraries:

• Need to reach more faculty members? Get the faculty members who already use your services to help advertise the library to their departments. Get them to share their stories and some valuable numbers on posters, or in meetings, or a special event.

- Trying to reach the college students? Perhaps they would be more likely to use the academic library if they see posters about the library in their classrooms or dorms that show what is available and show how other students use the library.
- Want to reach the administration? Connect them to the students and let the students share their library stories.

One way our library recently reached out to students was through SnapShot-PA. On October 28, 2009, Pennsylvania libraries took part in SnapShot-PA: One Day in the Life of Pennsylvania Libraries. The project was based on what had been done in other states, and it was launched through the Pennsylvania Library Association and the Commonwealth Libraries as a way of capturing the impact that Pennsylvania libraries of all types have on their given communities. Participating libraries were asked to keep statistics and capture events with photos or videos and comments. The information was compiled and posted online at www.snapshotpa.org. Our library decided to participate in this type of event for several reasons:

- To be a part of a statewide effort to show the value of libraries in a time of harsh budget cuts
- To gather a broad snapshot of our own library's usage on one particular day
- To gather input from our patrons about why they were using our library that day
- To use the quotes and images of the participants to entice others to use our library
- To use the event to publicize the library to the community

Our library decided to participate through videos. We advertised the event ahead of time, but received little feedback. On the day of the event, a rainy day at that, we asked the people who came into the library if they would like to participate by recording a brief video that told us two things: why they were in the library that day and how they used our library in general. Many said no, but in the end 54 patrons agreed to record a quick video. The footage was valuable for several reasons:

- It was a way for the state to capture how our academic library users were using the library on that particular day.
- It gave our university library a snapshot of why people were there that day and how they use our library in general.
- It also captured the busy nature of the library's Information Commons area in the background. Behind the person speaking was the traffic coming into the library, students meeting at the tables and chairs, and students working on computers or waiting for friends.

Although our gate count was collected and reported in the statistics portion of Snap-Shot-PA, it was never mentioned in the video. However, viewers can plainly see that our library was busy that day without knowing the exact number. We also learned a lot about our students and their use of the library beyond what was recorded. Patrons who decided not to record a message had a variety of reasons for not wanting to participate; feeling like a drowned rat from the rain was relayed by several students. One of the most surprising reasons that I heard from many students was that they were "just" there to use the computers, as if that weren't a valid reason for using their academic library. Perhaps we need to better market our library resources to those users, or perhaps we need to simply let them know that using the computers is a valid reason to come to the library. In any case, the benefits we gained through our videos were impressive enough that we are planning to do another video event this year during National Library Week to find out how libraries (including our library) have contributed to the lives of our students.

Flaunting It Online

Besides the numbers and personal stories, we must realize that if we want to reach a majority of our patrons in this technologically driven society, we need to go through technology to get there. It isn't enough to provide a website and have newsletters available online. Libraries need to branch out to blogs, Facebook, Twitter, and any other digital world to share information and "connect" with patrons. Variety isn't just the spice of life — it's the key to survival in a multimedia world.

1. Blogs

As often as technologies change and libraries adopt them as the new norm, it is difficult to keep track of when each new technology really embedded itself in our day-to-day lives. It seems like library blogs have been around for a long time, but in reality, it has only been a little over a decade. I started our library's first blog in 2005. Since then it has had spurts of activity based on the time someone (mostly me) had to write entries for it. We are currently in an upswing of activity thanks to the fact that I have a 40-hour-per-week public relations intern working for me this semester. This boost in productivity has led me to increase my publicity and visibility efforts for the blog and its entries as well.

The visibility for our blog posts has also gone through some ups and downs. At first, we were able to embed code in our website so that the first fifteen words of the five most recent posts would appear on the right side of the library's home page as bulleted news items. Then we changed to a different host company for the blog and couldn't get the code to work. At that point, our library's webmaster would just put the title of the post on the home page and link to that post in the blog. With the increase in posts, we now only have some of our posts linked on the home page and must work harder to get people to see our posts. We also push our blog posts to our Facebook page, which will be covered later.

The topics we have written about on the blog have been pretty varied over the years. We have included a wide variety of news, links, information, and events. A sampling includes:

- Library information such as an explanation on the differences between a database and a website
- How-to guides and information to highlight certain databases
- Information and links for current events such as Hurricane Katrina
- Election information with links to registration websites and candidate information
- Information about displays in the library
- Information for events in the library such as speakers
- Bibliographies and information that relates to campus events
- Information and links related to holidays, such as entries we did for Samhain and Earth Day

- Highlighted information about famous people (dead or alive) on their birthdays
- Special library hours during break sessions and finals week

Many of these entries, especially lately, include links to related library resources. For example, in a recent entry on Ayn Rand, we included links to information in library databases, online reference works, and our online catalog. We also link to e-books and streaming videos when appropriate to highlight the library's great wealth of both virtual and tangible resources.

In addition to the library's blog, a few years ago I decided to go in a new direction with the Curriculum Materials Center (CMC) website. I was tired of our old site and wanted the feel of a blog to share information with our education faculty and students, so I created a new WordPress blog for the CMC. The main page is the blog, with news and updates. However, I also created additional pages on the blog for things like databases, handouts, websites, standards, etc. I'm very pleased with it and find it easier to manage than the old site. I also like the ability to add widgets that benefit our particular audience.

2. Facebook

In 2007, we felt it was time to navigate a bit further into the world of Web 2.0 and created a Facebook group page. We advertised it and slowly gathered a group of "friends." We tried to get some conversations going with students regarding what they thought about the library and what they would like to see here. We did have two success stories through our group page. The first of these success stories began when the students asked to see recycling bins placed in the library. I forwarded the information on to our Dean of Library Services, and soon our custodians placed bins throughout the building. That same year, we had some complaints about the lack of food options and a request for vending machines. Working with the students' requests and the permission of our Dean, I was able to contact the people responsible for vending services on our campus and secure both a soda machine and a snack machine for the library that were installed later that same semester.

About a year later, I created a Facebook page for the library that allowed us to do a bit more than the Facebook group. One of the big benefits to the new page was that it allowed us to push our blog feed into Facebook. We had another avenue for news and information without having to repost everything. With shrinking personnel and tight budgets, making the most of the work you already do is a huge advantage. When we create events on our Facebook pages, we can also link back to the more robust information in the blog. That way we can play to the strengths of each media.

Another benefit to the Facebook page is that I can now change my profile to share items as the library's profile rather than my own. This is a recent addition to Facebook and is nice when you find news or want to share something that you see elsewhere. I can post it as the library and it goes to the news feed of anyone who "likes" us.

3. Twitter

In addition to blogs and Facebook, you can't go very far into a discussion on social media without touching upon Twitter. We also created a library Twitter account, but I never seemed to find our niche for that outlet. We did post a Word of the Day for a while with one of my graduate assistants, but that only lasted until she graduated. Last year, I set our account to pull in our Facebook posts to our Twitter feed. I recommend that libraries take advantage of the way that social media sites work together like this.

While I was tweaking the tweets for our library account, our cow began to tweet as well! Yes, you read that correctly. We have a tweeting cow. You may be thinking that our mascot must be a cow. Not true. Our school mascot is the Golden Bear. Our "Elusive Sea Cow," which is life-size and stands in our lobby, is from a Cow Parade competition in our State System of Higher Education. It found a home at our library and is a common meeting place for students. In fact, the cow is even a stop on campus tours. One of our librarians created a Twitter account for the cow and started tweeting for it as a way of communicating information about our information commons (jokingly referred to as the Cow-mons at times). We are just starting to push for followers for the Elusive Sea Cow and will have to see if students think it is cooler to "follow" the cow than to be seen "following" the library.

Local News Venues

Beyond Web 2.0 are all of the local news venues to tap into that can help spread library news and information. Public libraries know how important it is to be featured in the local paper as a way to advertise an event. The same goes for college campuses. Besides our newsletters and brochures, we regularly use the faculty listserv to post information about events, resources, and services. We try to keep a delicate balance of staying on the radar without becoming a nuisance and getting our messages deleted before they even get read. We also use the daily faculty news brief and the weekly student news brief to publicize news and events when appropriate. The student news is meant to be brief, and they mean it. The online form only allows for a 50-character title and up to 140 characters for the message. They also provide a space to put a link, so what we often do is send them to one of the blog posts for more information (and luckily, the link is not part of the 140 characters). Additionally, we use the closed-circuit TV system in our student union building where we can post information for events or speakers. The key again is to use a variety of marketing venues depending on what your message is in order to reach the most people.

Final Thoughts

We have all heard of the phrase "If you build it; they will come," which is actually misquoted from the movie *Field of Dreams*. It shouldn't come as any surprise that this quote no longer holds true for libraries. You can build the library. You can make it beautiful. You can have wonderful resources. However, if you aren't out flaunting what you have in a variety of ways, you're wasting time and money and energy. It's time for librarians to get out and get noticed. We don't need tricks. We are armed with wonderful resources and services that can do wonders for our constituencies. We just need to flaunt what we've got!

14

Your Own Best Advocate

How to Justify a Media Specialist's Position

MELISSA PURCELL

During these times of economic crisis and projected budget cuts in education, it is more important than ever to show how media specialists are a vital part of our schools. Library media center budgets are being cut, and media specialists are losing control over their designated funding. This allows school administrators to divert funds from vital media resources, which can ultimately result in media specialists losing their jobs altogether. In a perfect world, every member of the learning community would realize the importance of the school library and want to take full advantage of its fantastic resources.

Unfortunately, you will meet many high school graduates who proudly say they never used a library while in school. After I finish cringing when I hear comments like this, I try to calmly explain that they really did themselves a disservice by not utilizing the resources and services that media programs offer. Clearly, many people do not understand the importance of the library media center.

I don't know anyone who got into our profession just to be a promoter, but now that role is critical. We need to let everyone know all of the wonderful things we are doing in our media center programs. Now is the time to toot your own horn and toot it loudly!

Below I've listed the top 10 ways you can increase your presence in the public eye in order to promote your services, publicize your media program, and be your own best advocate.

10. Create Displays, Contests, and Posters to Promote Activities, Events, and Resources Going on in the Library Media Center

A great way to promote reading and various books in your library media center is to have students create different visual representations of their favorite books. Picture collages can be used to represent a book by having students include pictures for the setting, characters, themes, major events of the story, etc. These collages can also be made into screen savers and placed on computers throughout the school.

A fun and informative book contest can be set up using baby pictures of teachers next to a picture of their favorite books. Include a brief summary of the book. Students can guess the teachers by their pictures and the books they picked. Students love to see the baby pictures of their teachers and learn more about those teachers based on the books they chose (like when one of our science teachers chose a book about camping, which was another passion for him). Students are eager to check out the favorite book of their teacher, and different books in the library media center are highlighted by the short book synopsis and picture of the cover.

Other creative ideas include sending out e-mails to your teachers when new resources arrive and putting the resources on display in the library media center. Hanging up bulletin boards that highlight special events related to your library media center also helps spread the word about upcoming activities.

9. Create a Warm, Welcoming Environment by Using Feedback from Patrons

Do not be afraid to ask your patrons how you can better serve them through your library media program. A good motto to have is "there is no best, only better." Every media program can be improved upon, but evaluation is needed to identify areas for improvement. Post a survey each semester on the school's website (SurveyMonkey is free and user-friendly: www.surveymonkey.com) for patrons to complete. You may not be able to see the forest for all the trees, so you need an outsider's opinion of areas that may need improvement and areas that are really strong that you can highlight.

Use the results to better your library media center. If patrons are asking for a certain type of material or have complaints, be responsive to those requests and concerns. Also make sure you share a summary of the results and changes that were made with patrons and administrators.

Every student in the school should feel welcome and safe in the library media center, regardless of past offenses. By having a shelf of discarded and donated books for students who are not allowed to check out books due to fines or overdue materials, all students can feel wanted in the library media center instead of being isolated and turned away.

At my school, we keep a "book swap" shelf so students can always have a book. It is based on the honor system, and they are to bring that book back or bring another one to swap out in its place. Most of the books on this shelf are donated books that teachers, parents, and other students brought in when they heard we wanted to start a swap program. Students love it and they never have to leave the library media center empty-handed.

Make sure you involve parents and community members in the media program. A few suggestions for involving all members of the learning community include:

- Have a parent section in your library.
- Invite community members to participate in your book discussions or book blogs.
- Host a Technology Night once a month and provide Internet safety instruction, tours of Facebook, YouTube, the school website, etc.

- Ask community members to read to classes.
- Invite parents to bring a bag lunch and provide a monthly parent information meeting about what is going on in the media program.
- Encourage community members to tutor small groups of students in the library media center after school.

8. Make Yourself Seen on Campus and in the Community

There are many ways to maintain a high level of visibility outside the library media center. Stand out in the hallways between classes and make a point to say "hello" to the students as they walk by. Ask department leaders if you can attend their next departmental meetings in order to find opportunities to collaborate on classroom instruction in the different subject areas. Know your collection so that when the department members are discussing lessons, you can recommend library media center resources they can use to support the lesson.

Serve as a faculty mentor to show you are truly a member of the teaching community. Serving as a mentor allows you to make friends and form close bonds with your co-workers. Also volunteer as a student mentor. Just as with serving as a faculty mentor, volunteering as a student mentor will help you develop a close bond with students and allow them to see you in another role on campus. You may be fortunate enough to mentor students who never expressed a desire to read, but working closely with these students, you will have the opportunity to open up the world of knowledge and imagination through books and other resources in your library media center. Before you know it, your mentees will be checking out books faster than you can put them on the shelves.

Sponsor a club on campus. Reading clubs can encourage students to form friendships with others who share their passion for reading. These clubs can meet before school, after school, or during lunch. Broadcast clubs can teach students new technologies and cultivate a productive outlet for students' enthusiasm for technology. Green teams can work to recycle paper and ink cartridges from around the school and local businesses. Clubs allow you to know your students on a more personal level and learn more about their interests outside of school.

Volunteer to be on key committees such as leadership, technology, school improvement, and grant writing. Don't forget to send a monthly report to your administrators letting them know about all of the hard work you are doing on campus and in the community. While you really are your own best advocate, it's important to make sure that other key advocates for your job are kept in the loop.

7. Create a Library Media Center Website

Post a monthly newsletter to your website detailing all of the wonderful literacy events happening in and around your campus, school system, and state. Use weekly posts with catchy titles like "Wednesday's Website" and "Tuesday's Technology Tip." My favorite is the "Friday Fun Fact." It includes an interesting fact and tells which library resource it came from. This can be used to promote different resources available for check-out while highlighting different areas of study. Print these weekly posts and keep them in a notebook so patrons can have easy access to them when they visit the library media center.

Make your book talks accessible to a larger audience and more interesting to tech-savvy students by creating podcasts of the book talks. These podcasts should be put on your media center website so anyone can access them. The only equipment you'll need is an inexpensive (less than $50) MP3 recorder with a built-in microphone. In addition to podcasts that you create, whole classes can take on the project, or individual students can volunteer to create podcasts of their favorite books. The books with book talks will probably stay in constant circulation as patrons get "hooked" by the podcasts and cannot wait to read the whole book themselves.

Create a virtual tour of your library media center to use as an introduction during orientation and to show any new students entering the school. Post this tour on your library media center website so anyone who is not able to physically visit your school can at least get a virtual tour of your program. A very simple tour can be created with still pictures and written descriptions using PowerPoint. More elaborate tours can be created with video and recorded narration using MovieMaker (or other video creation software).

6. Teach Professional Development Courses, Give Library Media Center Orientations, and Present at Conferences

Orientation for teachers involves introducing new resources and the completion of a survey to see where they stand with their technology needs. Appropriate professional development technology trainings can then be planned and take place throughout the year. A technology skills list is an easy and efficient way to organize any ongoing technology training program at your library. Technology skills or competencies are the technology-related abilities, qualities, strengths, and skills required for the success of the teachers at your school.

Orientation is a perfect opportunity to:

- Introduce the students to the media staff
- Share valuable resources available in the library media center
- Show students the services that the media program offers
- Describe the purpose and mission of the media program
- Allow students to learn rules and regulations that will help them to be successful while in the library media center
- Explain how to properly care for library resources
- Allow students to experience the comfortable, welcoming atmosphere present in the library media center

Since all students in a school should attend the library media center for an orientation at some point, this is a good time to issue them their school identification or library cards, as well as usernames and passwords for online resources.

A parent orientation night can provide parents with the same information students receive. This allows parents to benefit from the services provided and to learn about the resources available to help their children be successful in school. Orientations are also important for media specialists because they:

- Allow the media staff to meet all the students in the school
- Provide opportunities to connect with teachers on a more personal level
- Give a chance for media staff to become more familiar with the needs of their patrons
- Let staff prove their willingness and desire to work with all the patrons in their learning community

Although orientations can be time-consuming (and also exhausting), the benefits well outweigh the efforts and the work involved.

Since technology is a rapidly changing field, you should work to stay up to date in areas that are vital to school performance. A great way to find out about current best practices in the field is to attend professional conferences. If you cannot find the time or the money required to travel to conferences, check into the numerous free webinars available online, or attend other classes offered for free in your area.

Print business cards from your home computer or use www.vistaprint.com to print free business cards (you pay the shipping). Have these business cards ready to hand out at conferences or classes so you can better network with colleagues. You can also hand them out to parents as a way to encourage community outreach, and to students who many need mentoring or extra media help. A business card is a great way to be recognized as the professional that you are.

5. Write Articles for Professional Journals and Magazines

Try your hand at writing for a professional magazine or journal. Writing for your own profession is an excellent way to share good ideas, and it can lead to professional networking opportunities. *Library Media Connection* and *Knowledge Quest* are two professional magazines that specifically address issues related to school library media programs. Both of these magazines accept unsolicited manuscripts on a variety of topics.

4. Apply for Grants and Other Recognitions

Seek special recognitions by applying for awards. A state exemplary media program award is just one example. Even if awards come with no monetary gain, you will receive great publicity from the recognition. Many states have an exemplary media program award with a detailed rubric. Even if you do not officially submit an application for the award, completing the application is a great way to evaluate your library media center.

Work to get extra money for your program by seeking donations from local businesses, applying for writing grants, and participating in fundraising activities. Not only can this result in real money for your library media center, it will also show that you are struggling to help get the school through these tight financial times. Seek free resources through different venues such as the We the People Grant (www.wethepeople.gov) for $350 in free books, and the Picturing America Grant (http://picturingamerica.neh.gov) for 40 posters and a teaching guide. Plus, if you become a book reviewer, many publishers will let you keep the books you review for free!

Volunteer to serve on a reading committee for grants or other awards. You will learn what a quality winning application looks like, and then you can take that information and apply for your school next year. Serving on one of the reading committees will also give you ideas for improving your media program and the services you can offer your community. Learning about exemplary media programs and practices is a great way to become more aware of your own strengths and weaknesses.

3. Use a Blog to Set Up an Interactive Discussion

Blogs are used by millions of people to discuss their lives and the news of the day. Forward-thinking librarians are incorporating blogs into their libraries. The one-way flow of information from basic web pages to patrons is limited; patrons need the ability to interact, and a blog is one of the best ways to facilitate that interaction. There are many different free educational blogs that are easy to use, such as www.blogger.com, www.21 classes.com, and http://edublogs.org.

One example of a blog would be a book blog for students at your school to comment on books that they have read. Although my school has a book club that meets once each month, not everyone who wants to be a part of it can attend. A book blog provides another avenue for students to share their love of reading — it is still a book discussion group, just online.

2. Use Twitter to Set Up a Communication System

A system should be set up to communicate with parents and other community members who may want to take advantage of the library media center services but are not in the school on a daily basis. Twitter is immensely popular right now, and it's a great way of letting your community members know what is happening in the library. Is there an excellent new resource that you want your patrons to know about? Is there a great program you are offering after school? Let patrons know about your updates automatically through your short (140 characters or less) tweet posts.

1. Work on Securing Newspaper Articles That Publicize the Great Things Happening in Library Media Centers

Local newspapers are often interested in printing articles about students' accomplishments. Do you have a reader who has an extraordinary amount of Accelerated Reader points? Is there a student who volunteers to read at a nursing home or another school? Did your students compete in a reading competition? All these topics could make good newspaper articles.

Plan and publicize different reading events. You might have high school students visit elementary schools to read to children in their after-school programs. High school students and elementary students would benefit from this, and it's newsworthy.

During summer vacation, reading lists or book recommendations are great things to print in the local newspaper when they may have areas to fill, like the space they normally use to list the weekly cafeteria menu.

Conclusion

Change does not happen on its own. It takes forward-thinking librarians to bring school libraries into the twenty-first century and make the library an essential part of the school it represents. We are no longer "just librarians" checking out books to students who happen to walk through our doors. We each have the power to reach our students by using new technologies that enhance learning experiences, by using social networking to get our voices and the voices of our students heard, and by using available online resources to open up a whole new world.

You need to set yourself up as an indispensable asset to your students. You need to network with others and market yourself inside and outside the school. That way, if your position ever ends up on the chopping block, then administrators, teachers, parents, and students will fight to keep you. Therefore, it is extremely important to get out there and make yourself seen not only in the library media center, but also on campus and in the community.

15

Successful Publicity for the 21st Century Library

Blending Traditional Library Marketing with Recruitment to the Profession

SHEILA SMYTH

The current campaign of marketing library services matches in prominence the drive earlier in the decade to recruit librarians to the profession. Both are responses to very real fears: the marketing of libraries is a reaction to the belief that, with digital searching and the supply of information at everyone's fingertips, the library has lost its purpose, whereas the earlier recruitment drive was triggered by the expected shortage of librarians with the retirement of the large baby-boomer cohort.

The most solid foundation on which to build any marketing effort is the excellent librarian who foresees, selects, and makes available high-quality sources of dependable information and guides the patron in their use. Exceptional performance in regular library tasks continues to play an essential and ongoing role in public relations, since the satisfied patron — as a member of the general public, as a student, or as a faculty member enjoying good outreach from a subject librarian — is the library's best advocate and defender. Think of the recent eloquent defense of British public libraries by the author Philip Pullman, affirming how libraries remind us that "there are things above profit, things that profit knows nothing about ... things that stand for civic decency and public respect for imagination and knowledge and the value of simple delight" (Pullman 2011). More prosaically, the student who benefited from relevant general library literacy instruction when preparing assignments will feel well disposed towards librarians and will appreciate that this is indeed a useful profession. Similarly, the student interested in history may be surprised to discover the breadth of librarianship when exposed to specialized subject instruction. I am thinking of an undergraduate's comment after a session introducing students to the political underpinnings of font changes in German printing towards the end of the Second World War: "I had no idea that librarians research such interesting topics and teach about them." And indeed, as Shannon has emphasized, it is important in countering habitual negative stereotypes that librarians not only be knowledgeable and competent but also be welcoming, and be seen to have fulfilling work (Shannon 2008).

Given the importance of quality service in supporting any effort at marketing the library, it follows that recruitment cannot be a numbers game. The 2002 call to action by then ALA president John W. Berry, spurring every librarian to "recruit at least two new librarians a year," epitomizes a kind of over-reaction we must avoid (Berry 2002). This proposal would have us triple the number of librarians *every two years*—the length of time it normally takes to qualify as a librarian! Do we really need that many librarians? And what about quality?

It seems to me that in order to recruit high-caliber candidates with the necessary range of ability, experience, knowledge, and skills, we need to cast a wide net, making a broader population aware that librarianship is a rewarding profession with its own realm of expertise and that it requires specialized training. Indeed, even among those who vaguely realize that specialized training is needed, few are aware of its nature or duration. Programs to spread this information should be active in all libraries at all times, not only in universities with library schools and not just when such efforts are trendy. Recall the astonishing revelation that most career offices do not carry information on the profession of librarianship (Jeong 2006).

Tight budgets are now forcing libraries to concentrate their energies on dealing with immediate concerns, and indeed some would even say on survival, so that recruitment to the profession has become secondary. Marketing library services following the 4Cs model of "Customer, Cost, Convenience, and Communication" has become essential to demonstrate the continued relevance and value of libraries in the modern world (Ashcroft 2010). These efforts strive to make libraries attractive to their target audience, to the supporting institution, and to prospective donors. The general idea is to increase library use and thereby strengthen the case for financial support in an environment of competing demands on limited resources.

Marketing Approaches Used by the University of California, Irvine (UCI) Libraries

• Keeping the UCI Libraries online presence up to date and multifaceted: Facebook, the UCI Portal, YouTube tutorials (e.g., www.youtube.com/user/UCIrvineLibraries), new features and events highlighted on the library's home page, QR Codes providing information on call-number ranges for devices such as iPods, NextGenMelvyl (UC version of WorldCat), and a mobile version of the library's home page.

• Marketing reference services by means of effective in-house signage and spotlights on the library's home page.

• More generally, promoting awareness among librarians of the added value gained from introducing patrons to the full range of services available in the library. Recommended techniques to achieve this are "cross-selling," such as familiarizing a patron at the reference desk with interlibrary loan services, and "up-selling," such as promoting workshops on repositories or on preservation services at the library (Germano 2010).

• Annual library scavenger hunt for new students at the beginning of the school year to familiarize them with the library and its services. In the most recent event, students had the opportunity to use their mobile devices to navigate throughout the building.

• Regular exhibits highlighting individual collections to stimulate interest in the libraries.

• The UCI-Space Repository online, managed by the libraries, now highlights and publicizes outstanding collections in the UCI Libraries. (http://ucispace.lib.uci.edu/community-list).

• During *National Open Access Week*, a library booth near the Student Center provided information on the advantages of and opportunities for publishing scholarly work in refereed open-access journals.

• Radio presence on the campus radio station KUCI, with volunteers recounting their experiences in seeking research assistance and publicizing some of our popular resources in UCI Special Collections, such as the archives of the philosopher Jacques Derrida or the collection on Immigrants from Southeast Asia.

• Maintaining a newspaper and magazine presence. In addition to the UCI Libraries regularly publicizing library services and events in the university newspaper, the UCI Libraries Southeast Asian Archive, for example, was highlighted in the *OC* (Orange County) *Weekly Magazine* as the best archive in Southern California (www.ocweekly.com/bestof/2010/award/best-college-archives-828868/).

• Participation in the national *Banned Books Week: Read Out!* public readings at UCI. This was publicized in the *Orange County Register Online* article of 9/30/09: "OC Observes Banned Books Week" (www.ocregister.com/articles/books-213139-school-banned.html?pic=1).

• Organization, in cooperation with the Orange County Public Libraries, of the *Literary Orange* fundraiser, in which Orange County authors speak on their work.

• SPIRIT (School Partnerships in Research and Information Technology) is the UCI Libraries ongoing outreach program to area middle schools and high schools, with primary emphasis on low-income districts. The goal is to encourage students to become interested in science and technology and pursue higher education.

Most of these efforts will naturally generate awareness of the wide range of library services as well as greater understanding and respect for librarianship. With the increased realization that libraries are at the forefront of applying and promoting technological advances, some users will develop a new appreciation for the technical expertise of the modern librarian. Through their emphasis on technology, librarians will be seen as forward-looking in their dissemination of knowledge, not least in their promotion of institutional repositories. Participation in the readings of the *Banned Books Week* signals the cultural awareness and open-mindedness of the professional librarian, while a library-organized literary festival reminds the general public that libraries provide both social and intellectual services to the community. As for the SPIRIT program, the practical help provided by librarians to the young beneficiaries is bound to generate at the very least goodwill, if not spark their interest, recognizing librarianship as a possible career if they pursue higher education.

These aspects of our marketing are essential for promoting the library and indirectly librarianship, but they cannot be the end of our efforts to secure the future of our profession: practical information and guidance are important in career choices. At UCI, this type of practical assistance has been provided for some 15 years by the Academic Librarianship Committee (ALC), part of the Librarians Association of the University of California (LAUC).

My knowledge of ALC recruitment activities spanning the period 2006–2010 stems from my membership on that committee, from my term as Chair (06–07), and from information generously provided by subsequent Chairs, Pauline Manaka and Kristin Andrews:

• Three *Panels on Librarianship*, in which several librarians described their own career paths to an audience of UCI students and interested UCI staff. To impress upon those making career choices — for the most part young and tech-savvy — that librarians use the latest technologies, one of our guest speakers made her presentation using *Second Life*. ALC created flyers and brochures to publicize these panels, which averaged over 20 attendees each.

• Collaboration with the California Library Schools at UCLA, San Jose State University, and California State University Fullerton, procuring up-to-date information on their programs and facilitating contact of prospective students with the appropriate institutional representatives.

• Publicizing the possibility of enrolling in an online library program while working at UCI, as well as the UCI Libraries' internship program offered to library school students.

• Collaboration with the UCI Career Center, providing information and publications on librarianship to which students can be directed.

• A mentoring program in which UCI librarians volunteer to meet members of the campus community seeking information on librarianship, on the availability of scholarships and grants, and on the library school application process itself. It was noted that several undergraduate referrals to these library mentors originated with professors who had a close working relationship with their subject librarians.

• Booth at the annual Graduate School Fair, in collaboration with the UCI Career Center, providing information and signing up students interested in meeting with a practicing librarian to answer their specific questions and describe a day in the life of a professional librarian.

• Booth with a similar function at the annual UCI Library Student Worker Appreciation Picnic, in collaboration with the Library Development Office.

• UCI Libraries staff and student workers currently enrolled in library school or interested in the profession are encouraged to join the *Library School Interest Group*, furthering the exchange of information and practical assistance.

Many factors contribute to individual decisions, so that it is impossible to quantify how many new careers in librarianship are triggered by any one recruitment program such as the effort at UCI. The purpose of these endeavors is to expose the full spectrum of undergraduates, who are often in the process of considering career options, to the possibility and implications of becoming a librarian and thereby to broaden the variety of experience and subject expertise among librarians. The simplest measures for assessing the success of the program are attendance at events, the number of inquiries at information booths or from mentors, and the number of referrals to mentors from teaching staff and others. For the future, an obvious refinement would be the collection of data on the subject specialties of participants.

• During the four-year period under consideration, that is, since 2006, at least 10 graduates and employees of UCI have attended library school in California. This information was provided by the library schools in California, the UCI Graduate Division, and the UCI Alumni Association, so that it does not include those who availed of instruction programs on the web or attended library programs elsewhere in the country.

• Sign-ups for in-depth information averaged 70 annually, whether from attendees at the above panels, from the Graduate Career Fair, or from the UCI Student Worker Appreciation Picnics. Respondents to a survey for the 2007 panel registered a 90 percent approval rating for that informational session, and such comments as "I particularly enjoyed hearing the librarians' own professional histories" were noted.

• There are about 12 UCI mentors for those interested in librarianship, some advising up to four students annually.

Now some may argue in these times of financial restraint: why assist young people in joining a profession with uncertain employment prospects? Why encourage them to join a demanding profession with modest financial reward? In my view, programs concentrating on recruitment are necessary in libraries, even in times of financial hardship. As John Huber noted, while more libraries are looking to become "lean" and sustainable, watching their bottom line, they cannot afford to lose sight of their most valuable asset: the high-caliber librarian who is essential to the survival of libraries (Huber 2010). Libraries have changed dramatically and call upon levels of expertise unimaginable only decades ago, and the trend continues, accelerating, if anything. Librarianship is an ancient and noble profession, but in the public eye, it is often either romanticized or trivialized. More than ever before, there is no single model of librarianship: the profession encompasses a myriad of distinct, non-interchangeable functions and specialties. Some of the necessary skills are found in abundance in fields from which few librarians have come in the past: science, engineering, business, law, classics, and, of course, foreign languages. Moreover, students in these areas who might be drawn to the profession often know neither how to go about it nor what is required.

In these days of globalization and rapidly expanding technology, we can no longer depend on the traditional ways in which our ranks have been replenished, that is, on the humanities and the social sciences spontaneously supplying the next generation of librarians. We need to target the full spectrum of the undergraduate population if we hope to maintain libraries as vibrant players on the social and intellectual scene.

A search of the literature reveals that the need to broaden the target for recruitment to the library profession has already been noted, and several programs are in place aiming at specific demographics (Pellack 2006). Many public libraries organize career events geared to young people and include information on librarianship. Some university libraries support initiatives to attract minorities to the profession, such as Washington University, St. Louis, which launched an internship program in 2004 to attract minority students from nearby Lincoln University to the profession of librarianship (Jeong 2006). Some universities try to interest young people in librarianship even before they enroll in college. Thus in summer 2002, the library at Cornell University instituted the *Cornell University Library Junior Fellows Program for High School Students* (Revels, LaFleur, and Martinez 2003). Also in 2002, the University of Notre Dame, Indiana, launched its *Summer Program to Recruit the Next Generation of Librarians* aimed at minority seniors from the local high schools (King 2010). Such programs are important, but what I am advocating in this paper are widespread, sustained, and systematic recruiting endeavors that appeal to the entire undergraduate population, like the recruitment program at UCI. Marketing is vital for libraries, but when we have weathered these present hard times, we must have a reliable cadre of professional experts to take over the reins in the library of the twenty-first century.

Appendix: A Step-by-Step Plan for Carrying out Recruitment

• Check if there were any recruitment efforts at your institution in the past.

• Gain the necessary buy-in from the library administration and/or supporting institution by providing a proposal indicating the goals/outcomes, cost, participants, staff time, location, and dates for proposed events.

• Do not reinvent the wheel. Check what initiatives and publications national and state library organizations/agencies (e.g. Labor Department, ALA, ACRL, CARL) offer on recruitment. For example, check out campaigns and informational resources from the ALA that include "Become a Librarian" (http://delicious.com/alalibrary/becomea librarian), "Frontline Advocacy" (www.ala.org/ala/issuesadvocacy/advocacy/advocacy university/frontline_advocacy/index.cfm), and "Your Major + Academic Librarianship = A Great Career! @ your library" (www.ala.org/ala/mgrps/divs/acrl/issues/recruiting/ recruiting.pdf).

• Do a literature search to see what other libraries are doing on recruitment, including libraries associated with a library school.

• Survey your population and see what they know about librarianship and from what sources. Also make sure you are aware of the trends and perspectives of the current youth, especially those entering college (www.beloit.edu/mindset/2014.php).

• Investigate which types of functions and skills are needed most in libraries at present and for the foreseeable future, so you can focus recruitment efforts on those areas (e.g., technology, science, modern languages).

• Collaborate with state or regional library schools.

• Collaborate with units on campus such as the Registrar's Office, the Career Center, and the Graduate Division. The idea is to make students aware of the profession as early as possible. As already mentioned, even career centers do not usually have information on librarianship, so it is no surprise that a survey showed that 56.6 percent of respondents first heard about science librarianship after college or in graduate school (Jeong 2006).

• When planning a recruitment event, assess the cost (e.g. speakers, renting space and/or equipment, publicity, food). Identify possible sources of funding, such as library donors, Friends of the Library, the library board, businesses, and cities. Recruitment events generally require no more than a small budget to be effective.

• Determine the most effective methods for publicizing the event: brochures, posters, signage, highlights on the library's home page. Thanks to computers, this is now relatively inexpensive.

• Whenever possible, contact campus, local, or state media outlets such as newspapers, television, and radio, to publicize the event to a wider audience (Shannon 2008).

• Alert all colleagues in the library to your recruitment events/program and provide them with some easy resources and information they can give to patrons making inquiries about librarianship. If at all possible, create a *Recruitment Page* on the library's home page.

• · Survey your library colleagues and those who participated in the recruitment program to help in evaluating the success and usefulness of the recruitment events.

• Re-assess the recruitment program annually.

• Document your results and provide them to your stakeholders (e.g., administration, donors, endowment office) and document the relevant information in your library's accreditation report to national library associations such as ALA, ACRL, and PLA.

Works Cited

Ashcroft, Linda. 2010. "Marketing Strategies for Visibility." *Journal of Librarianship and Information Science* 42 (2): 89–96.

Berry, John W. 2002. "President's Message: Addressing the Recruitment and Diversity Crisis." *American Libraries* 33 (2): 7.

Germano, Michael A. 2010. "Narrative-based Library Marketing: Selling Your Library's Value During Tough Economic Times." *The Bottom Line: Managing Library Finances* 23 (1):5–17.

Huber, John. 2010. *Lean Library Management: Eleven Strategies for Reducing Costs and Improving Services.* New York: Neal Schuman.

Jeong, Sarah H. 2006. "Why Didn't I Hear About It Sooner? Recruiting Undergraduates into Science Librarianship." *Science and Technology Librarians* 27 (1/2): 113–119.

King, Dwight. 2010. "The Next Generation: Partnering with High Schools for Future Minority Librarians." *College and Research Libraries News* 71 (4): 201–204.

Pellack, Lorraine J. 2006. "Uncle Albert Needs You! Individual Recruiting Efforts Are a Necessity and an Obligation." *Science and Technology Librarians* 27 (1/2): 55–70.

Pullman, Philip. 2011. Quoted in "Mr. Pullman's Compass." *New York Times* Feb. 1, A24.

Revels, Ira, LeRoy J. LaFleur, and Ida T. Martinez. 2003. "Taking Library Recruitment a Step Closer: Recruiting the Next Generation of Librarians." *The Reference Librarian* 82: 157–169.

Shannon, Donna M. 2008. "School Librarianship: Career Choice and Recruitment." *Journal of Education for Library and Information Science* 49 (3): 210–229.

PART V

Media Matters

16

Gaining Coverage

Connecting and Communicating with the Media

ANNA CANGIALOSI *and* SARA WEDELL

Introduction

The Chelsea District Library serves 14,000 people in Chelsea and nearby townships in Michigan. We connect with our community through print and digital media as well as extensive community partnerships. Our experience refining our message and constantly seeking new and better ways of reaching our users has helped us establish a successful approach to media relations. Libraries cannot afford to let marketing become an afterthought. It remains crucial that librarians embrace the task of promoting their value to their communities, and effective marketing is an ideal way to do that. By creating a strong message, defining what is newsworthy, developing good media contacts, creating effective press releases, matching the best media venues with specific events and services, and finding partners outside the library to help in the marketing process, libraries can emphasize their relevance and continue to draw in new users.

Establish Your Message

All communication with media outlets should reinforce your library's message. Communicating your library's message is something every staff member should be able to do, and each person should be able to do so in his or her own natural style. Rather than constructing an overall message for all staff to use, everyone should be able to relay a message that feels comfortable to them and relevant to the service they provide, from pages and circulation clerks to librarians and managers. They should also be dynamic rather than static, changing throughout the year to highlight seasonal programs or new services, eventually building up a portfolio of messages and stories from which to draw. The message is a conversational approach to marketing, and staff members can incorporate their own personalized views into it.

For example, our library has recently established a partnership with the Chelsea Area Wellness Foundation to create a five-year community read event focused on health and wellness. The committee is developing talking points to develop a brief, consistent message that will help harness word-of-mouth power to promote the project and partnership.

The Chelsea Reads Together talking points that will form the backbone of each committee member's message look like this:

- Chelsea Reads Together (who, what)
    Partnership between the Chelsea District Library and Chelsea Area Wellness Foundation to create a multi-year community read project
- This year's book: *Blue Zones* by Dan Buettner
    Offers a prescription for living a longer, more beneficial life
- The goal: (why)
    Create a culture of wellness in Chelsea
    Engage people emotionally, intellectually, and improve the quality of life in the community
    Promote awareness of health and wellness issues
    Inspire community involvement to create a more healthy Chelsea
- How does it work? (when, how)
    Community participates by reading the same book to stimulate dialogue and the exchange of ideas.
    Takes place in October each year
    Interact with other community members in a series of events relating to the book

The talking points above are an example of the development of a timely message the community read committee can communicate with their networks to convey the news and goals of the partnership. It can create buzz for the event and help to relay consistent information to the media.

What Is News?

Be selective about information that qualifies as "news." Each event that your library hosts does not constitute news. Making the distinction yourself will save you time submitting events to your local newspaper that end up being ignored or relegated to the weekly events calendar. Notify your media partners only to promote events that actively reflect your library's creativity and innovation. This way, editors will connect library press releases with good potential stories, which will net better coverage. All other events should be submitted regularly to media event calendars.

Think creatively about what events and services to showcase at your library. Special events are good candidates for media promotion: author visits or high-profile speakers are often deserving of news coverage. When promoting them, be sure to reinforce unique benefits to the community or significant partnerships that made them possible. Two examples of these are also two of the Chelsea District Library's biggest annual events: Authors in Chelsea and the Midwest Literary Walk.

Authors in Chelsea features three authors and illustrators of young adult literature who spend the day in the schools giving workshops and assemblies, followed by an evening book signing event at the library. Promotion for the event also emphasizes the partnership with local schools and how the library is filling a need for student activities. The Midwest

Literary Walk is a daylong event featuring readings by poets and authors at a range of venues throughout Chelsea's historic downtown. Its promotion incorporates the many partnerships with businesses and arts organizations that host readings. These events are scheduled to coincide with April's National Library Week, which provides an additional opportunity to reinforce our message about our role in the community.

Aside from costly special events, your programming lineup may already have promotion-worthy events that just need the right framing to give them media appeal. For example, the Chelsea District Library has strong attendance at weekly Baby Time and Story Time events. But as standard weekly programming, they didn't have enough "pop" to generate media interest. When the Youth Department partnered with a local children's bookstore to offer a series of workshops teaching literacy skills to parents of young children, we took the opportunity to promote the specialized workshops, the new partnership, and Baby Time and Story Time as ideal next steps for developing reading skills.

Wait for a compelling reason to notify your media outlets, such as establishing a new community partner for programming, introducing a new service to patrons, or sharing a human interest story about your staff, volunteers, or donors. These are examples of your library's high service standards and community connections — put them to use promoting your library.

Newsworthy topics may include:

- Special events
- Statistics and trends in services and programs: E-book/computer usage
- Spotlighting donors and volunteers: "Why I donate/volunteer"
- Fundraising drives
- New partnerships
- Operations: Adding Blu-ray to the collection, unveiling a strategic plan
- Leadership: Introducing new hires, staff speaking engagements
- Awards and grants

Create a Quality Media List

Creating a quality media list takes time, but pays off by ensuring your message is getting to the right media connections. Start your list with major and local papers and specialty publications in your area. Become familiar with their coverage areas and note the bylines, updating your list on a regular basis. Think about the audiences each publication attracts and take care that your submissions will appeal to their demographic. Seek out connections in the digital media world; contact local bloggers and neighborhood news sites like Patch.com. The next step is to contact the people on your list and confirm that you have the correct person and subject coverage. Ask them how they prefer to receive information from you, physical vs. digital, as text in an e-mail or sent as an attachment. This is also an opportunity to make a personal connection and become more than just a name on an e-mail signature line.

Stay up to date on media coverage of your library and events. A simple way to do this is by creating a Google Alert using keywords that relate to your library, services, and events. You are immediately notified when your terms are published online. This helps you measure your success rate and track the outlets from which you receive the best coverage. Keep current on community news and make connections between community needs and trends and what your library has to offer.

Don't be afraid to ask your community partners to share their media contacts. Not all of their contacts may be universally relevant to spreading your message, but opportunities may arise. For instance, the director of Chelsea's Chamber of Commerce has a monthly spot on a local radio personality's morning show. Knowing the library's interest in promoting our new local history website, he offered the library his air time one month. The history site saw a surge of hits on the day of the broadcast and for the week following. Now we have our own established relationship with the radio personality, an understanding of the topics she covers in our community, and proven results linked to appearing on her show.

Put the following actions to use creating or improving your media list:

- Include major area newspapers, state and local specialty publications.
- Develop a list of local blogs to follow.
- Monitor media relevant to your industry.
- Verify contact information and titles.
- Make contact with the people on your media list.
- Confirm preferences for receiving content.
- Send notice of all events to multiple community calendars.
- Share media lists with your networks.

Effective Press Releases

At many libraries, one person becomes responsible for writing all press releases. This ensures consistency, but gets complicated when writing up releases for events they haven't planned. At the Chelsea District Library, we've created a press release input form to save time and share information directly. The person responsible for the subject of the press release is asked to answer the questions on the form, which can then be adapted into an accurate press release.

The basic questions are these:

- What are you announcing?
- What is the goal of this announcement?
- When should this announcement be made?
- Why is it newsworthy?
- What are one or two key messages you want to convey?
- What is the most unique feature about this event/service? How will it benefit the target audience?
- Who are the target customers?
- Are there any industry/library firsts to note?
- List any relevant/technical details about the program/service/collection.
- Are there any third parties that can be quoted in the release? Provide contact name, company, telephone, e-mail address.
- What publications/media should we target for placement?

Editors receive numerous press releases each day, and many will be skimmed over and discarded. To stay out of the recycling bin, it's important to convey the gist of your release quickly and clearly. Create a compelling headline that incorporates your basic information and keeps their attention. Keep your headline under 20 words, creating a subheading if necessary. Your headline should contain a hook, something important that conveys the value of your story.

Think of a press release as an overview of your story, so keep it under two pages and focus on hitting the main points. Start your press release off strong, frontloading it with the most important information in the first paragraph. Lead with the basic five Ws: who, what, when, where and why. In the second paragraph, include a quote from someone connected to the subject: the library director, programming librarian, community partner, etc. The rest of the release should convey the remaining details in order of importance, ending with a standard boilerplate section that serves as a brief "About Us" for your library. This is generally done in a smaller font, to indicate that it is background information. Use "-MORE-" at the bottom of the page if it is a multi-page release, and use "###" to indicate the end. You can see a sample press release from the Chelsea District Library in the appendix at the end of this chapter.

Format plays nearly as large a role as content does in maximizing the efficacy of your press release, so observe these tactics:

- Include keyword phrase in headline.
- Create hook.
- Repeat keyword two to three times in body of release.
- Bold keywords.
- Include quote(s) from partners.
- Write in an active voice.
- Avoid jargon and acronyms.
- Use inverted pyramid format:
  Include the five W's in the first paragraph: who, what, when, where and why.
  Include quote in second paragraph.
  Expand on the five Ws in subsequent paragraphs.

Press releases need to be available digitally. Most media contacts will prefer to receive them digitally, and then they should be available on your library website. When e-mailing press releases to media contacts, the safest way to go is to paste the complete text into the body of the e-mail and add a catchy subject line. Don't send the release as an attachment unless requested; it's more likely to go unread.

A few additional steps will make your release more search-friendly:

- Keyword phrase is in the headline or subheading.
- Use keyword phrase two-three times in the body.
- Emphasize the keyword phrase in bold.
- Provide hyperlinks, which help search engines index your release.

Generating Coverage

Building relationships with local reporters is an important step in generating coverage. It's an opportunity to get on their radar and inform them about what your library has to offer. Use story suggestions, subject expertise, or just a "welcome to the community" as ice-breakers. These relationships can be mutually beneficial. For example, inviting a reporter to lunch turned into a brainstorming session that resulted in several story ideas, giving our library great coverage and the reporter valuable leads.

Make receiving and viewing your content as convenient as possible. Ask your media contacts how they prefer to receive their content and be sure to comply. Some prefer text in the body of an e-mail with no hyperlinks. Others prefer text in the body of an e-mail and photos as attachments. The easier you can make publishing your content, the more you will get published. Always remember to follow up and thank them when a story gets published.

Be prompt. Reporters are always on deadlines, so make your response to their inquiries your first priority. If you are asked for a quote, respond immediately before another story takes precedence. Understand that at times your story will get bumped if space is limited and breaking news occurs. Little can be done to prevent this except making every effort to provide stories that are as newsworthy as possible.

Emphasize local angles that connect to your story. By staying up to date on a reporter's stories through their publication and professional social networking accounts, you can stay current with topics they are covering. That information can help you frame your story because relevance is a necessary part of every press release submission or story pitch. Think about how your story relates to your community or exemplifies a trend.

Know your audience. Think about which demographics are more likely to read the content online or in print and submit story ideas accordingly. For example, we have had good results from submitting stories that appeal to an older audience to the local newspaper, which has strong print circulation to our senior community members. When we were promoting the premiere of the library's WWII documentary, we got the most response from a write-up in the newspaper, followed by the library's e-mail newsletter, which is primarily read by adults who are 40 and older. The result was a heavily attended premiere that was standing room only. In a similar case, we received coverage for a St. Patrick's Day party at the library that was co-sponsored by an active teen service organization. Since few teens read the paper in print or online, we had minimal registrations that likely came from parents signing up their kids. Despite good local coverage, social media, particularly Facebook, was by far the most effective communication tool, resulting in attendance of over 100 teens.

After you take the time to establish a relationship with your media contacts, take these steps to help make it a high-quality connection:

- Build mutually-beneficial relationships.
- Be receptive to reporters' preferences.
- Localize your story.
- Highlight relevant community connections.
- Know your audience.

Building relationships with the media takes time. Make the effort to reach out to your local media representatives and go the extra mile to provide content in a manner convenient for them. Give thought to the subjects of your press releases and consider if the audience you are seeking is a demographic of the media outlets you are contacting. Keep your media connections alive by staying in touch via social media and showing your appreciation for good coverage. Finally, have a clear and consistent message that firmly demonstrates your library's goals. Show the connections between what your library provides and the needs within the community. Strong relationships with the media accomplish more than just bringing people into a program; they are essential to keep your library and its mission at the forefront of community awareness.

Appendix: Sample Press Release

FOR IMMEDIATE RELEASE

CONTACT: Jane Doe | Head of Youth and Teen Services
PHONE: 123–456–7890
E-MAIL: jdoe@yourlibrary.org

March 17, 2011 | Chelsea, MI

**Award-Winning Authors to Hold Intensive Workshops at Chelsea Schools
Authors in Chelsea is Back for Second Year**

The Chelsea District Library will hold its 2nd Annual **Authors in Chelsea** event Wednesday, April 13 as part of National Library Week. **Authors in Chelsea** is a daylong event sponsored by the Chelsea District Library and the Friends of Chelsea District Library, bringing three nationally known authors and illustrators to do workshops in Chelsea schools, free of charge. Children and their families are also invited to the Chelsea District Library in the evening to meet the authors and get books signed. This year's line-up includes **Gail Carson Levine**, author of Newbery Honor book (and motion picture) *Ella Enchanted,* Michigan cartoonist and Chelsea District Library's Artist-in-Residence **Jerzy Drozd,** and **Johanna Hurwitz**, author of many books for young readers, including *Class Clown* and *Teacher's Pet.*

Authors in Chelsea provides children close contact with nationally known, award-winning authors and illustrators to explore the art and craft of writing and illustrating in order to encourage students to read and appreciate literature. "**Authors in Chelsea** will help students see that writing is a viable option for the future: real people write these wonderful books, someday they could too!" says Patrick Little, Principal of Beach Middle School.

Through intensive workshops with the authors, students will work to improve their creative writing, drawing, and reading abilities. The library is donating books by each author and illustrator to the participating school classrooms. "The visit to North Creek in March of 2010 by illustrator Mr. Frankenhuyzen was an exciting opportunity for our 2nd graders to meet an expert and learn illustration techniques. Teachers and students alike were appreciative for the **Authors in Chelsea** Program," says Beth Ingall, First Grade Teacher at North Creek Elementary. This program aims to inspire students to excellence by exposing them to high-quality authors and illustrators and perfect for all ages who have a love of children's literature. "Last year the Authors in Chelsea program gave our 2nd graders an up-close and personal experience with an experienced illustrator. The students were able to interact, ask questions and create illustrations alongside Mr. Frankenhuyzen," says Beth Newman, 2nd grade teacher.

Each author will be visiting Chelsea schools on April 13 to do writing and drawing workshops in the morning and afternoon with all the classes in 2nd, 4th, and 6th

-MORE-grades. The public is invited to the library's McKune Room in the evening to hear a brief presentation from each author, ask questions, and then get book(s) signed from 6:30–8:00 P.M. Wednesday, April 13. Books by each author will be available for purchase at the library, courtesy of Chelsea's *Just Imagine* bookstore. This is an all-ages event, and registration is not required.

About Us: The Chelsea District Library is a nonprofit organization whose mission is to provide equal access to quality resources that serve the lifelong cultural, educational, and informational needs and interests of all people. The library currently serves 14,000 residents in the Chelsea district–City of Chelsea plus Dexter, Lima, Lyndon, and Sylvan townships, and more than 20,000 individuals visit the library each month. The library's state-of-the-art facility is an access point for information including: books, periodicals, DVDs, CDs, audiobooks, downloadable e-books, subscription databases as well as access to the Internet. In addition to providing dynamic services to complement and support local schools and other important community needs, the Chelsea District Library strives to present timely, interesting, and high-quality programs and events to engage and enrich the Chelsea community.

###

17

Interacting with Other Entities Using Social Media

Michaela D. Willi Hooper
and Emily Scharf

Introduction

Social media is the place to see and be seen, not only for individuals, but for organizations. Early occurrences, such as ICQ and SixDegrees.com, allowed individual users to find and communicate with one another (Boyd and Ellison 2007). Now, sites like Facebook encourage people to network with one another and share their interests and loyalties. Businesses and nonprofits soon caught on to the enormous potential of social media for niche marketing. From Twitter's inception, businesses have leveraged its ability to allow them direct communication with their clients. Social media allows organizations to market to interested individuals instead of to stereotypes (Blakely 2010). Now, marketers can not only target clients who live in their geographical area or belong to a certain demographic, but also to those who share certain interests, activities, and beliefs.

Businesses have long understood the benefit of cross-promoting. An amusement park offers a discount on a soft drink can; a movie ticket offers 15 percent off at a nearby restaurant. Libraries and other nonprofits are even better poised to cross-promote because they have the same goal: to benefit the community, be it a city or a university. Examples of existing cross-promotional activities with libraries abound: a university history department and a university library co-sponsor a lecture; a local art cooperative displays its work in the public library.

The power of social media marketing facilitates this synergy. The local YMCA may post library events on its physical bulletin board and on its Facebook wall. The University of Michigan "tweets" about an author talk happening at the Ann Arbor District Library that may interest its students, faculty, and alumni. When organizations connect online, they increase individual awareness of their brands. A coffee lover may not realize the public library had a Facebook page until she sees her local coffee shop share a link about a lecture at the library entitled "Origins: Coffee." The "Geek the Library" campaign, sponsored by OCLC, reminds patrons that the library has resources for every hobby and interest. You can reach these special interest groups and hobbyists by working with the organizations that serve them.

Interacting with Other Entities Using Facebook

In 2010, Facebook overtook Google as the most visited website in the world (Saba 2010). What began as a social networking site for college students became a web within a web, where anybody and everybody has a profile page, including major corporations and nonprofit organizations. These public profile pages — belonging to shops, banks, universities, and public figures — can be seen by anyone, and are great opportunities for marketing. Sections of a profile (denoted by linked pages on the left side of the main page) include a wall, info, discussions, photos, videos, and events. Photos and videos are self-explanatory. The "wall" is the default page where most interaction takes place in Facebook. People can then comment on or "like" a post. For example, the "Geek the Library" campaign posted a link on their wall about the Shelbyville-Shelby County Public Library and individuals were then able to respond. "Info" is a more static page, comparable to the "about us" section of a traditional website. Some pages will have additional sections, like games and information on special products.

When two individuals connect on Facebook, they are called "friends." Each can see information about the other that is not available to the general public. The language is different when an individual connects to a public page. When Susan "likes" the Internet Public Library, several things happen: her friends can see that she "likes" the IPL, she will see updates from the IPL in her newsfeed, and the IPL can send her notifications. The IPL, however, cannot see the information about her that is not public.

In addition to a list of the individuals who "like" it, each institution can also have a list of favorite pages. For example, someone looking at the Poem In Your Pocket page might see the New York Public Library listed among other public New York City pages and decide to "like" it as well. Connecting with other institutions is a great way to expand your user base.

Once you have created your page, it is a good idea to find other entities in your region or with similar interests and add them as "likes." This will encourage them to do the same for you. Some suggestions might be other departments in your university, other branches of your library, other nonprofits in your city, and other venues that host events. A word of caution: remember that this is not your personal Facebook page, and not a place for you to express your beliefs. You should avoid "liking" "1,000,000 strong against eating animals" unless your institution includes vegetarianism in its mission statement.

Games ("applications") such as Farmville were very popular on Facebook for several years. The requests to "Help Suzy raise a barn" frustrated some Facebook users. At an institution where one of the authors worked, we were amused and horrified to find that an administrator of the library's Facebook page had installed an application on our page that allowed students to "Give the Library a Beer." The design of Facebook has since changed, and these applications have become less prevalent, but it is important to control access to the login information for the library account and to regularly check the page for spam. Not monitoring your page regularly will result in fewer individuals and organizations interacting with it.

In addition to the above-mentioned parts of a Facebook page, there is sometimes a Discussions section. This allows any user who "likes" the library to post a comment, similar to any other online discussion board. Monitoring what people are saying about your library is essential, but the Discussion board can also be a helpful place. You can get feedback about programs because Facebook users are able to post longer blocks of text.

You do not need to "like" this page to do cross-promotions. You can mention any entity or individual in a post on your wall. This will be seen in the newsfeeds of all individuals who "like" your page. To hyperlink on Facebook, begin by typing the "@" symbol when you are entering a post. As you type, Facebook will suggest entities and individuals in a dropdown menu who already have a Facebook account. Choose the appropriate suggestion offered, and when you enter your post, this name will be hyperlinked. Your status will appear on their wall, and, depending on privacy settings, be seen by both your "likers" and the "likers" of that institution. For example, Washington University Libraries-Olin Library posted a trailer from the Washington University Film and Media Archive, linking to the archive in the status.

Events, especially, lend themselves to cross-promotion. Many libraries choose to promote events on Facebook by linking to the calendar of events on their regular website. There are benefits to using the Facebook Events function, though. It allows individuals to see who else is attending, including which of their friends have said they will be there. Facebook Events also allows other organizations and individuals to "share" the link, expanding publicity beyond the library's own fan base. If you are having an author come in who has written a book about music, you could send a message to the city symphony orchestra asking them to share the event as well, since it might be of interest to their fan base. Individuals will be "reminded" of upcoming events to which they have been invited. Facebook will even recommend events that their friends are going to.

Facebook tends to tweak its interface frequently. Some of the technology tips above may become obsolete in the future. The best way to keep up is simply to use your page to interact with your patrons and other institutions. Facebook will notify you about the "upgrade." It is a good idea to look to other libraries with active pages for best practices. You can search for a particular library at the top of the page. A search for "library" yields a list of possible matches, along with how many people "like" each page, indicating their popularity.

Interacting with Other Entities Using Twitter

Twitter began in 2006 as a social network where users can send short posts. Posts, called "tweets," are limited to 140 characters and can include hyperlinks, often in the form of shortened URLs (more on this later). A tweet can be something as simple as, "I'm off to the public library to get some new books," or it can be the start of a conversation. As libraries strive to market to users in the Millennial Generation, social media has become an important way to reach out (Connell 2009). The opportunity for interaction between libraries, communities, and other Twitter users is great because of the nature of two-way communication (King 2009). Social media has allowed for a dialogue between customers and those providing service that has never been so immediate. Libraries can take advantage of Twitter's two-way communication by promoting events, discussing new books, sharing reviews, and much more.

When a tweet is sent out, other Twitter users can reply. The conversation described next highlights several Twitter features. A user tweeted about Cleveland Public Library's website and tagged the library using the @ symbol. The library responded with the @ symbol and the username of the person who had the problem. The library's response was able to include information about solving the problem. Similar to Facebook, Twitter uses the @ symbol to link to other user names.

In March of 2010, Webster University Library joined Twitter. Many other entities involved with Webster University had Twitter accounts; this included the president, an official university Twitter stream, many deans, various extended campus sites (the library is on the main campus in St. Louis), student groups, the school's mascot, and more. Many universities have multiple entities using Twitter accounts. These can include both groups and people. Webster Library was already being mentioned on Twitter in positive and negative ways; one user tweeted how beautiful the snow was outside the windows, and another user tweeted his concern that he could not connect to the Internet.

At Webster University, interactions through Twitter fall under the social media guidelines (www.webster.edu/socialmedia). The official Webster University Twitter account is maintained by Patrick Powers, interactive media manager. Mr. Powers responds to users who make negative comments about the university or other aspects of campus life, normally with a simple "How can I help?" Letting the user know that a real person is at the other end of the "twitterverse" sometimes helps Twitter users get assistance. Often, users respond to @websteru with a question or a comment for the specific office with which they are having trouble. Users can leverage Twitter to get an answer from a university-affiliated person.

Responding to user feedback on social networks in a timely manner is important. It is a fast-paced world, and waiting a week for a response is not going to cut it. There is no way to make everybody happy, but letting angry or frustrated Twitter or Facebook users know they can get help and providing them with a name, e-mail, or phone number of someone who can help is a good first step. Sometimes Twitter users ask a question that makes it easy to respond. For example, "How come the printers at Webster Library print double sided, also why only 2 scanners?" This is a straightforward question that was answered in 140 characters, and the user was able to engage in quick two-way communication. Short conversations like this are perfect for Twitter.

Interaction can occur as a conversation, or by pointing out something another user would like. The Gorlok, Webster University's mascot, tweeted an article from The Chronicle of Higher Education to the library using a shortened URL. Many different URL shorteners exist and are a way to share links on Twitter without using too many of the 140 characters allowed for each post. The URL shortener takes a long web address with many letters and numbers and shortens it to a manageable-sized URL. Common URL shorteners available for free on the web include bit.ly, tinyurl.com, is.gd, and dft.ba.

Twitter uses the term "hashtag" to refer to a topic that is discussed using tweets. These hashtags can be very beneficial for organizing the information on Twitter. They begin with a pound sign (#). Follow a Library Day on Twitter was October 1, 2010. The librarians behind Follow a Library Day (http://followalibrary.blogspot.com) got two well-known librarians to support their cause and thus got the word out to many librarians and libraries using the hashtag #followalibrary. On October 1, Webster Library tweeted about the event and the official Webster University Twitter account did, too. Thanks to the promotion, Webster Library's Twitter account gained approximately five followers. Hashtags can also be used for advocacy, like the #SaveLibraries hashtag, which is promoted by the

American Library Association (www.ala.org/ala/aboutala/offices/cro/getinvolved/saveyourlibraries.cfm). Some hashtags are used to identify your topic or geographical region. Some universities have their own hashtags, and some cities do, too. At Champlain College in Burlington, Vermont, students, faculty, community members, and more use the hashtag #campchamp. This hashtag can be used by local businesses to market specials to students or by the library to highlight displays, for example. The tweet by the local bistro also uses a city hashtag for Burlington, Vermont, in the form of #bvt. Hastags can account for successful cross-promotion across a community because users can easily search for their location or university.

Libraries can use Twitter for cross-promotion with community organizations, nonprofits, other media entities, and more. In any city or town, there are multiple entities using Twitter. Using information from Twitter feeds can highlight your library collections as well as your local paper, for example. As another example, a book review was retweeted by Buffalo/Erie Public Library and promotes both the book in the library's collection and the story from Buffalo Rising Media. Other libraries invite local organizations in for tours and engage in cross-promotion that way. The Vancouver Public Library was mentioned in a tweet by a local YWCA regarding a job-search tour. Countless examples of community organizations working together exist on Twitter to reach out to people who will likely enjoy the activities of both parties.

HootSuite (www.hootsuite.com), a social media dashboard, is a website that allows Twitter users to more easily keep up their Twitter accounts without using http://twitter.com. HootSuite gives users the option to schedule tweets, so when preparing what to post about your library, you can take time on a Monday morning and plan out tweets for the rest of the week. HootSuite will post these messages for you on a designated date, at a certain time. HootSuite also allows users to include shorten URLs with their tweets and has a built-in URL shortener (ow.ly). Another nice feature of HootSuite is the ability to gather statistics regarding these URLs. You can see how many people have clicked on them and from which geographical region. The downside to this program is that it now operates on a "freemium" model, whereby for one user, it is free, but for many advanced features and institutional accounts, there is a monthly cost to use HootSuite.

"Following" an account on Twitter is the equivalent of "friending" on Facebook. Libraries take different approaches to following users. Some university libraries follow anyone who mentions the library in a tweet, anyone who is affiliated with the university, and other university entities. Public libraries face a different challenge, because following patrons can be tricky. The public library users are not officially related to the library, like students, faculty, and staff are to a university. A good rule of thumb is to follow those who mention your library in their tweets and also follow community Twitter accounts for other libraries, businesses, and organizations. This will increase the visibility of your account and not offend any patrons because you have followed them without knowing them. Not all libraries follow that plan, however. According to a *Library Journal* article about following patrons or potential patrons, one librarian says, "We started by proactively seeking out locals and following them ... [w]e want to keep focused on using Twitter as a platform for interaction with our community" (Oder, Blumenstein, Hadro, and Miller 2010).

Like Facebook, Twitter is helpful for up-to-the-minute news about the library. If the campus is closed due to a snow day, for example, updating the library's Twitter account to tell patrons the status of the library can be helpful. Due to the 140 character limit of

Twitter, it should not be used as the only social media presence of your library, but it is certainly something to think about for your library.

In addition to the above-mentioned uses for marketing with Facebook and Twitter, libraries might benefit from using both social networks together. Reminding Facebook friends that you have a Twitter account and mentioning to Twitter followers that you have a Facebook page are easy ways to start doing this (Levy 2010). You can also link the accounts together so they update with the same information. There are different applications you can use to do this, including the Twitter application for Facebook which will update your Facebook status with your tweets and vice versa. The possibility to interact with other entities is lessened by doing this, because you are broadcasting the same message to all groups. By limiting your Facebook posts to the Twitter minimum of 140 characters, your marketing message might be diluted. Then again, if you do not have much time to market with social media, this is an easy way to get your library "out there" on both Twitter and Facebook.

Conclusion

We have delved somewhat into the technical language and functioning of two popular social media sites, Facebook and Twitter. The main purpose of this writing, though, is to illustrate how libraries can reach users by cross-promoting between institutions. Social media changes quickly, and books written about Twitter today will likely be obsolete in five years. Whatever new media is on the horizon, it is likely that some principles will remain the same.

• It is important to understand the functions and etiquette of each platform. Knowing the Twitter "hashtag" for your region, for example, is essential if you want to be "retweeted."

• Choose the organizations and individuals you interact with wisely. Who is part of your physical community that might also be online? Just as in real life, there may be vandals leaving "graffiti" on your "walls." You will need to decide what is vandalism and what is a valuable user contribution.

• But, do not be afraid of social media! Social media only serves to illustrate that which we should already know — everything is about relationships.

Libraries were intrinsic parts of their communities long before the advent of social media. Cross-promotional relationships existed and still exist in the analog world. Before we were "tweeting" responses to patrons, we were answering questions at the reference desk; before we were publicizing our new e-book collection on Facebook, we were hanging flyers for a Friends of the Library book sale on the bulletin board in the local senior center. Social media is just another opportunity to interact with your community instantly, transparently, and globally.

Works Cited

Blakely, J. 2010. *Social Media and the End of Gender* (TEDWomen, December); 8 min., 27 sec; from TEDTalks. SWF http://www.ted.com/talks/johanna_blakley_social_media_and_the_end_of_gender.html (accessed February 23, 2011).

Boyd, D. M., and N.B. Ellison. 2007. "Social Network Sites: Definition, History, and Scholarship." *Journal of Computer-Mediated Communication* 13 (1). http://jcmc.indiana.edu/vol13/issue1/boyd.ellison.html (accessed February 23, 2011).

Connell, R. S. 2009. "Academic Libraries, Facebook and MySpace, and Student Outreach: A Survey of Student Opinion." *portal: Libraries and the Academy* 9 (1): 25–36. http://www.infosherpas.com/libr246-11/files/Project%20Muse.pdf (accessed February 23, 2011).

King, D. L. 2009. "Creating Community at the Digital Branch." *Library Technology Reports* 45 (6): 30–33.

Levy, J. R. 2010. *Facebook Marketing: Designing Your Next Marketing Campaign.* Indianapolis: Que Publishing.

Oder, N., L. Blumenstein, J. Hadro, and R. Miller. 2010. "When Libraries Rack up Twitter Followers." *Library Journal,* April 15. 135 (7): 16.

Saba, J. 2010. "Facebook Tops Google as the Most Visited Site in the U.S." *Reuters,* December 30. http://www.reuters.com/article/2010/12/30/us-facebook-google-idUSTRE6BT40320101230 (accessed February 23, 2011).

Blinding Glimpses of the Obvious

The Simple Things That Will Unleash Your Library's Star Power

JOANNE KING

Every library needs good publicity. It helps bring awareness of valuable library services and programs to potential users and funders. It builds community goodwill. But it is not easy to come by in most communities. Most of us are competing for attention with businesses and nonprofits that can afford to outspend us. The traditional media landscape is shrinking, with fewer daily newspapers and locally-programmed television outlets. Most libraries do not have professional public relations people. And — let's face it — the library world is short on the glitz and glam that makes headlines.

Despite the challenges, there are many successes to be had by applying simple, low-cost outreach strategies along with a serious dose of common sense.

Queens Library is one of New York City's three public library systems. We are in the same media market as some of the highest-profile institutions and events in the world. We are handicapped by being geographically distant from the heart of the action (Manhattan). Yet, we score a lot of press coverage by making the optimal use of the tools at hand.

The Rules

1. Be accessible and responsive. Answer your phone. Pick up your voice messages. Read your e-mail and your text messages. Respond in a timely manner. It sounds foolish, yet many opportunities are lost because no one answered the call. In the "olden" days, business etiquette required every phone call to be returned the same day. If you couldn't do it yourself, your assistant or colleague called and said, "I apologize, Mr./Ms. X is tied up today and will return your call tomorrow. Is there something I can help you with in the meantime?" It is a good practice. Empires have probably been lost because no one bothered to return a phone message.

2. Now means "*now.*" Right now. This instant. Journalists and media people work on deadlines. They have a gigantic content void to fill. Now. As you certainly know, news moves at lightning speed, and that speed is being accelerated all the time. When a media representative contacts you, you need to grab the opportunity *right now*. In a couple of hours, they will move on to something else. Andy Warhol famously predicted that "in the future, everyone will be world-famous for fifteen minutes." If he could have foreseen the twenty-first century information landscape, he might have predicted only fifteen seconds worth of fame.

3. Say "yes" first, figure out the details later. When a media outlet calls and wants to send a reporter to cover something at the library, say "yes." Do not hesitate. Do not take time to think it over. Do not say, "I am not sure, I have to ask Ms. So-and-so." Say "yes." Figure out how you will handle it *after* you hang up.

4. Before that ... be *empowered* to say "yes." Media outreach can and should only be handled by someone in your library whose judgment is beyond question and who is armed with full, pertinent information. If the senior management or the board or municipal overseers (or whoever is at the top of the reporting structure) prefers to control information and access at a higher level, then wherever that might be is where the media inquiries must go. There is not time to ask "may I?" up the ladder, wait for an answer to come down the ladder, and still take advantage of opportunities that will shine positive light (or avert negative light!) on your library.

5. Meet the journalists' needs. Media people need input to do their jobs. If they do not get it from your library, they will simply get it from somewhere else. Whether the news is good or bad, you want to be in control.

Example of bad news: there was a small smoky fire in the library, caused by an antiquated coffee pot. The media phoned for information, but the library has decided not to comment (always a big, big mistake). What does the journalist do to meet his need for a comment? He stands out front and asks a passer-by, "Did you know there was a fire here yesterday? Don't you think that is careless and a disgrace?" And the passer-by, primed by the negative way the question was framed (and flattered to be inside the drama), says, "Of course it's a disgrace! Half the town could have burnt to the ground! I'm lucky to still be alive!"

A good news example: a B-list author is doing a book signing at your library. Normally, the media would not bother, but it is a slow news day and they have a void to fill. It is your lucky day. Unless ... you don't answer the call promptly (rule #1). Or you drag your feet before agreeing (rules #2 and #3). Or you do not meet their needs when they arrive (rule #5).

What does the journalist need? The journalist needs the pertinent information about the event. He needs to interview the principal and at least two others. He prefers a picture, if at all possible. A quote from the library is always held in high esteem. In the case of the B-list author's book signing, that means a brief bio of the author and a list of other publications, an interview with the author, a chance to ask two library customers what they like about the book, and a quote from the library director or the president of the Friends of the Library about how honored they are to have such a celebrity in their midst, and inviting customers to check out all the titles at the library, available in multiple formats.

Where are you getting all of this information on the spur of the moment? You are a library person, for heaven's sake! This is what you do! If a customer walked into your library and asked for a brief bio of the author, a list of his other publications, etc., you would hand over a list of resources in a heartbeat! Be your own library customer.

If the journalist gets what he needs easily, he will readily think of the library next time he needs editorial. If you make him pull teeth, he won't be back.

6. Think about the big picture. The single best weapon in your media arsenal is a good picture. "Good" means visually interesting as well as high quality. If it also has motion so it makes usable video, it will increase your coverage exponentially. An example: your library is opening a new wing. A photo of the outside of the building is of minimal interest. A photo of three individuals dressed in suits, smiling in front of the library is minimally better. Those same individuals shaking hands with people as they enter is a bit better because they are moving. Dress those same people in colorful costumes from favorite storybooks and you are on the right track for TV news coverage. The more drama you can dream up, the better.

Picture quality is very important. Digital cameras have excellent quality, are affordable, and easy-to-use. The pictures must meet minimal specifications. For purposes of print media, you need a resolution of at least 200 dpi (dots per inch). For online use, 72 dpi is sufficient. A picture taken at 200 dpi is perfectly usable online, but not vice versa. A word about fluorescent lighting: if your camera does not have a special setting to deal with it, buy a small piece of "minus green gel" at a camera store or online. It is a thin sheet of pink-colored gelatin. Simply tape it across the lens of your camera with a bit of masking tape. It will get rid of that ugly green tinge that plagues photos taken in fluorescent lighting. Total cost: under $5.

7. The more mud you throw at a wall, the more sticks. Getting good publicity for your library is a numbers game. The more you pitch, the more you get. Truly, no matter how worthy the story is, you will get a very small percentage of hits. Do not become discouraged and stop because "they never use it anyway." Every pitch builds awareness of the library with the media, whether they pick it up or not, and contributes to your ultimate success.

8. "Everybody knows" is among the world's most useless phrases. It's right up there with "don't worry" and "calm down." No, everybody does *not* know what your library does. If they once knew, they may have forgotten. And you have introduced new services and programs. You constantly need to re-introduce your most basic services and programs to your target populations. New people move into the service area. Young parents have forgotten what is available for toddlers. Recent retirees never knew the scope of what's available to them because they have never had the opportunity to access it during the day. You probably are great about announcing new whiz-bang services when they first are introduced. Then what? The programs and services that build the greatest value for your community are the ones that are going to be there for decades, precisely because they are so valuable. They deserve the spotlight every now and again. Re-brand them in a fresher way.

9. "Everybody texts" (or keeps in touch via Facebook or reads their paper mail) is an equally useless phrase. People absorb information from many sources simultaneously. The more often they hear it, read it, see it, and from the biggest variety of sources, the better they will remember and accept it as truth. If you want to get the word out about an event or service, you need to use every single communication channel you can possibly think of, all at the same time. The more, the merrier. They are not redundant.

10. Look forward more than you look backward. Too many library publications and newsletters rely on photos and stories about events that have already happened, because the event was successful, and of course, people enjoy seeing the photos. If your purpose is to encourage the public to utilize and think well of your library, you have to spend most of your promotional effort on programs that have not happened yet. Look at the for-profit world for inspiration. Think about the last sale booklet that you received from a department store. Their purpose is to lure you into their physical or online store. They have spent more money than anyone in the library world will ever see to find the right formula. If they had photos of happy shoppers enjoying last week's sale, would it make you want to rush in? Do you see photos of the store's board of directors? A message from the store manager? Obviously, a library is not a retail store, and there is ample reason to make the board and staff feel appreciated. Nevertheless, there is a lot to be learned by modeling after the retail sector. Paradise-yet-to-be-found is more compelling than paradise lost.

The Tips

What do you have to tell the media about your library? You have plenty to say, and it is right under your nose. Here are some ideas to help you look at the bounty in new and exciting ways.

• **Recycle and re-brand.** This is a lot like cooking with leftovers. Take what you already have, give it a great new name, then announce it and suddenly — a star is born. Take your cue from of-the-moment buzzwords you are hearing in popular culture. Echo the same language. The odds are that you are already doing this in the form of topical book displays. The only additions are A Name and An Announcement.

An example would be during an economic recession. You know from library customer inquiries that people need financial assistance and help in managing their money. You have an opportunity to pull together your financial literacy print resources, photocopy the online resources list, put a sign over the stack, and send An Announcement to the press that you have opened the Financial Literacy Center. Your press announcement has a quote about how important it is to the community and what kinds of resources customers can find. Although you haven't spent a dime, it appears that you have a new, relevant service and a reason for the press to cover your library. You can just as easily have Family Game Night Center, Emergency Preparedness Center, Parenting Center, even a light-hearted Zombie Survival Center. It does not last forever. When the sign and the need get dusty, roll out something else. Or ... if you have the desire and the time, you can leverage any of these into extra resources by approaching a relevant business for funding. The First State Bank Financial Literacy Center has a weighty ring to it and might include some programs on the topic funded by the bank.

The Announcement and The Name are what makes the difference. Half a shelf of books on health are just that: half a shelf of books on health. Half a shelf of books on health with A Name and An Announcement are the Community Wellness Resource, and a genuine media opportunity.

• **More about The Name:** In order to feel relevant and "now," choose language from popular culture and use terms that customers can relate to, even if they are less correct than the professional terminology. Yes, "Multimedia Center" is correct, but "DVDs, CDs and Video Games" is a better communication. Resist library-speak.

• **Manufacture photo opportunities.** Anything that delights the eye will delight the media. The more unusual you can make it, the more compelling it will be. Play "dress up" with your events. If you always have a defensive driving course for over 55-year-olds, at the last session, provide borrowed academic caps and gowns and let the customers "graduate" for the camera. It upgrades an everyday program into a potential media event.

• **What if they don't come?** It is entirely possible that you will have handed out those caps and gowns, but the media do not come for any one of a million reasons. You did not waste your time. *You* will take the picture and send it out and get more coverage than you could have imagined. But — and this is very important — it has to be done right now. Now. The pictures cannot sit locked in the camera for two weeks until someone gets around to it. Now. E-mail it now. (See Rule #2).

• **A word about elected representatives.** They love to have their pictures taken. They *live* to have their pictures taken. Admittedly, they will often be boring pictures; nevertheless, you will make it up in goodwill. Invite your elected representatives to come to the library for every imaginable reason.

• **Take advantage of slow news periods, and understand what an "evergreen" story is.** Media people are regular people. They have too much to do during the holidays. They have children with head colds. They want to take time off and get away from the daily grind. If you facilitate for them, they will come back to you again and again.

News has natural rhythms that mirror the business world and the weather. Barring a real disaster, hard news naturally slows down during holiday periods, a few days before long weekends, in the depth of the winter, and the height of the summer. This is because newsmakers are going on vacation and/or distracted with their own lives. At the same time, the need to fill the newspaper or broadcast goes on. These are gilt-edged golden opportunities for libraries. Stories that might never see the light of day suddenly become viable.

"Evergreen" is the term the media use for a story that is not nailed to a specific date or event. The opening of a new building happens on the date that it happens. A profile of the artist who painted the mural in the children's room, however, is equally relevant whenever they run it. It is "evergreen."

When you provide evergreen story ideas to the media that they can use during slow news periods, you have created an ideal environment for news coverage. Think ahead. Three weeks before Thanksgiving, for instance, you dream up two or three evergreen story ideas. Maybe you found a bunch of photos of winter sledding in the late 1800s from the local history collection or you suggest they profile Ms. Smith, who is 98 years old and has been a library volunteer for 70 years. The stories must be evergreen. Why? The media people are going to be taking time off and they need to do the story in advance, then run it during the holiday period.

Send a very brief pitch off to a couple of media outlets and tell them to contact you whenever they are ready. Specifically use the term "evergreen story ideas." Then sit back and wait. Have all your ducks in a row because inevitably, you will get the call at the least convenient time. (But you will say "yes," per Rule #3.)

The weeks grind by. The reporter is exhausted. Her children have head colds and she has to bake for the holidays, plus she has to file *two* columns so she can take the holiday week off. What to do? What to do? The library! She has your pitch! Those stories are evergreen! She is saved!

Then it gets better. Once the story appears, other media representatives, also exhausted and looking for low-hanging fruit, see it and do stories about the library. It becomes a landslide of positive media coverage and you are a media darling.

• **Redefine who "the media" are.** Once upon a time, daily newspapers were the authoritative voice. Then, broadcast radio and television became the 800 lb. gorillas. That has all changed. Media is highly de-centralized. Blogs written by anonymous nobodies carry enormous weight in the public perception. To make your library a star, you have to broaden your perspective about whom you should contact. Taking a 360-degree approach will yield the best results, because each media outlet has a tiny slice of the pie. Newspapers and broadcast outlets are still very important. So are ethnic media, blogs — especially the micro-local ones — online-only news sources, bulletins of local houses of worship and community groups, social media, and a million outlets that will become important tomorrow but haven't been invented today. The point is: you may be very successful in the media even when you do not get the front page of the daily newspaper. Smaller hits are equally valuable, and even more influential among certain demographic groups. Define success by how well your library is known and loved, not by which media got you there.

• **Lose control.** The biggest obstacle to making your library a star is fear, because you can never be 100 percent certain of what will be written. Inviting the media to wantonly have their way with you is inherently risky. Libraries, boards, corporate attorneys, City Fathers and Mothers worry about letting customers make unfiltered comments about the library. They worry that staff will say something unflattering. What if the photographer shows the messy corner in the basement? What if...? Do not throw the baby out with the bath water. Good, consistent media coverage is overwhelmingly beneficial to your mission. To get it, you are going to have to loosen up and place some trust in the universe. Libraries are inherently good places that do so much good for the community. That will always shine through.

Loosen up! Let your imagination fly! Throw open the windows, and try something new! Headlines await.

PART VI

Using Community Partnerships

19

Community Outreach

Downtown Scavenger Hunt and Business Holiday Discounts

Mary Lou Carolan

In the summer of 2007, I was faced with a dilemma. As the children's coordinator for the Wallkill Public Library, I had just received a 2' by 3' cardboard standup display of "Ike the Detective Dog," the mascot for that summer's reading program, for use as a promotional item. As I looked around our very small library, I couldn't imagine where I would place "Ike" where he would be enjoyed but not tripped over. It was at that moment that I had an idea. This attention-getting display would be much more effectively used out in the community rather than sitting stationary in our children's room. I decided to create an opportunity to encourage people to stay and explore downtown once they had visited the library, and "Ike" was going to help me.

Our library sits in the heart of the hamlet of Wallkill, a small rural community in New York with a downtown business area of mom and pop stores struggling to survive. Traffic to the businesses suffered greatly when the local grocery store closed and families stopped coming downtown. I often wondered how the library could help bring families back to the main street as we always had a pretty steady stream of customers. The advantage a library has is much like that of a traditional anchor store — it is a destination place that experiences repeat visitation, on a weekly or bi-weekly basis, and offers unique products and services to people of all ages.

However, not everyone sees the library as a place of influence with intrinsic value and relevance to the community. We have a unique opportunity to enhance our image in this way if we are persistent, creative, and begin to think more strategically, like entrepreneurs. Developing methods to emphasize our impact by sharing impressive annual usage statistics, unique collections, children's programming, and digital services with the community makes good business sense. Consider summarizing this information on bookmarks and handing them out to business people, town council members, school officials, and other decision makers. Add it to your website and train your staff to understand and communicate this information to your customers.

Having a 20-year career in the nonprofit sector taught me a very valuable lesson: the major reason people don't give to an organization or a cause is that they simply have not been asked. I have applied this principle to the marketing of all of our library programs. In the library world, we need to become comfortable asking our community to get involved and help us out, to take the initiative, step outside of our comfort zones, and introduce ourselves to everyone we can as a library representative and let them know what we are doing. Let them know how effective we are at creating an educated and informed citizenry while building a strong community.

It's also important to consider our requests for support from the business owners' perspectives. Think about questions they might have. What's in it for them? Why should they care? What difference could it make for their business? Make sure you have considered these questions and have solid responses developed before you venture out. People will generally be interested if they can feel your enthusiasm, if you show that you care about them, and if you let them know that you are making a reasonable request. Small business owners want to hear about free advertising for their business, the potential for increased traffic to boost sales, an opportunity to promote their business as "family-friendly," or ways they can be affiliated with other local shops that may have been around longer and are more established.

It was armed with this reasoning that I ventured out into our community on a warm afternoon in late spring of 2007 to promote our summer reading program. I walked from business to business toting the cardboard display. I asked the business owners if they would be interested in hosting "Ike" in their store for one week and be part of a library scavenger hunt. I informed them of our marketing strategy for the program and estimated the number of kids who would participate in the game, thus visiting their establishments. Then, we promoted it like crazy.

Eight businesses enthusiastically jumped on board. Each of the eight weeks of the summer reading program, participating kids (234 in all) came to the library to pick up a clue which described the business of the week in a playful rhyme. The kids and their families then wandered around downtown, using the hints from a rhyming clue, to find where "Ike" was hidden. The bakery/collectibles shop, named after Elsie the cow of Borden condensed milk fame, was found using this clue: "Coffee, bagels and homemade jellies, this place has stuff that's good for our bellies; it also has fun stuff and old stuff too; and its name is inspired by the one that says, 'Moo.'" The ice cream store/Christian gift shop could be located with this clue: "I do, you do, we all do, for this...? Find Ike hiding in this 'divine' place downtown." The local barbershop in the little red house could be found with this silly rhyme: "Fro hawks, Mohawks, a flat top or a buzz. You come to this place to get rid of some fuzz. Just look for a building that is little and red, and think of where you might go to do something good for your head!" You get the idea. It's not Walt Whitman, but it's fun.

Businesses were encouraged to hide the Ike display away from their windows so the kids and their parents had to come inside to find him and have their clue slip signed by the store owner. Our goal was to connect families with business owners, encourage people to see what the businesses offered, and ultimately support their local merchants. It worked. Each business welcomed between 35 and 40 new visitors per week. Store owners held their own promotions and welcomed the families by handing out lollipops, homemade cookies, balloons, discount coupons, and goodie bags. The kids and their parents grew more excited with each week of the game. They enjoyed walking downtown, getting to know the store owners, marveling at the fact that we had an old-fashioned hardware store, a flower shop, a gift shop, and more.

The owner of the small soft-serve ice cream shop remarked: "We had so many new customers that week that I wished we could adopt Ike for the summer. Here we were thinking we were just helping out the library, but it turned out the library was actually helping us!" That was the beauty of the program — it seemed to bring a lot of people together to become more of a community. Libraries have a unique capability of taking a leadership role in helping to build and strengthen downtown communities; they can become places that anchor community life and bring people together.

Taking on the role of entrepreneur and marketer, however, may not be something that all library staff are necessarily comfortable with, prepared for, interested in, or knowledgeable about. Therefore, finding the right person to deliver the message is just as important as the message itself. Ideally, the director or head librarian would take on this role, but perhaps the children's librarian or other outgoing, fun, and personable staff member may be the better choice. Challenging the stereotype of the "bun-toting, shushing librarian" is a formidable but necessary task if we are to progress boldly as a profession into the twenty-first century. Improved marketing and outreach efforts can have a significant impact on enhancing public awareness and perception of libraries, repositioning the library as the heart of the community as well as an essential service.

It's important that libraries leverage the economic contribution that they make just by being in the community. Once patrons leave the library, they can choose to use other services such as restaurants, banks, grocery stores, and coffee shops in the immediate area. In our community, we have been fostering this behavior by featuring a "support your local business" section in our front hall, posting flyers for new businesses and new menus for cafes, as well as business cards, brochures, and special sales event notices. We have encouraged local cafes and coffee shops to provide our story time parents with coupons and offer children's specials so the parents will be enticed into gathering there before or after programming. We sell discount cards for the school band program, benefit dinner tickets for the Lions Club, cookbooks and local history guides for the historical society; we've handed out free white pine tree seedlings for the town environmental committee and hosted Girl Scout cookie sale booths and veterans' ceremonies for the American Legion. There is no other organization in town that is capable of doing this on a daily basis, as well as on nights and weekends. It is a service we actively seek out and promote to our community.

During the holiday season, we worked out an arrangement with 25 small businesses in Wallkill to offer a discount to customers who showed their library card when making a purchase. We were overwhelmed by the support and received generous offers of discounts on deli sandwiches, hardware store purchases, insurance quotes, haircuts, car service, wine sales at the liquor store, and complimentary gift-wrapped candles from the local gift and antique shop. We were also aware that some businesses were really struggling financially, so when they said all they could offer was a free cup of coffee, we told them that was great and added them to the list.

The patrons have enthusiastically embraced this effort and enjoy the value-added benefit their library card brings. One patron told me she visited every single store on the list just because they were supporting the library, even sitting through a 40-minute free insurance consultation! Another told me she went into the hardware store for the very first time and told them she was there only because of the library discount program and opted not to use the discount with her sale. She just wanted the store owner to know how much she appreciated his support of the library.

After the holidays, I ran into a member of the fledgling business owners association who commented on how successful the library card discount program was, and remarked, "Why didn't we think of that?" I didn't know. I do know, however, that the idea of building community doesn't come naturally to everyone. It's a bit like the concept of sharing when you're a toddler. The idea may sound appealing, but only if there is a direct benefit to you and you don't have to give that much in return. The role the library plays in this scenario is the creative catalyst. I like to think that we are sweeping away the cobwebs in the minds of those in town who have run out of fresh ideas, inviting them to join us in trying something refreshing and new.

Consistent invitations go out to our businesses partners to participate in events we are hosting. The kick-off event for our summer reading program often attracts over 400 people. Imagine the exposure a small local business can get at an event like that if they set up a space advertising their products or offering samples? Equally as important as the invitation is the thank-you. After the summer event, we send along a thank-you note with candid photos taken of kids and their families enjoying the scavenger hunt and other activities. Often we will try to get photos of the kids and the business owner, and I have noticed those photos posted on the wall of the store, along with our letter, long after summer has gone.

After the holiday discount program, we hosted a card-making workshop for kids, and I asked each one to make an extra card that I could use to send a thank-you note. On a snowy February morning, I hand-delivered these homemade valentines to all participating business owners for their support. On the back of each card it read: "Lovingly made for you by one of the children from the Wallkill Public Library." These cards were proudly displayed for weeks on the counters of the local stores. This good publicity works well for the store and for the library.

Awareness of the positive impact a library can have on a small community may have a big impact on local funding decisions in the future. A great library reflects the needs of its community. Determining those needs develops and strengthens the relationships among patrons, community members, and library staff. Through the years, I have learned that it's all about relationships — forming them, building them, and keeping them. You'll never have to make another cold call to ask for support if you know someone, or someone they know, and have a little bit of information about them to strike up meaningful conversation.

To determine the needs of the community, library staff need to take the time to ask what people want, what they like, and what they want to see the library offer in the future. This information can be gleaned from informal but directed conversation, or solicited by conducting written or electronic surveys. Understanding the needs of patrons and being able to demonstrate that the library is meeting those needs is critical to survival. Additionally, the community at large should be aware that your library offers something of value, whether it's public access Internet service, Wi-Fi, fax and photocopying, art venues, live performances, workshops, opportunities for social interaction, educational children's programming, or free access to extensive print, media, and digital collections. Is your community aware that during challenging economic times like these, library usage soars as people seek connections, job search assistance, computer access, free children's programming, and personal enrichment? Use local outlets such as weekly newspapers, cable television stations, and social media to keep your community informed of the services, whether they use the library or not.

Libraries also connect people to their communities by serving as civic information centers. Information on community events, entertainment, workshops, youth sports, and arts programs, the best businesses to patronize, and other noteworthy destinations, can welcome visitors and help locals to understand and better appreciate their community.

My years of nonprofit training helped me to bring innovative, fundraising, and marketing strategies to the library in order to build audiences and dedicated patrons while fostering community. I have learned that no matter how great one's idea is, there are 10 more coming down the pike from someone else. The most important thing is to take action. Timing is everything, and there's always a good time for something. Libraries have to stay in the public eye to show their relevance and value. With so many entities vying for coveted taxpayer dollars in these tough economic times, libraries must identify, promote, and leverage the impact of the programs, collections, and services they offer. Inviting collaborations with local businesses provides a vital link to emphasizing the economic value a library can have, especially in a small community.

So when you are planning the next library program or introducing a new concept, collection, or idea, I encourage you to ask, "Who else needs to know about this?" Ask this question of your staff, your board, the Friends group, and your patrons. This collective input may yield some unexpected results and engage others in thinking bigger than books and programs within library walls. Unique marketing strategies can help change the perception of the library and position it as a catalyst, an innovator, and a leader in community and economic development. Most importantly, it can transform the library to be seen and experienced as a vital resource that your community cannot live without.

Quick and Easy Marketing Tips for Libraries

There is no need to reinvent the marketing wheel. Here are a few tools and ideas you can implement today to begin developing outstanding community outreach strategies for your library:

• Use the library calendar of events (National Library Week, Children's Book Week, etc.) to develop fun and unique marketing opportunities for your library. Invite the community to get involved and help with promotions. Ask businesses to underwrite the cost of an event, provide coupons, or contribute raffle basket items. Always list them as supporters of the library event.

• Show the impressive return on investment (ROI) to your patrons by having them compute what they save annually by using your library. The **Library Value Calculator**, created by the Massachusetts Library Association, is available on the American Library Association website (http://www.ala.org). Our library used this exercise during National Library Week, and we gave staff members a sticker with their annual savings written on it. For example: $2520.00. Each time they were asked about the "price tag," staff replied: "This is what I save each year by using the library. Would you like to see what you save?" Patrons couldn't wait to find out their savings, too, and get their own price tag to wear! Each time patrons determined their savings, they wrote it on a slip of paper that was added to a raffle for discount certificates and store coupons. We were amazed at some of the savings that came up ... and so were the patrons! Take that, Barnes & Noble!

• Take advantage of a free marketing program being offered nationally called **Geek the Library**, a community awareness campaign created by OCLC (Online Computer Library Center, Inc.) and funded through the Bill and Melinda Gates Foundation (http://www.get.geekthelibrary.org) This marketing campaign is open to libraries across the country and offers free, eye-catching promotional materials as well as professional support and training to customize the effort for your community. The goal is to use tested marketing and community outreach strategies to enhance public awareness, perception, usage, and funding of public libraries. It's a perfect way for cash-strapped libraries to access high-quality marketing tools that can be easily personalized and reproduced at minimal cost. Our small rural library was the first New York State library to register, and now over 20 other NY libraries have joined us. It is a fun and refreshing way to promote library use while finding out what our community members "geek," (meaning what they love to do, learn, experience) and to let them know their library supports them!

The Why, What, Who, When, and How of Library Community Partnerships

JENNIFER L. HOPWOOD

Sometimes You Need More Than a Friend

Libraries by definition are places where different types of media may be found for entertainment, education, and research purposes. However, many libraries have seen a shift towards outreach and community education programs. Programming is a necessary tool for introducing the library to the community, which in turn will improve attendance and circulation. Sustaining services many times means doing more with less while still providing an enjoyable experience for the patron. Programming will draw the patrons in, but it also means a drain on both time and manpower when faced with having to get it all done with fewer people and limited budgets.

Having a Friends of the Library group is a wonderful thing. They provide both manpower at programs, fundraiser backing to purchase materials for these programs, and speakers for events. Of course with budgets tightening up, many have moved towards purchasing books and the shelving to keep those books. If you have a Friends group, then you are very lucky; if you don't ... well, don't worry. Sometimes you need more than a Friend, and this is how you go about it.

Reaching out to the community for programming support and partnerships can be beneficial to the library and to the supporting business or community group. The library can receive aid in the form of donated product, funds, or even time while the business or group receives increased traffic or sales. This is a win-win situation because both parties will receive additional publicity and community recognition through the partnership. How you market it, or how you present your request, can make a big difference between obtaining the help you need and being denied.

Social Responsibility: Why Do Others Want to Help?

Ever walk into one of those big warehouse chains and seen that list of local schools with dollar amounts listed on the wall? Or maybe you have noticed the little league photos posted on the wall at your local pizzeria. This is one way that the business is advertising its social responsibility to the community. All of these teams and schools received some form of sponsorship or support from the business. In other words, there is a partnership that exists between the two.

Many national chains have a percentage of profit, product, or time that they must donate towards community programs each year. It is part of the company's charter or business plan. Some of these companies will partner with other organizations, like the American Library Association, to distribute aid in the form of one-time grants. Other companies manage their own giving programs. Some of these companies include:

- Target (www.target.com)—five percent of the company's income goes to support local communities. The Early Childhood Reading Grants may be used to sponsor library children's programs that promote reading. This program is run through an online application.
- Sam's Club / Wal-Mart (www.walmartstores.com)—Sam's Club and Wal-Mart both sponsor local community giving programs. These programs are administered on a local level and you must see store managers for more details.
- Best Buy (www.bestbuy-communityrelations.com)—Donates up to 1.5 percent of profits back to the community through local store giving programs. See store managers for more details.

Local businesses are also willing to help, especially when it is pointed out that sponsorship will also promote their businesses. Community groups often just want to get their name out there in the community. School volunteer groups are especially useful because they may have members who are working towards scholarships and are in need of a certain amount of hours to fill their community service requirements.

Determining Your Needs: What Are You Asking for and Whom Do You Need to Ask?

Marketing a product doesn't only mean that you are promoting it. That is only one part of it; the first part is your market research. When it comes to library programs, there are several parts to that research. Analyze your community; take a look at your market area to see if your program or concept is even needed. You may have the best idea in the world, but if it is something that is not suited to your area, then even the best idea in the world will flop. Take a look at the programs that have worked in the past. Were there any sponsors for that program? Do your patrons approach you with requests for certain topics? If you can't sell it to your community, then there is little chance you will be able to sell the idea to a sponsor or partner.

Next, determine what you need to accomplish your goals. When dealing with community partners, you can't just ask for undefined help. You need to be specific to get results. Does your program have a theme? Is there a gap in your collection that needs to be filled? Can you use a product donation or are you asking for cash to purchase the items on your own? If you are asking for a monetary amount, make sure that you do your research to find out how much you will need. Try to be as specific as possible in what you may need; companies like to know where the money is going. Keep records of everything you purchase so you can refer back to them if needed. This is also helpful if you should decide to host a similar event; all the research has already been done.

Once you know what you need, do some research to determine whom you should contact. Does your summer reading program have a water theme? Then you might want to try contacting your local pool supply store or water park. Are you doing a program on graphic novels? Try contacting your local comic book shop to see if they might be willing to talk at your event. Call the store to determine the name of the owner or manager. Make sure that you have accurate contact information for them. Do they prefer snail mail, e-mail, phone calls, or face-to-face. Just like querying a publishing house for a manuscript, you get better results when you direct your request directly to the person who can help you, rather than an open "To Whom It May Concern."

Chains and franchises can be a little bit more difficult to work with. If you don't have a local store or office in the area, proving that a relationship would be beneficial may prove rather difficult. If the group or business does not have some stake in the area, then there is little chance that they will be willing to help. Analyze the group's mission statement or charter to see which of their goals mesh with the program you are trying to establish. They may not have a presence in the community now, but if you make your argument appealing enough, they just might decide to take an interest.

The donation request process at every business is different. Some allow their stores to make donation decisions on a local level, and some of them require that you apply to a corporate office. The best thing to do is ask your local manager which procedure you need to utilize.

The exceptions to these are national chains that have a presence in the community through third parties. For example, if your local store sells a particular brand, try e-mailing the company to see if they will be willing to donate product. Check out the company's website. Many companies will have a contact form on their site for general information. Send a simple e-mail requesting the contact information for the representative who is in charge of donation requests. Some companies may even have a request form specifically for that purpose. If the company has a "Frequently Asked Questions" page on their website, take a look at it. The answer to your question may have already been answered. If you find the information, make sure that you read all the requirements before making requests. Some companies have policies regarding donating only to established partnerships, communities that their employees live in, or to groups that fall under certain IRS requirements, like 501(c) nonprofits.

Timing: When Do You Ask?

Timing when to ask for donations can be tricky depending on what you are asking for. If you have a deadline that you need materials or commitments by, make sure you mention that in your correspondence. Some companies also have deadlines that they use when making decisions. Requests usually have to go through some form of approval process before they are granted or denied, and that must also be taken into consideration. A good rule of thumb is to give the other party at least two months, unless they already have an established timeline that must be followed.

How to Get It?

First impressions are lasting impressions; this partnership is important to you and should be reflected in your demeanor. Prepare what you are going to say in advance. A smile can be heard in your voice, even over the phone; remember to be courteous and polite. If you are making the request in person, dress professionally. Also, make sure to call ahead or observe when the location has a slow moment. You would not want to make a request at a restaurant during lunch: their busiest time. The manager would not have time to talk to you, and the visit could result in more animosity than goodwill.

However, when you are trying to solicit a programming request through an e-mail or letter, it all comes down to the numbers. Statistical information is a valuable tool for making requests because it is shows that you have taken the time to do your research, and facts appeal to shareholders while adding credibility to your request.

Below is an example of a typical programming request letter. First, take a look at this example for the information that should be included in your request.

Dear Mr. Joe Smith:

We need your help! The staff at the XXX Library and the XXX Library are planning a stellar summer reading program for the children in our community. Located in Big City, Florida, we serve a community of over 106,000 residents. Last year we had over 1,000 children and teens participate in our program and hope to exceed that number this year. Our goal is to get kids reading and learning for pleasure.

Creating a sense of challenge as well as fun, we would like to offer incentives to keep the participants reading all summer. We would also like to have drawings at the end of the program for big prizes. Because of our limited budget, we cannot afford to offer this without help.

We appreciate any donation you care to make. Possible donations include items to give away as prizes, small toys, coupons, free goods or services (admission tickets, fast food coupons, etc), or cash to buy prizes. Your business will be recognized as a proud sponsor of the XXX Library's Summer Reading Program.

If you can help us in any way, please contact me at the Youth Services Department xxx-xxx-xxxx or my e-mail: abc@libraryemail.org. We hope to include you in our summer plans. Many thanks!

Sincerely,

Paige Turner
Youth Services Librarian
XXX Library
1234 Library St
Big City, FL XXXXX
XXX-XXX-XXXX
Fax XXX-XXX-XXXX
abc@libraryemail.org

The above letter begins by directly addressing a specific person. It then proceeds to give a demographic description of relevant information like the location of the library and the number of residents that are served by this program. This information can be found online through the U.S. Census (http://www.census.gov) or the Public Library Geographic Database (http://www.geolib.org). Both of these websites are examples of market data research that can be used to appeal to your target audience. In this example, the focus has been placed on the size of the community, but if the goal of the request was to appeal to a different market segment, then other statistics can be utilized like the median age, residents with children, or ethnicity. Next, internal information, like the number of previous participants, is included in the letter. If this is the first time that you have held this program, you may want to include an estimate of how many participants you expect. However, be realistic in your estimates. It is better to exceed your goal than to fall short of it.

Then the letter clearly states the goal of the program. What is trying to be accomplished by the program? Why is the sponsor being asked for assistance? These are important questions to answer. Remember that this information should appeal to the sponsor while also giving examples of how the resources will be used (e.g. offering incentives as prizes).

Finally, be specific in what you are asking for and what you will do in return. In the case of this request, the letter is asking for small items that may be used as incentive prizes. Examples are given, but the request is kept open enough for the sponsor to have an idea of what is being looked for while giving them room to generate their own ideas. If you are looking for a guest speaker, you might want to explain the theme of the program and ask for suggested topics that the speaker would be willing to cover.

As mentioned in the letter, all partners should be acknowledged for their sponsorship in some form. Everyone who donates, no matter what the service, receives a "Certificate of Appreciation" thanking them for their involvement in the community programming. Depending on the event, they might also have their logo or information printed on publicity flyers. It is a good idea to give the sponsor copies of all flyers so that they can promote the event or partnership at their location.

Strike! A Real World Example

For the past three years, the Franklin T. DeGroodt Memorial Library of Palm Bay, Florida, has partnered with a local bowling alley in offering free games to children who met their reading goals in the Summer Reading Challenge. In the second year of the partnership, this relationship was expanded to include every library in the county as well as a sister site for the bowling alley. The bowling alley printed out coupons at no cost to the library system. This year-to-date, they have redeemed a total of 130 coupons between the two bowling centers. They estimate that each of those coupons generates at least an additional $10 in profit for them from other sales like the snack bar and parents or siblings bowling. That is about $1300 profit from customers who might not have visited if not for the free game coupons they donated to the library.

Outreach: Giving Back What You Take

Before you ask for anything, you need to know what you are willing to give back. Partnerships mean that you are working together with someone. This is a give-and-take relationship, so make sure that you plan on disclosing the work or product that the library will give in return. Are you willing to place advertisements for the company on display? Will you be able to give a program at their location? Before you ask for anything, make sure you know what is in your power to give back as well.

One of the best ways to seal a partnership is to agree to a program outside of the library. This is known as outreach programming. Outreach programs can be as simple as doing a booktalk at the local community center or as elaborate as participating in a community festival as a storyteller. Some outreaches can be done on a weekly basis, like a storytime program held every Tuesday night at your local chicken fast-food restaurant or a one-time visit to a school's open house night.

Outreaches benefit the library because they expose the library to stakeholders who might not know where the library is located, let alone have a library card. Just as the bowling coupons in the previous example generated traffic to the bowling center, an outreach program can also generate traffic to your library. It is just another form of advertising what you have to offer. Remember that the sponsor is helping you out, so it pays to be flexible.

Evaluate!

When you researched what had worked in the past, you may have been looking at information gleaned from evaluations. Evaluating a program or partnership is one of the most important parts of the mix because this is where you learn from your successes and your failures. When evaluating the success of your program, you need to look first at how many people attended the program or used the service. If your attendance was low, look to see why it failed. Did you offer it at the wrong time of day? Was there another event or service competing for your patrons' time? If your attendance was high, what feedback did you receive from your patrons? This last question is important; your event may have yielded high attendance, but was it a success? The success of a program can be gleaned from what people are saying about it.

At the end of every program or service, offer a survey to your patrons. For the best results and feedback, surveys should be distributed and collected before the patron leaves the program. On your survey, you should list questions regarding how much the patrons liked or disliked the program, where they heard about the program, but also what programs they would like to see in the future. This last question helps for future programming development, but also gives you something that you can show your partners. It is your validation of a successful partnership both now and at a later date.

The last part of the evaluation process is to contact your sponsor and see how everything went on their end. Maybe they had problems with redeeming donated coupons or they heard customer complaints about the program. The sooner you contact the other party, the easier it is to fix any problems.

Endless Possibilities

Many grant applications will ask for information regarding other participating parties or sponsors. Having already formed partnerships with local groups or businesses means that most of the work has already been done for you and you now have the contacts for future partnerships. Keep in mind the idea of networking. It is a good concept to utilize because additional contacts can be made through a partner's partnership.

When time and money are at a premium, there is no harm in asking for assistance. Once a partnership has been established, it becomes easier for future partnerships. The process of soliciting a partnership can be time-consuming; if you have a good group of volunteers, perhaps even ones made through a school partnership, this may be something that you can delegate. Keep in mind that the price of your time can be made back twofold in the rewards you will gain through this community support. Partnerships are worthwhile endeavors that create lasting connections to the community you serve.

21

Reaching Out to the Campus Community Through a Student Advocacy Group

CYNTHIA M. AKERS *and* TERRI PEDERSEN SUMMEY

Academic librarians often face challenges reaching out to students and gathering feedback about the library. As Kuhlthau (2004) discovered, the information seeking or research process contains a strong affective element. Students may experience a diverse range of emotions when confronted with the unfamiliar territory of the library, including anxiety, isolation, and frustration. The library can be intimidating for them, and some students will mistakenly think that they are the only ones having difficulties. They may be inhibited from asking for assistance, especially from library staff who appear to be older, more knowledgeable, and more confident. Feeling overwhelmed and suffering from a lack of confidence, students may avoid the library altogether, never becoming fully aware of the wide range of library resources and the services available to them.

Although librarians work hard to "spread the news" about library resources and services, they interact mainly with other faculty outside of the library. Interactions with students are often in a more formal library instruction setting or one-to-one at the library service desks when students are brave enough to approach someone. Often, students may seek out other students, including student employees, as informal peer mentors. "When a student sees a classmate working in the library, there is an existing relationship upon which communication can be built. If the questions posed by our anxious student are met with good answers, a bridge to the library has been built" (Baird 2006, 4).

The idea for a student advocacy group emerged during a strategic planning session where participants felt that creating such a group would allow students to effectively market the library directly to their fellow students. The organization, dubbed the ESULA (Empowered Students for University Libraries and Archives), has accomplished this initial library marketing goal and beyond. After several years in existence, the members of this group are not only campus-wide advocates for the library, but they also sponsor social activities within the library, assist with library tours and other library-sponsored events, and serve as a sounding board for the library administration and staff. This chapter analyzes the origin of the organization, recruitment of members, the types of campus activities they participate in, lessons learned, tips for setting up a similar organization, and a review of resources for further exploration. Although this chapter focuses on the experience of a student advocacy group in an academic library, this concept could be adapted to other libraries, especially those in an educational setting.

Background and Information on the Organization at ESU

Emporia State University is a medium-sized university located centrally in the eastern half of Kansas. Initially founded as the Kansas State Normal School, ESU continues to have a strong tradition of teacher education while also offering a comprehensive education in a variety of other schools and colleges. Although ESU has several nationally known distance education programs and a Metro Center located in Overland Park, Kansas, the university is still primarily a resident academic institution. The population at ESU is approximately 6,000 students with 350 faculty members. Library services for the university community, regardless of location, are provided by the University Libraries and Archives (ULA), which employs eight to 10 librarians and about the same number of staff members.

In January of 2006, in order to provide a future direction for the purchase of library resources and the provision of library services, the ULA administration and staff held a strategic planning session. This all-day event also included library student employees, student government representatives, and faculty from a variety of schools and departments.

One of the emphases that emerged from the planning process was the need to raise awareness about the resources and services offered by the University Libraries and Archives. In order to move forward with this emphasis, a Marketing Task Force was established. A faculty member from the School of Business was asked to lead the group. Throughout the remainder of the spring semester of 2006, the Marketing Task Force met to achieve their stated goal: to develop a marketing plan with strategies for the ULA. During a brainstorming session about how the ULA could better articulate and market their resources and services, the idea of creating a student organization emerged. ESU already had a student advocacy group for the campus, the ESU Ambassadors, and its organizational structure provided the inspiration for how the Libraries and Archives group was put together.

As the planning continued, the name ESULA was created, which stood for Empowered Students for University Libraries & Archives. The stated purpose of the ESULA was to raise awareness of the ULA, to serve as an advocate for the organization, and to be a peer resource or mentor to other students on campus. The Marketing Task Force believed that students could participate in a variety of activities, including presenting programs about the ULA to students in the resident hall, giving tours of the library, and making presentations to new students. They would also participate in activities for the William Allen White Children's Book Awards celebration, National Library Week, and Banned Books Week.

Because students are busy, the task force felt that incentives to join the group needed to be provided, such as an ESULA polo shirt to wear during events, dinners with the Dean of the University Libraries and Archives, a personal letter of recommendation from the dean, opportunities to interact and network with library and archives faculty and staff members, enhanced library privileges, and complimentary food. In exchange, the students who became members of the ESULA organization would provide at least four hours of service each month to the organization and the University Libraries and Archives. Their service hours would include member training, book awards activities in October, National Library Week in April, and monthly meetings.

It was quickly determined that such a student-centered organization would work best if it were officially endorsed by the university. Depending on the structure of a college or university, such an approach provides not only publicity assistance to the organization, but also enables financial support via a student government or center for student involvement (Akers 2011, 126). The spring semester of 2006 was spent gathering student signatures on a "Petition to Seek Recognition" from ESU's Associated Student Government, creating a draft constitution for the organization, and finally realizing the approval of ESULA as a university Recognized Student Organization (RSO) in late spring 2006 (Akers 2011, 126). Membership is open both to undergraduate and graduate students, and currently ESULA has representation from student assistants employed in the library as well as students who share an interest in library services activism.

ESULA's Role in Library Advocacy: The Student-Centered Style

The name "ESULA" implies advocacy as a student-centered concept. "Empowered Students for University Libraries and Archives" focuses on the word "empowered," emphasizing that ESULA members actively engage in promoting library services and resources within and beyond the context of the physical library building. A sample of these activities includes:

• Hosting a table at the fall and spring ESU Activities Fair, not only to recruit potential members, but also to hand out bookmarks, brochures, and other materials about the library. In addition, ESULA members encourage attendees to sign up for a "Semester Survival Kit" giveaway and provide information about upcoming ESULA-sponsored events.

• Sponsoring a monthly "Game Night at the Library." This idea was first proposed in spring 2007 by ESULA, and since that time it has become a popular venue where all students can relax, enjoy games and refreshments in the library building, and experience the library as an inviting space and place. Some game nights feature a variety of traditional board games, while others focus on a theme such as Harry Potter or, most recently, a scavenger hunt to tie in with National Library Week.

• Participating as student leaders for library tours at an introductory level for English Composition I and international students. The ESULA advisor provides basic training for these tours, but true to student advocacy, also seeks input about the types of services and resources that would best interest other students during tours. Such methods are crucial for gaining "a fresh, unique student perspective regarding use of the library. As a result, the library can focus upon what is important to students and implement services that they want" (Dubicki 2009, 176).

• Assisting with events that, while considered outside the library context, still relate to the library's promotion and outreach. Examples include ESULA's help with the William Allen White Children's Book Awards ceremony and the State Library of Kansas/Kansas Center for the Book's "Kansas Reads to Preschoolers" yearly program.

• Creating and overseeing fundraisers for ESULA's continuing promotional activities and support of travel to regional and national conferences. The most popular fundraiser is a Book and Media "sale," in which gently used books, CDs, DVDs, and related materials are made available twice a semester to the ESU community for monetary donations. Visibility for ESULA is greatly heightened when the Book and Media fundraisers are held in the ESU Memorial Union. The location of the fundraiser is alternated during the semester with the library lobby to emphasize the library building as a friendly, welcoming place.

• Fostering an environment for ESULA members to develop and hone essential leadership skills for their future careers. As a Recognized Student Organization, each year ESULA elects a Chair, a Vice Chair, and a Financial Chair. Each officer works closely with the ESULA faculty advisor, but at the same time, meeting agendas, short-term objectives, and long-term objectives for the group are set by the officers and members. In addition, ESULA members have participated in a panel discussion about the organization's founding and mission at the Kansas Library Association Annual Conference. These opportunities collectively offer student advocacy group members the chance to learn more about "time management, adaptability, goal setting, leadership, networking ... [a]ctive members also strengthen personal traits such as responsibility, dependability, strong work ethic, initiative, self-confidence, and self-awareness" (Carnes 2007, 49).

One requirement of an RSO is a to have a faculty advisor who serves as just that — an advisor who facilitates the student organization's ideas into reality, not someone who dictates the direction of the group. It is particularly rewarding to note that the ideas for game nights and book and media fundraisers came from ESULA members. The ESULA advisor, a faculty member from the library, attends twice-monthly meetings and aids in the progress of ideas from concept to reality. The advisor also serves as the go-between with ESULA members and the library's dean. Allowing students to feel comfortable in brainstorming initiatives is a "self-teaching" enterprise that permits students to feel "more relaxed to discuss the content ... as well as present arguments and suggestions about the initiative[s]" (Hasty 2001, 36).

Lessons Learned / Tips for Success

From the conception of the program until now, much has been learned by the library faculty, staff, and students involved in ESULA. In this section, lessons learned by the University Libraries and Archives and tips for creating a successful program will be shared.

• Furnish incentives for membership. From the beginning, those who created the idea for the ESULA organization recognized that incentives may be needed to encourage individuals to join ESULA and to offer needed motivation to help with sponsored activities.

• Provide opportunities for free food and drink. Deuink and Seiler (2006) recommend serving food to the members of the student advocacy group at their regular meetings (20).

• Find forums outside of the library to recruit students. Recruitment of student members has been a challenge. ESULA has many library student employees who join the organization, but finding venues to recruit students who are not connected to the library is important. Seek out and utilize activity fairs, tables in the student union, and other places that may provide opportunities to recruit a diverse group of members.

• Make recruitment of members a year-long activity. Recruitment in the fall semester is important, but new students may be overwhelmed by the college experience and opportunities available to them. Continue recruiting in the spring and summer semesters to add members to your group.

• Build on the enthusiasm of the current members. Use student members who are excited about the group and its activities to spread the word and recruit others (Deuink and Seiler 2006, 19).

• Training is essential. If the student organization is being used as an advocate and marketing tool for the library, educating group members about the services and resources offered by the library is a task of paramount importance, particularly if the organization is providing library orientation or information sessions. Overall training can help the student advocates in acquiring the "big picture" of the library to see how the various library units interact and fit together. In addition, a key strength of student advocates is that they are embedded in classes throughout the university and may be able to provide information about the library when research or class projects that involve library use arise.

• Listen to the student group. The members have a stake in the library and often will have good ideas about resources and services. Provide opportunities for them to offer their input and suggestions and then take action on their ideas. Group members may become frustrated if they provide ideas that they feel are not taken seriously.

• Deuink and Seiler (2006) emphasize that libraries with a student group should "show enthusiasm for the club," allowing the students to express their ideas and think creatively about what they would like the organization to offer and how their mission is accomplished (20).

• Allow the student members to provide direction for the group. Since the purpose of a student group may be to market the resources and services of the library, student members should be empowered to help determine what activities they want to participate in or sponsor during the year.

• Seek out collaborative opportunities or partnerships with other groups or entities on campus. As mentioned earlier, the ESULA group at Emporia State had been sponsoring game nights. Recently, they were approached by the President of the ESU Chess Club to coordinate the timing of their next game night with the chess night sponsored by the club, resulting in a fun event that drew in more people for both activities.

• Stay in constant contact with the members of the organization. One way to do this is to hold regularly scheduled meetings.

• Recognize that an advocacy group is "a program rather than a one-time experience. At best, it is inclusive, ongoing, and promotes open inquiry. Through ... open dialogue, we are able to align [students'] learning with our desired outcomes and are better able to see how their values may be expressed in the workplace" (Baird 2006, 16).

• Research to learn more about the culture of one's library; for example, a college or university library, like ESU's University Libraries and Archives, may be eligible for sponsorship of an association via a student government or union. Partnerships between libraries and other academic departments can offer funding for student training and could be more appropriate for a specific organization (Holliday and Nordgren, 2005, 282).

• Willingness as librarians to let go of the notion that we know the best types of services and resources that will appeal to our students or other constituencies. Student advocacy groups fit wonderfully with the idea of assessment as a continuous cycle, and also serve as "a powerful marketing tool ... [offering students] the opportunity to present ideas to enhance the library and make it more student-friendly" (Deuink and Seiler 2006, 21).

• Rethink the concept and mission of the library. Many libraries are moving towards the idea of "library as place" instead of "libraries as storage." Use the student organization to reach out to the extra-curricular interests of students, like gaming, sports, and social networking.

Conclusion and Resources for Further Information

Student advocacy groups can result in changes badly needed in a library that may not be recognized by the library staff. A student advocacy group can be relatively informal or, as in ESULA's case, an approved university organization. The Library Student Advisory Board at Pennsylvania State University's Schuylkill Campus, for example, is a mirror of a "public library's 'friends group' ... developing ideas for creating a better student experience at the library, and acting as peer advocates of the library to encourage student use." (Deuink and Seiler 2006, 18). Also, the Library Peer Mentor Program at the Utah State University Libraries utilizes students at the reference desk and in the classroom "as a way to engage USU students and make them more comfortable using USU Libraries" (Holliday and Nordgren 2005, 282). And, as evidenced at Monmouth University, academic librarians can tap into business and marketing curriculums to collaborate with students in promotional case studies, raising awareness of library services (Dubicki 2009, 164). Whatever the approach, information professionals would do well to consider the power of student advocacy for promoting the resources and services available at their libraries.

WORKS CITED

Akers, Cynthia. 2011. "ESULA: Changing Perceptions of the Academic Library through Student Activism." *Reference Services Review* 39 (1): 123–131. doi:10.1108/00907321111108150.

Baird, Lynn N. 2006. "Students as Story-tellers: Advocacy from the Ranks." *PNLA Quarterly* 70 (4): 4, 6–17.

Carnes, Lana W. 2007. "Student Organizations: Gateways to Professional Opportunities and Skills Development." *Business Education Forum* 62 (2): 48–50.

Deuink, Amy, and Marianne Seiler. 2006. "Students as Library Advocates: The Library Student Advisory Board at Pennsylvania State-Schuylkill." *College and Research Libraries News* 67 (1): 18–21.

Dubicki, Eleonora. 2009. "Business Students Chart a New Course for Promoting the University Library." *College & Undergraduate Libraries* 16 (2): 164–179. doi:10.1080/10691310902958459.

Hasty, Douglas. 2001. "Student Assistants as Library Ambassadors." *Technical Services Quarterly* 18 (2): 31–40. doi:10.1300/J124v18n02_03.

Holliday, Wendy, and Cynthia Nordgren. 2005. "Extending the Reach of Librarians: Library Peer Mentor Program at Utah State University." *College & Research Libraries News* 66 (4): 282–4.

Kuhlthau, Carol Collier. 2004. *Seeking Meaning: A Process Approach to Library and Information Services.* 2nd ed. Westport, CT: Libraries Unlimited.

PART VII

Event Planning and Implementation

22

Library Services Fair
Putting Friendly Faces with Valuable Services

KALEY DANIEL *and* KIMBERLY VARDEMAN

Long gone are the days when the Texas Tech Library housed a card catalog protected by shushing librarians. Today, the Texas Tech Library is the happening hub of academic resources for group study and collaboration and scholarly research. Seeing more than three million visitors per year, with a physical collection that would span the distance from Lubbock to Austin (more than 400 miles) and 24/7 access to millions of e-resources, it's no longer your grandfather's library.

When walking through our doors with the stereotypical library in mind, the cutting-edge technology and the multitude of services filling our enormous building can be intimidating. When students are brave enough to ask for help at the service desk, they are excited to see that what we have can really benefit them. Without some user instruction, however, they will likely have significant challenges in utilizing the plethora of free services available through the library.

Seeing the need for proactive outreach, we wanted to capitalize on the opportunity to organize a fun, hands-on event for students where we showcased all that the library has to offer. We did not want the students to walk into the lobby, grab a flyer and a drink, and then leave. We wanted them to see the resources and services. We wanted them to interact with the librarians. How better to achieve this than through a Library Services Fair? However, instead of setting up tables to only hand out brochures and promotional items, we needed to take advantage of hosting *our* fair in *our* building, showing students where to go and who to ask for help.

Goals of the Event

We wanted to show students that we are approachable and that we have the expert knowledge to help them. It can be intimidating for students to use a database if they have not done so before, so the fair would provide students the opportunity to meet their Personal Librarian (subject specialist librarian) who could offer walk-up demonstrations of databases or who could answer questions on a more informal and personal level. Most importantly, we wanted to be hospitable and welcoming, putting a friendly face with the students' research lifesaver. Therefore, we set the following goals for our fair:

- Increase student awareness of virtual research assistance
- Increase interaction with Personal Librarians
- Increase utilization of e-resources
- Increase library staff visibility
- Increase students' familiarity with navigating building
- Increase students' knowledge of borrowing procedures

Planning

The Director of Communications & Marketing and the Personal Librarian for Reference became the lead coordinators for the event since marketing was just as critical as the execution of the event itself. Planning began in May, allowing four months for coordination and marketing preparation. In the initial planning stages, one of the first decisions to make was which library departments to involve in the fair. Public services departments such as Reference and Circulation were an obvious choice, but we also wanted to feature other departments and services that would be attention-grabbing or completely new to most students.

Next we needed to choose the time and date for the fair. We decided this would be a great event to hold at the beginning of the fall semester, when thousands of new students arrive on campus. We scheduled the fair for Tuesday, September 14, from 10 A.M. to 3 P.M., which allowed sufficient time for marketing and promoting the event after the students overcame the first days' jitters, found their groove, and settled into their routines. Hosting the fair during those hours capitalized on the peak traffic flow through the building.

Once we finalized the date, we reserved the room and equipment and then asked specific departments to organize a booth or table for the fair. Almost everyone accepted the invitation. As soon as we had a final count on the number of booths, we began drafting the floor layout with these goals in mind:

- Placing booths expected to draw the highest traffic on the perimeters of the room, in view of passersby. We strategically placed the tables with swag and promotional items tied to the marketing in direct sight.
- Ensuring electrical outlets were in reach of tables that would use multimedia displays.
- Keeping traffic flowing through the fair. The plan included greeters at corridors near entrances to guide people inside and provide directions, and fair workers were instructed to help facilitate traffic flow.

As an example, the Mango Languages booth — one of the biggest draws of the fair — integrated marketing efforts with eye-catching, color-coordinated giveaways. There was a matching language-learning database display unit as well as librarians wearing bright orange or lime green t-shirts, making it an ideal choice to place near the entrance.

When it comes down to it, you find yourself facing that old adage "the best laid plans...." Prepare to be flexible about the physical arrangement, even up to the day of the event. You may find that some groups need more space or additional tables as their enthusiasm for the event grows.

A major step in the planning phase was to muster the troops, so to speak. We arranged a meeting several weeks before the event and invited all the staff members who agreed to participate in the fair. This provided a chance to share our goals, theme, and vision with them. We wanted to get everyone involved together in one room to talk about the setup and flow of the fair and how each department's booth would contribute to the success of the event. The marketing team previewed the fair concept designs for signage and set the deadline for departments to request their specific marketing material needs for their tables. Each group had leeway to be creative about what they wanted to display and hand out to students. The meeting gave staff the opportunity for brainstorming, discussion, and to ask questions.

Put Your Best Face Forward

The trick here is not to send fair participants away with jargon-filled, multiple-page documents. We wanted to provide them with quick-and-easy descriptors for each service area and/or simple instructions on particular services (e.g., setting up an ILLiad account) they learned about while at the fair. We learned there are two important pieces of information to include on all of your marketing materials. The first is an easy and efficient way that customers can get back to the service you spoke to them about. The second is the most direct channel for asking questions and receiving prompt answers. Below are the materials we supplied from each table:

- All tables: Libraries General Brochure, services fair survey, library-branded pens, sticky books, and ID/wallet key chains
- Mango Languages Database: smoothies, mouse pads, t-shirts, reusable bags, suckers, bookmark, flyer, table tent
- QR Codes and Social Networking: flyer, Facebook and YouTube bookmarks
- Digital Media Studio: "What You Can do in the Digital Media Studio" Flyer
- ARTstor and Architecture Library: ARTstor postcard, Architecture Library Brochure
- Personal Librarians: LIBR 1100 Flyer
- Digital Collections: business cards (with digital collections, electronic repository, and electronic theses and dissertations web pages), sheet with QR codes resolving to collections, and sign-up sheet for announcements regarding new releases
- Document Delivery: ILLiad Account Setup Flyer
- Circulation: Return Books Flyer

Marketing the Services Fair

Before crafting your marketing message, you need to know who your audience is. More often than not, the primary audience at our library is undergraduate students, particularly freshmen and those new to campus. Use words that appeal to their sense of logic, understanding, and, most importantly, fun! To put it simply, use a clear, concise message that explains "what's in it for me?"

Once you've figured out your message, you need to make sure you reach your audience where they live:

- Since our building draws more visitors than all of our athletic venues combined in one year, we knew to take full advantage of all of our interior signage opportunities.
- Outside our doors, we knew from our market research that the next most frequented channels "visited" by our audience included the Student Union Building, the campus buses, and the university newspaper.

After you've determined your message and your distribution channels, it's important to set a deadline for your marketing pieces launch. But sender beware:

- You don't want to launch your campaign too far from or too close to your event date.
- A good rule of thumb is to launch a couple weeks before your event and pulse pieces like ads (with set "run" dates) throughout this timeframe targeting the "most read days" (e.g., our research shows our university newspaper to be most widely read by students on Tuesdays and Thursdays).

Below is a listing of our integrated, strategic marketing pieces and their "run" dates:

1. E-communications
   - E-mail for faculty liaisons to send to professors: send two weeks out and one week out.
   - E-mail for graduate school distribution list: send two weeks out.
   - E-mail signature: distribute to organization three weeks out.
   - University-wide e-mail announcement: send two weeks out and one week out.
2. Digital Signage
   - Multimedia Display Unit (MDU) slide: post two weeks out.
   - TV wall slide: post two weeks out.
   - Digital signage in other participating academic buildings: send three weeks out.
   - Public computer wallpaper: post two weeks out.
   - Residence Life Cinema slide: send three weeks out.
   - University marquee: run two weeks out.
3. Web Communications
   - Facebook profile posts: pulse beginning two weeks out.
   - Facebook profile event: send invite two weeks out.
   - University library website news story & thumbnail: post two weeks out.
   - Library events calendar: post as soon as location is reserved.
   - University events calendar: post as soon as location is reserved.
4. Print Ads — full color, quarter page first, then half page: run twice the week before; run twice the week of (day before and day of)
5. Large-Format Signage
   - Interior banner: hang morning of event.
   - Window cling: hang morning of event.

- Fabric display panel banners for each station/table: set up day before.
- MDU frame: install day before.

6. Print Publications
   - Flyer (color, 8.5"w × 5.5"h, front only): distribute at IS 1100 classes & LIBR 1100 classes during summer/beginning of semester; hand out at graduate school orientation at beginning of semester.
   - Poster (color, 22"w × 28"h): post in library and student union building two weeks out.
   - Library door/elevator sleeve (8.5"w × 11"h): install two weeks out.

7. Public Relations/Events
   - News release for local media: send two weeks out.
   - Event advisory: send two days before.

One of the most important aspects of our marketing was that each table's promotions and their marketing designs and messaging continued and remained consistent throughout the year for ease of student recall. The fair served as the marketing campaigns' launch pads.

Don't Be Just Another Face

Since one of the major goals of the fair was to introduce students to research resources available to them, Information Services (reference) librarians were out in force greeting students and conducting live demonstrations of several e-resources. The booth for these Personal Librarians had an MDU on which librarians showed students how to navigate to subject-specific resource guides on the library website. They educated students on how to get help by using the "Ask a Librarian" chat and e-mail services. The librarians have a "Roving Reference" cart that they take around campus and answer questions at the point of need, wherever the students may be. On the day of the fair, the cart was parked in the library, but librarians told students about the cart and to be on the lookout for it if they have questions.

One of the most successful parts of the fair was the Mango Languages language-learning database booth. The librarians working the booth wore their Mango Languages t-shirts and the giveaways on their table were also colorful and reinforced the theme, including bookmarks, mouse pads, and a candy bowl that held mango-flavored Dum Dum Pops. An adjoining MDU had basic and advanced language lessons queued to play for curious students. Librarians also had a blender, ice, and mango smoothie mix, and served up smoothies in small cups decorated with cocktail umbrellas. Having candy and drinks at the booth enticed many students into the fair. The coordinated Mango promotion continued throughout the semester in a "Where will you Mango?" campaign.

One of the booths featured a department that was unfamiliar to many students, the digital collections. Librarians from the Digital Services group who did not normally have occasion to work with students face-to-face taught users how to navigate and search the library's Local Digital Collections. They created a slideshow of images from the *La Ventana* yearbook digital collection that holds the complete collection of Texas Tech yearbooks in high-resolution and is searchable in full-text. For example, students could find pictures of relatives who attended Texas Tech decades before or see the current chancellor back in the days when he was a student at the university. They also trained students interested in music on how to access a streaming sound music collection.

Another table hosted by architecture librarians promoted our sizeable art and architecture image collections in our ARTstor database. All of these collections are certainly valuable resources for students, but unless someone provides instruction in accessing them, they will most likely pass under the radar of most undergraduates. The librarians demonstrated the high-resolution images and the ability to insert them into Microsoft PowerPoint among other features on an MDU.

The Digital Media Studio had plenty of equipment available for checkout at their table. Students are able to check out digital cameras and camcorders, lighting kits, iPods, projectors, voice recorders, and more. A sample of those products, plus DVDs and audio books, were on display for students to be able to feel, touch, and demo.

The Document Delivery (Interlibrary Loan) Department had a laptop at their booth on which they showed students how to create their ILLiad account and how to request items the library does not own. The Circulation Department talked to students about activating their library cards, checking out books, reserving study rooms, and how to avoid those dreaded library fines.

A novel idea for the fair was to have a demo of how to use QR Codes. QR (Quick Response) codes are two-dimensional barcodes that can be scanned by a mobile phone with a camera and a QR code reader app. After the user scans the code, the app interprets the code and automatically directs the user to a destination, such as a mobile website, video, contact information, or simply a body of text. Staff with different mobile phone platforms showed students how to download a QR code reader app and then practice using it via the table's banner and flyer. Students were then encouraged to find the QR codes throughout the library — in the stacks for online catalog searching, on equipment for how-to videos, at Personal Librarians' doors to save contact information, and at the reference desk for after-hours assistance. The booth also promoted the library's social media presence and invited students to connect with us on sites such as Facebook.

Tours of the library building began every half hour from a point near the fair's entrance. Additionally, short workshops (30 minutes in duration) were provided. One was on how to use EndNote Web. Another was entitled Mining Uncle Sam's Data (covering maps, government documents, Geographic Information Systems (GIS), and conducting patent searches). Both workshops were held in other rooms of the library.

Greeters stood near entrances and exits to invite students into the fair. We greeted students but did not pressure anyone to participate. Workers at all sites should be prepared to engage students instead of expecting students to approach them. After staff made the first contact, even reticent students asked questions and were open to receiving user instruction.

What Impression Did You Make?

Approximately 300 to 350 people attended the fair. We derived this number from the receipt of surveys, engagements at tables, and distributed smoothies. While we didn't set a goal for attendance, mainly because we weren't sure what to expect on our first attempt, we felt this was a respectable showing.

At the end of the year, we compared the usage of the resources in fall 2010 with previous semesters and found we achieved most of our goals.

• We observed a 73 percent increase in usage of our virtual research assistance services in fall 2010 compared to fall 2009, with a large spike in online chats and questions received via e-mail.

• We increased interaction with Personal Librarians, seeing approximately 10 percent more face-to-face meetings between students and librarians compared to the 2009 school year.

• The utilization of the Mango Database increased dramatically, from an average of 12 uses per month during January–August 2010 to 214 during the months of September–December.

• The ARTstor Database utilization saw a 150 percent increase to 8,260 sessions per month; the Local Digital Collections reached an all-time high in the number of visitors in the two weeks surrounding the fair, but visits to those collections returned to previous levels. The ARTstor Database and Local Digital Collections marketing messages laid in the foundation of the fair continued when these services were featured at an image workshop taught the week after the fair.

• We observed an increase of library staff visibility through a larger number of service desk contacts. There was a 150 percent rise in questions asked at service points in fall 2010 compared to fall 2009.

• Increasing students' familiarity with the building was less successful as the tours were not well attended.

• Any improvement trend of students' knowledge of borrowing procedures was difficult to analyze; however, the one-on-one, informal Q&A provided through the fair at least lessened the intimidating process.

While it was difficult to isolate the Library Fair from other marketing initiatives, it is important to note that the initial distribution of the services' messages occurred at the fair, and it was this foundation that provided the launch pad for further marketing campaigns.

During the fair, we found the easiest way to attain feedback was to have a short, three-question flyer at each table. When table representatives concluded their conversations with a customer, they asked the customer to fill it out and leave it with any representative at any table. By doing so, they would be entered in a drawing for the chance to win a 1GB jump drive. A majority of customers were eager to be entered in the drawing and didn't mind three questions. So, the trick here is to offer an alluring and functional prize and keep the survey short.

One of the questions we asked on our survey was how the customer heard about the fair. No big surprise since our building has more visitors than all of our athletic venues combined, 73 percent of the students said they heard about the fair as they were passing through. Our university-wide e-mail announcement drew the second-largest percentage.

We also asked customers if there was anything they didn't like or thought we could improve. Below is a sampling of the responses:

- Good friendly faces.
- Enjoyed the info and free stuff.
- Learned about library services.
- Learned about KIC scanners & the media place on the 2nd floor; everything was great; I learned about things I never knew existed.
- Enjoyed the goodies, on-screen demos; it was great as-is.
- Learned new info (QR codes and Mango); nice people.
- Pretty helpful; maybe needs some details about each service written on paper.
- Enjoyed learning about scanning services; enjoyed the space & time; let students borrow books to study at home; library is sometimes too cold.
- Enjoyed ARTstor booth, Mango (but no English, I need it); needs to be more attractive.
- Not everyone was very nice and taught things.
- Very informative; short and to the point.
- Loved the chocolate and sticky-note notebook; found out who my subject librarian is; loved it.
- Learned about personal librarians and Mango.

Lessons Learned

- Start planning well in advance of the event, especially when planning the first such event for your organization. It's good to stay in touch with the participants throughout the planning phase and up to the day of the event. Even if you're ready, they might not be.
- Our instruction sessions on EndNote Web and Mining Uncle Sam's Data were not well attended. This seemed to illustrate that our students are more interested in receiving short, quick pieces of information at an event like this.
- Tours were not well-attended, but this could have been because of a lack of signage and some disorganization in how they were operated.
- We observed how essential it is to have IT/technical support staff on standby for technical emergencies that arose on the day of the fair. You never know what kind of mood your technology will be in.
- Contact external service departments early and keep them well-informed and updated during the entire planning process as these are more than likely departments out of your control, and therefore, you're at their mercy.
- Food at events like this greatly enhances the environment and participation. It can serve as both an ice-breaker and a draw. An added plus is when you're able to link your service(s) with the food (e.g., our Mango smoothies and language-learning database). Creative techniques will aid in student recall in the future.

After the success of the inaugural Library Services Fair, we had more confidence to try new things and expand the showcase to include more services over multiple days. We plan to continue the fair annually as it was an excellent opportunity to promote the library, to educate our primary audience on its services, and to introduce the library and staff to students in a friendly, stress-free environment.

23

Selective (and Subtle) Marketing of Library Instruction

MARK AARON POLGER *and*
KAREN OKAMOTO

Introduction

Providing a library instruction class is not solely attached to giving a library tour, assisting in teaching the whole class how to do their research assignment, or giving an orientation about the library. A library instruction class provides a unique opportunity for librarians to showcase the plethora of print and electronic resources in their libraries, market their services to students, market themselves as key experts in locating information, and promote select resources that are specifically suited for the specific class in question. The actual class, albeit only one to two hours in length, provides students with essential tools so they can be more prepared when doing academic research.

What is marketing and why should libraries be concerned about it? Nims (1999) explains that marketing is the systematic and planned process of carrying out market research, creating new services and products, and evaluating programs to improve these services and products. The needs of library users are central to the concept of marketing. According to Nims, libraries should be concerned about marketing because they are no longer considered the sole or primary providers of information. Libraries are competing with the Internet, bookstores, and online booksellers as information providers. Nims further writes that marketing activities have often been the responsibility of instruction librarians because they interact with patrons and they create new services. Marketing, then, is no stranger to library instruction.

Readers are probably already familiar with and already performing (and perfecting) the marketing activities that we outline below. Academic librarians have been marketing libraries for decades without even referring to their efforts as "marketing." These activities are considered essential and integral to the profession. We present selective and subtle marketing techniques for library instruction sessions to raise the profile of your library and to make library instruction memorable to your students.

Before the Class Starts: Negotiation with Teaching Faculty

Contact the instructor about the objectives and desired outcomes of the library session. What does the instructor want his or her students to learn? Discuss what databases and topics should be covered. This is a great opportunity to market special library services and products to the instructor. For example, if your library has special collections or archives, you may want to work with the instructor to create course assignments that use these special library resources. Obtain a copy of the course assignment and review the approaching deadlines for assignments. Find out what the instructor has already covered in terms of the research process and available resources for the assignment. Look over the course syllabus to see what students are reading in that particular class. And last, but definitely not least, obtain a tentative list of student research topics. All of this information will be useful when planning and designing the actual library instruction session.

It is important to market an efficient system for requesting library instruction. Teaching faculty should be able to request library instruction with ease. Currently, many librarians make the process very easy by accepting requests via the telephone, e-mail, or in person. Giving multiple methods for faculty to request library instruction may give the appearance of flexibility on your part, but it may end up becoming labor intensive and inefficient. Develop a template to gather specific information from faculty members, and provide a consistent method for accepting requests. Providing an online request form on the library's website may be the most optimal way. This keeps a record of the date of the request, the teaching faculty member, the number of students in the class, the course number and section, the preferred times for library instruction, and the course assignment. Request forms can be transmitted via the library website and forwarded to the appropriate librarian who will schedule the library instruction class.

Academic departmental meetings are a great place for librarians to market library instruction. At the beginning of each semester, subject liaison librarians should inquire with departmental secretaries if they can speak at their meetings. If they are invited, this gives librarians a great opportunity to market library instruction to their faculty. According to Ardis (2005), inviting librarians to be "guests" in a class or departmental meeting gives them a platform where they can market the library to a targeted audience. At the meeting, librarians should bring key marketing materials like screenshots of the library website, sample subject guides, business cards, bookmarks, and brochures. Departmental meetings can be ideal venues for selective marketing of library services.

Tailoring the Class to Student Learning Needs

After determining the students' research and learning needs, it's time to prepare for the class. Identify sample database searches that use the students' proposed research topics. By incorporating student topics into the session, you can maintain their interest and demonstrate how library resources are relevant to their studies and academic success. If possible, skim through some of the assigned readings on the syllabus to identify what has been and will be covered. If your class is for graduate students, you may want to demonstrate how to save database citations by creating an account with the database vendor or exporting citations to a bibliographic management tool such as RefWorks. Graduate students may also be interested in creating e-mail alerts that notify them when new articles are published on their research topic. Consider other services and databases of interest to this user group, such as interlibrary loan and document delivery, databases like Dissertation Abstracts, and even quiet reading rooms and study carrels. For undergraduate students, easy, quick, and convenient database search tricks and library services could be the focus of your session. If you like to prepare slides for your library sessions, you may want to include the library logo on your slides and attractive images of the library. Include library contact information at the end of your presentation and encourage students to contact the library when they need help.

Your library might also consider redesigning the library's website for marketing and teaching purposes. For example, the library's home page and the entire website may be designed with library instruction and marketing in mind. Is there an area on the library's home page that features new and/or exciting services? Are popular and important links clearly visible on the home page? Is it attractive and user-friendly? An easy-to-navigate home page and website will make marketing the library during instruction sessions easier.

It is very important to know your audience before the class starts. If it is an ESL class, ensure that you use plain language in your handouts and in your presentation. It is important to speak slowly and repeat yourself often. For graduate students, we may assume that they have done considerable academic research and that they are familiar with the library catalog or with databases. However, it is important to determine beforehand their level of library knowledge. A graduate level accounting class that rarely visits the library may have students with limited information literacy skills. Accounting students may not write research papers, so they may not be aware of library services or resources. Science students may visit the library to study but not to make use of our vast collection of print and electronic resources. Librarians are fortunate, however, in that they can easily find out who their audience is. As Ardis (2005) writes, when librarians visit a class, they are guest lecturers who market the library to pre-defined groups of users; professors validate the importance of libraries and librarians by inviting them to speak.

Simple, Straightforward Handouts and Signage

Before starting a new semester of library instruction, evaluate the current state of your handouts and signage. Prepare a user-friendly handout that can be referred to after your library instruction session. It should contain just enough information for the level of the class, but no more. In addition to being a key marketing tool, handouts are educational, informative, and act as a quick and handy research guide when students and faculty visit the library. According to Jaeger (2009), key messages in handouts and signage should be short and simple.

Be consistent throughout your handout. For example, include the library brand (or logo) consistently across handouts and signage. Include the web address of the library website, and incorporate the major tools you wish to market. It is important to include a selection of resources that are relevant to the course. Keep the handout short, preferably no more than four double-sided pages. Handouts should be catchy and not contain too much text. Many students don't like to read more than is required. Include the most necessary information, such as search strategy tips and the name and description of key databases and websites. Include contact information for the library like the reference desk phone number and e-mail address. You may want to include your own e-mail address for individual research consultations, if you provide them. Use bold letters on key terms. Make bulleted lists. Include images and screenshots of database interfaces and search results. And do not be afraid to leave white space. Send a PDF file of the handout to course instructors beforehand, and if there is a course management system like Blackboard, see if they will upload the file to it.

Some library instruction classes are held in classrooms inside the library. Make sure signage is simple and straightforward. A simple font with plain language reading "Library Learning Lab" is a simpler term than using an acronym or a "high-tech" sounding term. It also results in a much simpler sign. Avoid trendy terminology such as "e-classroom" or "digital lab," and make minimal use of acronyms since students may not know them.

In order to ensure that students do not discard handouts, make them memorable. Preparing multi-colored handouts or handouts in a different paper color than white may be more catchy, and students may keep them longer. Promote selectively and only market what is relevant based on their learning and research needs. For example, freshman students love to know that we have free textbooks for loan (i.e. course reserves) and that we lend out laptops. Make enough copies for the class (including the instructor) and make five more copies for those students who are absent from the class. It is important to hand out your business card to the instructor and to put your contact information at the footer of each page of the handout.

When preparing handouts for a class, ask colleagues to see their handouts for more ideas. Each librarian prepares handouts and teaches in a different style and covers different material.

Online Guides

In addition to preparing physical print handouts, consider creating online tutorials or other online guides (Erazo 2003). Create tutorials and guides with a target audience in mind. For example, if you are targeting first-year students, you might want to create a tutorial on plagiarism and the importance of citing sources. Similarly, you might want to create a LibGuide that targets a specific, required course, such as a first-year composition course. Promote these online resources during your instruction class.

During the Library Instruction Class

One of the most important things we can do is effectively market ourselves. We should market our skills, expertise, and services. During library instruction sessions, we want to convey our enthusiasm for information, research, and libraries. Topics such as bibliographic databases, information literacy concepts, Boolean searching, and bibliographic control may not be immediately exciting to our students. By being energetic, prepared, enthusiastic, knowledgeable, and even humorous, we will do a great job of marketing not only the library as a welcoming and necessary place for students, but ourselves as well. Smile! Be the approachable and helpful person you are for your patrons. The library instruction classes allow us to market ourselves as expert researchers as well as information seekers. We need to emphasize that libraries and librarians are about more than just books.

Marketing During the Library Tour

Take the class on a tour of the library. While libraries are becoming an increasingly online resource, the library-as-place is just as relevant and important for students today. Students need a place to read, study, have group meetings, type assignments, check out physical books and, of course, get research help. The tour can highlight key resources and services, showing students what is physically available in the library. A tour may also make the library less intimidating and more memorable. Key stops for the tour could include the circulation desk, reserve collection, the reference desk, the circulating collection, computing facilities, study rooms, printing stations, and the reference collection. You can also incorporate a library scavenger hunt as part of the class. Students enjoy this fun group activity, which incorporates peer learning and discovery while marketing the library.

Marketing the Library and Select Resources

Ensure that the library instruction class is not a monologue with you marketing your key resources. We're not database vendors who wish to sell products to libraries. Our focus is not related to making money. Our goal is to educate our users and selectively market specific resources to specific users. We want our users to understand that our services are free, and we want to teach them how to use them effectively. Library instruction should incorporate humor and storytelling and should foster participation from the students. In sum, the library instruction class should follow a dialogue model, not a monologue model. For example, asking students to raise their hands if they purchase textbooks for their courses is an important beginning to market the reserve (textbook) collection we mentioned earlier. Students are happy to learn that many of our professors put textbooks on reserve for free, which means they do not need to purchase all their textbooks each semester.

An example of using humor in marketing the library is a colleague of ours who dresses up for a library instruction class held on Halloween. Another example is showing humorous websites like www.malepregnancy.com as examples of false information. But use humor with caution; it can backfire and is not always effective. Librarians should practice their "routines" with the awareness that not every class will be receptive. Humor is not 100 percent guaranteed, and library instructors should not feel discouraged if humor is unsuccessful.

Storytelling, on the other hand, tends to have a better success rate than humor. Storytelling is a more casual and personal way to connect with students and market resources. For example, when talking about the many channels of information in the world, you may wish to ask students where they were when they were informed that Michael Jackson died. You may want to tell students where you were when you found out the news of his passing. Ask students to generate a list of information resources that gave them the information of Jackson's death. This leads you to subtly market the New York Times database, which gives access to old New York Times articles from the 1880s. Connecting the course content with personal experiences and stories humanizes you as the library instructor, and it eases the tension of the class. It also makes the class less formal and evens the hierarchy between instructor and learner. When the hierarchy is evened out, there is more trust between learner and library instructor. When learners are more relaxed, it is easier to market select library resources because trust has been established.

Marketing your resources should be fun and not "pushy." Ask students about their experiences of trying to find an available PC workstation on campus. Many will express their frustration. This is an opportunity to market the "free laptop lending program" available at some college library campuses.

Emphasize that everything is free in the library, and all a student needs is his or her library card. Jaeger (2009) suggests developing catchy slogans or phrases to attract your users. Developing a catchy phrase for library cards like "your gateway to free stuff" may attract more users. For those libraries that provide free scanning and faxing services for library cardholders, mention to students that a library card acts a "free pass" to scanning and faxing.

Rockwell-Kincanon (2001) writes that marketers strive for simplicity in their messages. Students can only absorb so much in a single library instruction class. Try to target only a few, selected items. It is not recommended to market library instruction by citing the ACRL Information Literacy standards. Librarians should summarize their importance with a simplified message such as, "we help you succeed in your studies."

Mani (2008) writes about the mobile library instruction program she helped implement in her library. They used the catchy phrase "Library-On-the-Go" to attract users. The service comprised a laptop on a mobile cart with instructional materials. She also developed a logo that identified the name, service, and contact information. Brand recognition of this type is important in selective and subtle marketing.

Being employed at the City University of New York, a university with 23 college campuses, the authors know it is important to market the value of the library card. Many students are unaware that their library cards will work at all college campus libraries and that they can borrow materials at different locations and return them at their home library. Remember to bring your own library card to the library instruction class for students to see. Talking about things is not the same as showing them.

Bring an actual laptop that can be lent as well as reference materials, textbooks, newspapers, magazines, and academic journals. It not only educates users, it connects them to the content of the library instruction class. Much of the material presented in the class may be completely new to the students. Bringing in materials to show the class may decrease student anxiety and stress.

Since many students are accustomed to paying 10 cents for photocopies, it is important to market the scanners in your library, as the "free alternative" to photocopying. Market the scanning service as the " free" option and the way to save trees. This gives you an opportunity to market the library as a partner in being "green."

Books have traditionally been associated with libraries. Promote them! Bring books that are relevant to the students' topics and display them in the class. Pass them around and recommend relevant titles. Tell students how and where to check out and renew books, and if you have any special interlibrary or intercampus book loan and delivery services, market those as well.

After the Class Ends

The library instruction class may have ended, but ensure that students have not been forgotten. Some students may feel overwhelmed or dissatisfied because they now have an abundance of information but no idea where to start. Encourage them to make an appointment to speak with a librarian about their research assignments. Market your "consultation" service if you offer one.

It is also important to incorporate an assessment tool after the class. You may wish to include a questionnaire, a small quiz, or an assignment. It is important that we are making a difference in the students' learning experience. Even a simple feedback form would be helpful.

Ask instructors if they would like to add you to their Blackboard course (or any learning management system) next term, if there is an online component. Whether the course is completely online or hybrid, ask ahead to be included. This ensures that there is a constant presence of a librarian. In addition, inquire if there is any percentage of participation that can be attributed to a library component. For example, if the instructor has a 20 percent participation grade, ask if 10 percent can be allotted to a library assignment or quiz. This would ensure the importance of the library to the course. You can post information, answer student questions, and provide library links on the course site. To have a longer-lasting presence or impact on students, try "embedding" yourself in a department and hold office hours for students and faculty. If possible, correspond with the course instructor and follow up on student progress on their research assignments.

If you have a large budget for business cards, it may be a good marketing strategy to hand out business cards to both students and the instructor after the class. You may wish to staple it to the handout you give in class. Conclude the class by talking about the "Ask a Librarian" service that may include live chat, text reference, e-mail reference, in-person reference, and telephone reference. Ask instructors for a follow-up class towards the end of the semester if they have the time. Keep in touch with the instructor. This shows a commitment by the librarian to ensure student success, and it markets the library service as ongoing. Many students and instructors are disappointed at the "one shot" library instruction class. Marketing library instruction as "ongoing" and not limited to one formal class is an effective way to keep connected.

It is important to maintain good relations with teaching faculty. We want them to continuously show how valuable we are as a service. We also want to keep them abreast of new services and resources. One such example of keeping the momentum rolling is offering faculty workshops after the semester ends. According to Graham (2008), faculty workshops allow teaching faculty to get more acquainted with the physical facility and print and electronic resources that can meet their research needs. Graham also writes that faculty workshops offer an opportunity for subject liaison librarians to market themselves and subject-specific library instruction.

Conclusion

Selective and subtle marketing of library instruction is an ongoing and multifaceted process. It involves identifying the needs of students and addressing those needs by developing library sessions that introduce relevant resources and services. As Rockwell-Kincanon (2001) astutely points out, good marketers know how to attract the user's attention and how to make their services and products memorable by distilling these products into key concepts. Certainly, librarians have been developing focused and targeted library instruction classes for ages. However, by framing library instruction activities as a potential marketing opportunity, we can provide user-centered instruction that not only supports our students, but helps raise the profile of the library and our profession.

WORKS CITED

Ardis, Susan B. 2005. "Instruction: Teaching or Marketing?" *Issues in Science and Technology Librarianship* 42. http://www.istl.org/05-spring/viewpoints.html (accessed April 5, 2011).

Erazo, Edward. 2003. "Using Technology to Promote Information Literacy in Florida's Community Colleges." *Florida Libraries* 46 (2): 20–22.

Graham, Jamie M. 2008. "Successful Liaison Marketing Strategies for Library Instruction: The Proof Is in the Pudding." *Southeastern Librarian* 56: 4–8.

Jaeger, Paige. 2009. "Marketing Information Literacy." *School Library Media Activities Monthly* 25 (7): 52–54.

Mani, Nandita S. 2008. "'Library-On-The-Go': utilizing technology to provide educational programming." *Journal of the Medical Library Association* 96 (3): 230–232.

Nims, Julia K. 1999. "Marketing Library Instruction Services: Changes and Trends." *Reference Services Review* 27 (3): 249–253.

Rockwell-Kincanon, Janeanne. 2001. "Got Library?: Musings on Marketing Information Literacy." *OLA Quarterly* 7 (2): 16–17.

24

Lions and Tigers and Fairs, Oh My!

Ramona Lucius

San Antonio Public Library values community events, so much so that the library's three-person Outreach Office participates in an average of 80 events per year. These events bring us into contact with nearly 18,500 people.

That number alone is incentive enough for us, but participating in events brings plenty of other benefits to libraries. Public events provide the opportunity to speak to people from all walks of life and put library cards into their hands. Through events, librarians inform nonusers about new services and upcoming programs, thus dispelling the notion that libraries are no more than book warehouses. Event participation also shows that librarians consider themselves an integral part of the neighborhood.

At San Antonio Public Library, we seek diversity in the types of events that we attend, with the expectation that this will bring us into contact with diverse populations. We attend everything from baby expos to senior fiestas, from charity golf tournaments to resource fairs for military families. Sometimes our attendance makes a statement; for example, our participation in the ADA Celebration demonstrates our commitment to serve people with disabilities. Sometimes our attendance supports a cause, such as literacy. Sometimes we're there to promote our resources that relate to the subject of the event.

But San Antonio is a party-throwing city, and we can't attend everything. Participation costs the library in staff time and travel expenses. In accepting invitations to events, we look for opportunities to issue library cards and convey information. Events that draw primarily out-of-county crowds, such as rodeos and parades, we usually decline. If the event is expected to draw fewer than 100 people, we are unlikely to accept.

We seldom attend non-public events, with the exception of teachers' orientations. To maintain our objectivity, we don't attend events that have a political or religious purpose, although we will attend public events with a non-religious purpose (for example, reading rallies) that happen to take place at a church.

Your library's mission statement and your community's demographics can help you to determine at which events the library must have a presence. "Must-do" events for us are Feast of Sharing (a free holiday meal that draws upwards of 17,000 low-income individuals), and back-to-school events, in support of our system's mission of promoting childhood literacy.

Guidelines for Event Participation

In planning the library's involvement in public events, administrators should consider the following:

- What does the library wish to accomplish by participating in events?
- Will certain types of events take priority?
- Does the library require a minimum expected attendance?
- Will the library attend non-library fundraisers? Sports events? Events hosted by religious or political organizations?
- Will the library attend if an admission fee or vendor's fee is charged?
- Will the library attend events with restricted admission, such as teachers' conferences?
- Will the library attend if alcohol is served?
- Will library staff or volunteers be used?

From these decisions, guidelines can be written, such as these:

In keeping with San Antonio Public Library's mission, the Outreach Office seeks to participate in educational, cultural, literary, and community-building events held in Bexar County. We will not participate in private events or those that are political or religious in purpose, nor will we participate in an event at which we would be charged a vendor's fee.

What we can offer:
- an information table, including bibliographies relevant to the event's purpose
- story time and simple crafts for children
- on a limited basis: library mascot, bookmobile

1. A minimum of four weeks' notice must be given to schedule an appearance by the bookmobile or mascot.
2. A minimum of two weeks' notice must be given to schedule staffing for an information table.
3. A written request, made by a school official or official event organizer, must be submitted.

Intake Checklist

In deciding whether to participate in an event, it helps to have a checklist of required information:

- Date of call
- Caller's name, phone number, and e-mail address
- Caller's organization
- Event's title, date, times, and location
- Purpose of the event
- Audience for the event (e.g., families, seniors)
- Number of people expected

- The library's role in the event (information table, bookmobile, crafts, story time, mascot)
- Contact person and phone number for the day of the event
- Will most of the attendees be local?
- Will the event be held inside or outside?
- Will a table, chairs, and canopy be provided?

The To-Go Kit

Even a brief event requires quite a few supplies, and those supplies can be comfortably transported in a rolling crate or suitcase.

The well-appointed "to go" kit contains:

- Newsletters or program flyers
- Materials promoting the library's electronic resources
- Bibliographies of books, databases, and media relating to the subject of the event
- Library location maps
- Circulation policies
- Handouts listing the library's operating hours
- Pens
- A banner and/or table skirt featuring the library's insignia
- Binder clips or bungees to fasten the table skirt to the table
- A folding chair and a folding table (if not provided by event organizers)
- Library card application forms, attached to clipboards
- New library cards
- Acrylic literature holders and sign holders, with signs promoting card registration and programs
- Cell phone, with the name and number of event organizer
- Sunglasses, sunscreen, bottled water, and umbrella (if outdoors)
- Materials for library activities at the event (story time, crafts)

Staffing

Unless the event is expected to draw more than 500 or last longer than four hours, one staff member can probably work it alone. When staffing is a problem, perhaps volunteers could serve as the "away team." Check with your Human Resources Department to be certain no policies would be violated by using volunteers, then decide whether to pair the volunteers with staff or allow the volunteers to operate independently.

Whether a staff member or a volunteer, an effective event worker is a special person. He or she will be competing, albeit in a friendly way, with other vendors for attention. If a stage show is going on, the competition will be even keener. The larger the event, the less time the public is willing to give any one vendor, so the event worker needs a hook to bring people to the table and keep them there long enough to issue a library card or convey news about library programs and services.

The event worker needs:

- An outgoing personality
- Reliable transportation
- Thorough knowledge of the library
- Initiative, poise, and resourcefulness

And he or she will need training on:

- The library's goals for the event
- Procedures for issuing library cards
- The dress code
- Procedures for recording statistics
- Appropriate responses to questions
- Procedures for using equipment
- Instructions for games or crafts offered at the event

A dress rehearsal, followed by the chance to work alongside an experienced event worker, will help a newbie gain confidence.

Patter

To attract the public, the event worker needs to develop a patter, some ready-made but natural-sounding phrases that will capture attention. Each worker will develop a style that fits his or her own personality, but the content needs to focus on the event-goers' interests. Pander to the crowd! So if the passerby is:

- Accompanied by a baby or preschooler, start with an invitation to attend story time
- Accompanied by a school-age child, start with news about the library's homework assistance or summer reading program activities
- A young adult, start with mention of downloadable movies, music, and books
- A senior, mention the free programs and friendly reference staff ready to help with any question

Responses for a Tough Crowd

People say the darnedest things sometimes, but an experienced event worker will have a ready response.

PASSERBY: "I don't have time to go to the library."
STAFF: "These days, you can use the library anytime from your home computer. With your library card, you can access complete articles from more than 5,000 magazines and newspapers from all around the world. And you can download e-books, audiobooks, music, and movies, all free of charge."
PASSERBY: "My mother used to visit the library, but since her accident, she can't get out."
STAFF: "We have a free books-by-mail service that may be just the answer."
PASSERBY: "I owe a lot of money in fines."
STAFF: "We may be able to set up a payment plan that would allow you to keep checking out books while you pay a small amount each month."

PASSERBY: "The library is too noisy."

STAFF: "Yes, libraries have changed quite a bit in recent years. But we know that people still need quiet spaces, so our library has a no-talking room. Next time you're in the library, just stop by the front desk and I'll be happy to show you where it is."

PASSERBY: "I don't read."

STAFF: "Do you listen to music? We have 50,000 music CDs, plus downloadables, everybody from Lady Antebellum to Lady Gaga. How about movies? We have 100,000 DVDs, from the first Western ever made to the only horror film to win Best Picture."

The better prepared the staff member is, the more likely he or she can turn a complaint into a learning experience — for both parties.

Hooks

Draw in the children, and the adults will follow. So when the environment allows, we offer a story time, a craft, or a game. If the event is too busy or the weather too blustery for activities, we'll bring a small giveaway item, such as a bookmark.

When we have two or more workers, and when the noise level permits, we offer a 10-minute story time. We take an assortment of oversized, interactive Easy books suited to ages two–10 and allow the children to choose from them. It's usually not possible to follow a schedule, so when two or more children approach, we invite them to sit down for a story. Once we get started, other children will join the crowd. Meanwhile, as the reader engages the children, the rest of us talk to the parents.

Since for most events, we have just one staff member working the information table, we offer a simple craft or a game. We prefer crafts we can preassemble; for example, for spring and summer we take out "butterfly rings." We cut a large butterfly pattern with a die-cut machine, then punch two small horizontal holes in the center of the butterfly. Through the holes, we loop half a pipe cleaner. On top of the butterfly, we twist the ends of the pipe cleaner together and shape them as antennae; underneath, we form a ring, through which a child's finger will fit. Now the rings are ready for the child to decorate with stickers or crayons. Bats and snowmen can be used for other seasons. This craft works well at busy events since it requires little supervision.

At slower events, we may offer a literacy game. In one such game, we cut cardboard into playing-card sized bits, then paste on pictures of people or objects — for example, a sailor and an umbrella. We then place the cards into a colorfully decorated can. The child draws three cards and makes up a story about the pictures. This gives the child a chance to demonstrate narrative skills.

On-the-Spot Reference

If an Internet connection can be established, the library could offer on-the-spot reference service for adult events. Using portable electronic devices and bilingual reference librarians, San Antonio Public offered reference services at an international business convention. Questions we received were primarily directional. Conference attendees and organizers were impressed with this "value-added" service.

Bookmobile

A bookmobile, from a marketing point of view, is a large, moving billboard. From the viewpoint of outreach staff, it is a service vehicle meant for circulation. Either way, with a typical bookmobile producing 10 miles or less to the gallon of gas, taking a bookmobile to an event can be costly. For safety and security, a second staffer should accompany the driver, doubling the costs but reducing risk. Travel time — not only to move the bookmobile to and from the event, but also to move the staff to and from the bookmobile — must be allotted.

The bookmobile is an inviting place for a tired event-goer and a comfortable place from which to issue library cards and conduct story times. But if the bookmobile will be parked far from the vendors' tables, few event-goers are likely to stop in.

Event-goers need to be monitored when they come onto the bookmobile: often, they don't realize that bookmobile books are not giveaways. We position a staff member at the door, where she can greet everyone and inform them that if they have a library card, they can borrow books from us — and should return them before the due date to the nearest library. She then gives each person a map of library locations.

San Antonio Public Library's bookmobile makes ready for Senior Jamaica, a festival for those over the age of 50 (photograph by Barbara Celitans).

Once you offer your bookmobile for events, you may be overwhelmed with requests from organizers that perceive the vehicle as a free source of entertainment. We've even had invitations for the bookmobile to appear at children's birthday parties. Publishing your guidelines can help you to avoid difficulties. Here are ours:

"As scheduling permits, we accept requests for our bookmobile to appear at public events within Bexar County. No fee is charged for this service; however, please be aware that the number of special appearances the bookmobile can make is very limited, due to the bookmobile's service schedule. Visitors to the bookmobile can register for library cards, check out library materials, and place holds. Our 32-foot-long bookmobile requires at least 45 feet of parking space. Requests for appearances must be submitted at least four weeks in advance."

Mascots

A mascot can be an easily identifiable symbol: just ask any child who McGruff is. When the mascot appears at events, children will gravitate toward it, and the experience they have will leave a lasting impression. The mascot is an ambassador of goodwill.

For libraries that don't yet have a mascot, the choices are myriad. Several factors should be considered, however, beginning with the impression the mascot makes. Should your mascot be large and in charge, like Martin County (MN) Library's Tazz the Tiger? Should he be cute and cuddly, like Newark (NJ) Public Library's Corky the Koala? Or should he be unique, like Cold Lake (AB) Public Library's Boris the Book Hog? Some libraries choose mascots that make a connection to the local area or to the library itself. Omaha (NE) Public Library's mascot is Scamper the Prairie Dog, while the Maine Library System has Baxter the Maine Coon. Oakville (ON) Public Library reminds the public of the library's acronym through the mascot's name: OPaL.

Consider also how the mascot will be used. Will the mascot spend most of its time outdoors, shaking hands and giving hugs at fairs? Will it be inside, entertaining crowds at library events? Should it perform stunts? Mime? Dance? Speak?

A mascot working outdoors requires a costume that won't fade under exposure to the elements and frequent cleanings. If the costume has feet, those feet must have a sole thick enough to provide protection for the performer. The soles must be made of material that won't melt when the mascot walks across hot pavement, and they must be stitched securely to the fabric so that the soles don't separate from the feet.

If the mascot is to perform stunts or dance, the costume must be flexible and durable, with elements that won't fall off or pull apart as the performer moves. A cooling vest must be provided to keep the performer from overheating. If the costume includes a face covering, the performer must be able to see through it.

If the mascot will be used primarily with groups of small children, be aware that broad movements from a large creature can be frightening. Small movements made with the mascot kneeling at the child's eye level are less disturbing. The performer shouldn't reach for the child but instead offer open arms or open palms so that a hug or handshake can be the child's choice. And since the performer will spend quite a bit of time kneeling, the costume needs to stretch. Extra fabric around the knees, or knee pads, will ensure the performer's comfort.

Most mascots give silent performances since talking through a mask can be difficult. If your mascot is to speak, you'll need to prepare some lines that will not only be entertaining but also convey a pro-library message.

Finding and keeping the right performer is the most difficult aspect of mascot management. Ideally, the library would have a pool of performers, available for work on nights and weekends. But in addition to scheduling issues, so much is required of a mascot performer that the pool is likely to be quite small.

The mascot performer must be:

- Athletic enough to walk, bend, and kneel on all kinds of surfaces while wearing a 15- or 30-pound costume for 15 or 20 minutes
- Healthy enough to hold up under the intense heat that a costume can generate (especially when worn at an outdoor event in August)
- Gentle enough to ease the fright of a small child unused to seeing a large animal walking on two legs
- Extroverted enough to enjoy hugging strangers and posing for pictures
- Able to fit into the costume

In an ideal situation, the performer would be someone already on staff, someone you can depend on, perhaps an outgoing circulation attendant who would enjoy getting outside and performing.

San Antonio Public Library's Libro the Library Lion takes time out from his mascot duties to smell the flowers (photograph by Beth Graham).

Whether a staff member or a volunteer is used, the performer will need a little training. At San Antonio Public Library, we instruct performers on how to

- Put on and remove the costume
- Move safely through crowds
- Interact with children through gestures
- Respond to common problems, such as a crying baby or a lost child
- Hold a baby
- Touch a child appropriately
- Interact with other mascots

At San Antonio Public Library, our Number One mascot rule is that Libro the Library Lion never travels without a handler, and that handler is always a staff member. Libro's costume has a heavy head that reduces the performer's vision and hearing. With a handler walking beside him, holding his hand, Libro can move through crowds with confidence. The handler protects him from rambunctious toddlers who would pull his tail, from teens who might push him, from potholes that might trip him. The handler is also there to protect him against accusations of impropriety.

Before announcing that you have a mascot available for public performances, establish guidelines to ensure the performers' welfare, to protect the library's image, and to avoid being inundated with requests.

San Antonio Public Library has set these mascot guidelines:

Libro the Library Lion is a costume character portrayed by a San Antonio Public Library volunteer and escorted by a librarian. Libro appears at library-sponsored events and at public events. Libro does not speak or perform tricks.

Because Libro's purpose is to promote the library, Libro appears only at events at which San Antonio Public Library will be distributing information and registering the public for library cards. Requests for appearances by Libro alone will not be accepted. Similarly, requests for Libro to appear at private functions will not be accepted.

Because the costume is heavy and retains heat, Libro's appearances are limited to 20 minutes apiece, or 15 minutes for outdoor events. If scheduling permits, Libro may make two appearances at an event, with a 20-minute break between appearances.

A dressing room away from public view must be provided.

Maintaining a mascot can be a time-consuming and costly endeavor, but the goodwill created by a talented mascot can make the work worthwhile. A mascot is also a surefire way to get your library a photo in the local newspaper.

Post–Event Reporting

We maintain an online spreadsheet for the use of all our librarians. We use this spreadsheet for intake, when an invitation first comes in; for noting decisions, such as whether and how we will participate; and for debriefing, tracking the number of library cards issued and of people reached at the event.

This record enables us to know from year to year which events are "must-do" and which are "no go." It reduces incidences of duplication when an organizer sends the same request to multiple branches. And it enables us to perform analytical studies, to be certain we're reaching the underserved.

Conclusion

What libraries do for their communities is important and unique, yet we face a great deal of competition for the public's attention. Participating in community events may be just the attention-grabber you need.

25

The Crabby Librarian

Community Icon and Social Media Star

MELANIE A. LYTTLE *and* SHAWN D. WALSH

If we knew in early 2006 what we know now, perhaps things would have been done differently. We had no strategy when the character of the Crabby Librarian was created. In fact there was no "we" at all! The Crabby Librarian was Melanie's crazy idea born from the need to use felt crab hats her staff bought on a whim. The character and everything about her for several years was more a series of gut feelings, educated guesses, and dumb luck than a cohesive plan. By 2010, when Shawn took the Crabby Librarian to social media, there was a marketing strategy, and expanding the role of the Crabby Librarian in the community through social media was key. For libraries interested in creating their own characters or marketing themselves through social media, we hope our story and what we learned will help guide you on your way.

How the Crabby Librarian Came to Be

It was the spring of 2006, and Melanie Lyttle had just started as the new Head of Children's Services for Madison Public Library (MPL) in Madison, Ohio. She planned visits to the three elementary schools in town to promote an animal-themed summer reading program. Melanie's passion for summer reading, coupled with the knowledge of the power of school visits, meant MPL was going to promote its children's summer reading program in school with more energy and creativity than ever before. The problem was, Melanie needed a hook to interest the kids and entice them to participate. Without realizing it, Melanie was trying to develop a pull-marketing strategy. She needed something to draw children to the library.

Prior to Melanie's arrival at MPL, the staff had done an "impulse buy" from the summer reading catalog. The felt crab hats pictured there were so cute that the staff were sure they could be used somehow. These hats became the inspiration for "The Crabby Librarian," who embodies two prominent negative stereotypes: librarians are unfriendly, and they hate children. In the school presentations, Melanie assumed the grouchy persona of the Crabby Librarian. She insulted the children and called them names. Immediately the children responded with booing and heckling of their own. They realized right away that the reverse psychology approach used in the presentation was just a gimmick. There was no way anyone could be as horrible, mean, and rude as the Crabby Librarian. Whatever she said, the children knew to take the opposite meaning. Melanie ended each school presentation by separating herself from the Crabby Librarian persona with an "un-hatting" and an invitation. Without her crab hat on, Melanie talked about the fun of pretending to be someone she was not and expressed her wish that the children would visit her at the library. Even though most all the children already realized the Crabby Librarian was a gross misrepresentation of what MPL and its employees were like, it was good to make sure everyone, particularly the youngest children, realized Melanie was just pretending to be extraordinarily mean. As a result of the presentations, the library nearly tripled the number of children who participated in the summer reading program from 2005 to 2006. Somehow Melanie's unconsciously developed pull-marketing strategy not only worked, but it proved more successful than she or the rest of the library had ever imagined.

It was spring 2007, time to decide how to promote summer reading for that year. The theme did not immediately lend itself to a Crabby Librarian presentation, and the original plan was for the character to be a one-time thing. The children, however, remembered this character six, eight, and nine months later, indicating the Crabby Librarian should return to the schools. The problem was that in order to create a credible story for the Crabby Librarian, another character was needed. Children cheered the return of the Crabby Librarian and embraced the new character, Miss Dawn. This was simply MPL Children's Services Assistant Dawn Weaver being herself. Children who were regular library patrons already knew her, and the children who had not been to the library before embraced her. It was Miss Dawn who kept the Crabby Librarian from succeeding in her campaign to keep children out of the library and away from the summer reading program. That year's two-person skit was a success!

Since the duo of the Crabby Librarian and Miss Dawn had attained a certain level of notoriety in the community, it was logical that they would go to the schools and promote summer reading in subsequent summers. The presentation changed to incorporate each year's theme, but the structure remained constant. Employing reverse psychology was key, and they kept with that formula. The Crabby Librarian never wanted to "share" her summer reading prizes because no children were worthy of them; she did not want them to participate in summer programs because they would ruin her fun. Year to year the prizes and programs changed, but the message stayed the same, and the children loved it.

In 2009, the library suffered an approximately 30 percent reduction in state funding. Staff were laid off, operating hours were cut, and every library service was examined to determine its value and necessity. School visits to promote summer reading were evaluated as well. Coincidentally in 2009, Melanie and Dawn stopped visiting one of the three schools because it refused to let them make grade-level presentations. So that year the school only received promotional flyers. Unfortunately, there was a significant drop in summer reading sign-up in 2009, mostly from that school.

It would have been easy to blame the decline in summer reading sign-up solely on the one school's lack of visitation. However, it was more than that. For many in the community, the library was not a priority. It was not "the third place." It did not rank behind home and work as the next most important and influential place to be, particularly with the shortened operating hours. People did not gather there, and being a community center is exactly what "the third place" was. In 2010, the discussion of summer reading promotion broadened to the question of how to convince parents that the library was valuable. Children always seemed excited to see the Crabby Librarian when she visited them in school. What could the library do to reach the parents? It was the parents who had to spend time and gas coming to the library. MPL could not hope to compete with the soccer and softball fields as a place to gather if they did not capture the attention of the parents.

In the midst of discussing this seemingly insoluble problem, in early 2010 someone else joined the discussion. Shawn Walsh worked for the Northeast Ohio Regional Library System (NEO-RLS), and MPL contracted his services weekly to fix computers, do preventative maintenance, and provide guidance about technology for the library. He was invited to participate in the discussion about getting parents to bring their kids to the library and making the library "the third place."

Shawn saw a solution to the problem right away: use social media to reach the parents. However, he was not just talking about having a Children's Department Facebook page. He proposed a Crabby Librarian Fan Page on Facebook, a Crabby Librarian Twitter feed, and putting the presentation Melanie and Dawn did at schools on YouTube for everyone to see. Shawn knew about the Crabby Librarian, and he realized the character could be more than a summertime novelty.

The Crabby Librarian got a Facebook fan page at *www.facebook.com/crabby.librarian*. Posts ranged from "I hope everyone forgets that Monday is the first day of storytime sign-up" to "I can't believe someone ordered such-and-such book because now kids are going to want to come in and check it out." The fan list started to grow.

When the Facebook fan page had been in operation for a few months, Shawn was ready to tackle the next part of the plan. He was committed to putting the school presentation on YouTube as well as putting it on DVDs for children who did not see the Crabby Librarian in person at school. Recording the school presentation and providing DVDs for teachers to show during the last week of class was the solution to the school the Crabby Librarian could not visit in person. This way, no child was missed and parents could see what their children were talking about. Fortunately, NEO-RLS had a studio with various cameras, lights, and backdrops, as well as experience with producing videos. The library hired Shawn's services for a day, and Dawn and Melanie went to the studio to tape their presentation.

Barely into the recording session, both women realized taping for YouTube was nothing like visiting a school. Dawn and Melanie never rehearsed much for their school presentations. They never memorized a script. They always gauged how over-the-top to make their performance based on audience reactions. For YouTube, the current "school presentation" was too long. The script should have been memorized. Worst of all, they had nothing to gauge their performance by because there was no audience. This was in addition to worrying about wardrobe, makeup, and roasting under hot theatrical lights. Eventually, after about five hours, they got a nine-and-a-half minute video recorded that was in the same style and format as their school presentation.

As an incentive to watch the video, children were challenged to come to the library and answer a question about what they saw for a chance to win a prize. And the prize: the chance to throw water on the Crabby Librarian at the end of summer reading picnic! The video did what it was supposed to do. Children signed up for summer reading as they had in earlier years. Adults came and told Dawn and Melanie just how much they enjoyed finally seeing what their children were talking about. The video (*www.youtube.com/watch?v=9AjEFNfrEul*) never "went viral," but it was a good first attempt. The contest was a great gimmick as well. Several children were chosen to throw water on the Crabby Librarian, and their parents were amazed at Melanie's willingness to be soaked!

Months passed. It was early 2011 and time to think about summer reading promotion. Melanie and Dawn were ready. The video would be much shorter, about three minutes. Dawn suggested doing a completely different presentation. For five years, the Crabby Librarian's message had been the same. For the sixth season, tell a self-contained story, and through that story, show that Madison Public Library was a great place to visit. The summer reading theme for 2011 was a hodge-podge theme of birthdays and "looking back in time" as the library joined the community in celebrating the bicentennial of the founding of Madison Township. The concepts for the video were a mix of silent movies and birthdays. While this was not the usual formula, one thing remained the same: the Crabby Librarian ineffectively tried to stop the discovery of library fun. Again, a contest was tied to viewing the film on YouTube. This time, children needed to identify the difference in the endings of the school presentation and YouTube video. The school presentation was again available on DVD for children, including homeschool, private, and parochial students who did not see the school visits. The fabulous prize: the Crabby Librarian visiting the winner's birthday party!

The quality of the 2011 YouTube video (*www.youtube.com/watch?v=7Rv5GLWsUow*) was far superior to that of 2010. Shawn again served as the director, producer, videographer, and music arranger. He was able to replicate the feel of a silent movie through various film editing techniques, and he created a soundtrack from two songs Melanie's sister, Allison Lyttle, had written. This resulted in a very professional looking two-and-a-half minute video.

The reaction to the video was overwhelmingly positive from children and adults. Children wanted to talk about what they saw at school and then what they saw on YouTube. Parents marveled at Dawn and Melanie's improved acting abilities. The addition of a circulating DVD of the presentations meant anyone curious about what exactly was going on could be part of the fun as well.

The Crabby Librarian and Miss Dawn are definitely well known now! The 2011 YouTube video plays on a portable DVD player anytime the library goes into the community. Dawn, Melanie, and additional library staff members who either have been seen with the Crabby Librarian or resemble the two actors are treated as "rock stars." They get noticed and identified as being from the library by their "fans." Many of these fans have never actually been into the library building. Whatever happens next for the Crabby Librarian, she has been successful in making people aware of the fun library in their community!

Annotated Guide to Creating Your Own Community Icon, or How to Becoming a Social Media Star

Creating Your Main Character

• Find a willing actor or actress on staff. Look for someone with energy, passion, and a sense of humor.

• Give the character a recognizable outfit. The Crabby Librarian always has the same red headpiece with crab eyes, claws, and legs. She also dresses head-to-toe in red.

• Consider whether your character needs a foil. The Crabby Librarian has Miss Dawn. They are partners like Laurel and Hardy. Miss Dawn is like Stan Laurel, the straight man who keeps the story flowing. The Crabby Librarian is like Oliver Hardy, magnified and intensified. Children and adults recognize this familiar relationship, and they rally for Miss Dawn, the champion of the children, as she receives horrible treatment at the hands of the Crabby Librarian. Miss Dawn connects with the audience, and they know she cares for them and wants them to come to the library and have fun.

• Think extensibility. The Crabby Librarian is dynamic and ever-developing, adapting to the situations at hand. There are scripts for her school presentations, but she moves beyond them, interacting with children and behaving as the character.

• Plan for consistency. Fundamentally, the Crabby Librarian and Miss Dawn stay the same. The Crabby Librarian never wants children to come to the library, and Miss Dawn welcomes children with open arms. The situations both characters find themselves in change, but their reactions are always the same. And every summer poses the same question: "Will the Crabby Librarian keep children from coming to the library and participating in summer reading, or will Miss Dawn keep the Crabby Librarian in check?"

• Get staff buy-in. It is critically important that the front-line staff participate and play along with the story. At MPL, it is the circulation staff who talk with the children about their experiences with the Crabby Librarian. The staff builds upon the details children tell them to spontaneously create other "evidence" of the crabbiness of the Crabby Librarian. These adults legitimize the story of the Crabby Librarian in the eyes of the children.

• Get support from library marketing people and administration. Karen Gates, MPL's public relations person, embraces the marketing concept and incorporates the Crabby Librarian into published materials and signs whenever possible. The director, Nancy Currie, recognizes the ongoing value of relationship building and budgets for the Crabby Librarian activities each year.

• Make sure the character allows children to be "in on the joke." This happens in two ways for the Crabby Librarian. Melanie is the antithesis of the character she plays. For children who are regular library users, seeing Melanie's rude and disparaging antics is utterly ridiculous. Children who do not know Melanie also get the joke because her behavior is so over-the-top. There is nothing that is too crazy for the Crabby Librarian to do or say, and as a result, the children easily recognize the actual message.

Using Social Media to Share the Message with Your Community

• Choose your format. MPL tries to reach parents in the greater Madison community. Based on seeing what people use in the library, it appears that Facebook and YouTube should be the most successful outreach as Twitter or MySpace seem less used. However, format choices are always being evaluated to see if a change is necessary.

• Know your purpose for using social media. YouTube lets the parents experience the zaniness of a Crabby Librarian school presentation. Facebook allows the character to continue to use reverse psychology in her posts. As she "complains" about things, she is actually promoting new books or special programs that bring children and parents into the library.

• Identify your target audience(s). MPL was aiming primarily at adults, and Facebook works to reach that audience. Anyone can watch YouTube clips, and the expectation is that children will watch the school presentation on YouTube with their parents.

• Keep an active social media presence. Melanie, or someone else, posts on Facebook as the Crabby Librarian at least every 10 days, but sometimes once a day, depending on what information needs to get out. Currently, full-length Crabby Librarian videos are posted to YouTube once a year.

• Conduct conversations. The Crabby Librarian frequently comments on other people's comments on her fan page. Occasionally, staff members will write a comment to get a conversation going.

• Vary the types of posts made. On Facebook, sometimes there are pictures of library events, and other times there are links to the library catalog or program calendar. On YouTube, there are the formal, full-length videos from the summer, and occasionally there are informal clips of the Crabby Librarian doing things in the library.

• Let everyone know you are using social media. When the Facebook fan page first started, there were notices at the bottom of Children's Department flyers saying, "Follow the Crabby Librarian," and there were also promotions in the library. A notice was included in the library newsletter that went to all the homes in Madison. The URL for the YouTube video is always on all the summer reading fliers given to children at school. Melanie also has "Follow the Crabby Librarian" in the signature of her e-mails and on her business cards.

Tips for a Successful YouTube Video

• Get an understanding videographer. Anyone can film a movie and use editing software. It is because Shawn understands the goals of the YouTube video that it is successful. Shawn takes pride in his contribution to the process, and his care and understanding make the Crabby Librarian and Miss Dawn look fabulous.

• Get help from people familiar with working in film or theater. Melanie and Dawn made use of the library's relationship with a local theater arts organization. Actors gave advice on makeup, blocking, and body movements that made the 2011 video much better than 2010.

• Consider the lifespan of your video. YouTube videos can last forever. The 2010 video was incredibly specific to a two-month span of time in that year. The 2011 video, while related to the summer reading theme, can be used indefinitely as an example of the creativity of the library staff and its commitment to reaching customers where they are.

Concluding Thoughts

If nothing else, the story of the Crabby Librarian is one of evolution and collaboration. She was originally Melanie's creation, but the Crabby Librarian's longevity can be credited to Dawn's talents as well. For years the Crabby Librarian only appeared in the summer, but it was Shawn's vision that brought the character to more than just the children. Using social media, he introduced the Crabby Librarian and Miss Dawn to the parents and other adults of Madison. The opportunities for the Crabby Librarian in the future are endless.

With that said, it is important to remember the first audience of the Crabby Librarian is the children. They are growing up with the message that libraries are fun, dynamic places to be. Children continue to laugh at the joke they are in on, and they appreciate the continuity of the "reverse psychology" message. Whether or not all these children visit the Madison Public Library, they will remember their interactions with librarians with fondness. Someday, these children will be parents. Perhaps they will finally and unequivocally make libraries a beloved and necessary part of the community, "the third place."

About the Contributors

Zoia Zeresa **Adam-Falevai** is a reference paraprofessional for the Smith Library at Brigham Young University–Hawaii in Laie, Hawaii. She obtained her BA in Pacific Island studies from the Brigham Young University–Hawaii. She did her internship at the University of Hawaii with the Hamilton Library's Special Collection in 2004. She is a member of the Hawaii Library Association and is enrolled in the Library and Information Science Program at the University of Hawaii-Manoa.

Cynthia M. **Akers** is an associate professor and coordinator for information literacy, outreach, and assessment at the Emporia State University Libraries and Archives in Emporia, Kansas. She earned her MLS and an MA in English at Emporia State University. She also serves as the faculty advisor for ESULA (Empowered Students for University Libraries and Archives). Her research interests include assessment of library service quality, social networking, outreach initiatives for student and faculty populations, and library instructional technologies.

David F. **Andersen** is distinguished service professor of public administration and informatics at the Nelson A. Rockefeller College of Public Affairs and Policy at the University at Albany, State University of New York. His research focuses on public policy and public management, especially information systems and simulation modeling for public sector organizations. He spent the 2010-2011 academic year on sabbatical in Cholula, México, and Montréal, Canada, as a Carlos Rico Fulbright Scholar.

Deborah Lines **Andersen** is an associate professor of information studies and informatics, College of Computing and Information at the University at Albany, State University of New York. Her research focuses on public libraries and the choices they make in service delivery. She has served as a consultant for the Albany Public Libraries as they conducted a successful rechartering campaign, and spent the 2010-2011 academic year on sabbatical in Cholula, México, and Montréal, Canada, as a Carlos Rico Fulbright Scholar.

Bridget **Burns**, acquisitions, collections, and outreach team lead with LAC Group at the NASA Goddard Library, obtained her MLS from the University of Maryland. She served on the MLA Award Committee in 2006 and 2007. From 2007 to 2010, she was the ASIST representative to the Federal Library and Information Center Committee. She is a member of the Springer Government Library Advisory Board, and in 2006 was awarded an IIA Impact Award by her peers. She has also received awards for outstanding customer service (2003), process improvement (2006), and innovation (2008).

Anna **Cangialosi** is the marketing coordinator at the Chelsea District Library in Chelsea, Michigan. Her position involves managing, implementing, and assessing marketing campaigns and activities that promote library services and programs. She previously served as the community outreach intern at the Southfield Public Library and has a background in advertising, having worked as an art director at Doner Detroit. She holds an MLIS from Wayne State University and a BFA in communication design from the College for Creative Studies.

Mary Lou **Carolan** is the director of the Wallkill Public Library in the Town of Shawangunk, New York. She holds a bachelor's degree in political science and is working on an MLS from Clarion University. Her program, "Where's Ike?—The Detective Scavenger Hunt," won the Ramapo Catskill Library System 2008 Children's Program of the Year Award, as well as the Pride of Ulster County Award for creative and innovative community programming.

Kaley **Daniel** holds an MBA from the Jerry S. Rawls College of Business Administration at Texas Tech University in Lubbock, Texas. She has served as a communications and marketing professional for 10 years and is the leader of an internationally award-winning creative team as the director of communications and marketing for Texas Tech Libraries. She has presented at the Texas Library Association Annual Conference and has been featured in *American Libraries*.

Ann Marland **Dash**, electronic resources librarian with Zimmerman Associates, Incorporated, at the NASA Goddard Library, received her MLS from the University of Maryland, College Park. Her background in fine art and art history aided her when she became the lead of the library's marketing design group, which was charged with creating the new library logo and brand image. She has been performing outreach for libraries since 2006, when she started her library career by building partnerships with several local schools as a young adult specialist at the Howard County Library.

Becky Lynn **DeMartini** received her MLISc from the University of Hawaii–Manoa in 2005. After a short time at Hawaii Pacific University as a reference librarian, she joined the team at Brigham Young University–Hawaii, Laie, Hawaii, as the reference/technology librarian in 2006. She spends her time developing the Joseph F. Smith library's website and online presence and helping students and faculty with their research needs. She has enjoyed serving as the president of the Hawaii Library Association and is chair of the Faculty Advisory Council at BYU-Hawaii.

Paul S. **Edwards** has served as a generalist librarian with the Boston Public Library's Grove Hall Branch since 2009. He holds an MA in history from Arkansas State University and an MSLS from Clarion University of Pennsylvania. A second-career librarian, he has been with the Boston Public Library since 2005. He is the author of several articles, including work published in the *Arkansas Review: A Journal of Delta Studies; Encyclopedia of Arkansas History and Culture; Rural Libraries;* and *Bookmobile and Outreach Services.*

June **Engel** is a librarian and manager at the San Diego County Library, Imperial Beach Branch, in Imperial Beach, California. She completed her MLIS at the University of North Texas. She is a contributor to Imperial Beach's *Eagle Times* and has been awarded two grants: the State of California's Out-of-School Time, and Libros Sin Fronteras. Recognized by the California State Assembly for her work with the South Bay Community Change Project, she was selected for, and recently completed, the State of California's Eureka! Leadership Program.

Lesley S. J. **Farmer** coordinates the librarianship program at California State University Long Beach. She earned her MLS at UNC Chapel Hill and her doctorate at Temple University and has worked in school, public, special, and academic libraries. She serves as CSLA Research Committee chair and won ALA's Phi Beta Mu Award for library education. A frequent presenter and writer for the profession, her research interests include information literacy, assessment, collaboration, and educational technology.

Wayne E. **Finley**, business librarian/assistant professor at Northern Illinois University Libraries (DeKalb), earned his MLIS from the University of Illinois and his MBA from Western Illinois University. Prior to working at Northern Illinois University, he was the assistant director of a public library district in northern Illinois. His research has appeared in *Behavior and Social Sciences Librarian* and he has presented on library management at IFLA. His co-authored "Creating and Sustaining Community-Focused Programs" appeared in *The Frugal Librarian: Thriving in Tough Economic Times* (ALA, 2011).

Michael **Germano** is the library faculty member at California State University, Los Angeles, dedicated to the College of Business and Economics. He is primarily focused on teaching courses in financial information literacy as well as business information for decision-making. He holds a law degree from Temple University and a master's in information science from Simmons College as well as an MA in English from New York University. Prior to joining California State's faculty he worked at LexisNexis for 15 years in a variety of sales and marketing positions.

Vera **Gubnitskaia**, youth services manager for the Orange County Library System in Orlando, Florida, obtained her library degrees from Moscow Institute of Culture (Russia) and Florida State University. She worked as a librarian, a manager, and a library consultant, in public and academic libraries. Her articles appeared in *Librarians as Community Partners: An Outreach Handbook* and Florida Library Youth Program's *FLYP Forward*. She has extensive experience in marketing library programs and services to district schools, area businesses, government organizations, and community partners.

Kerol **Harrod** (MA, University of North Texas) works at the Denton Public Library in Denton, Texas. He writes and co-produces the television show *Library Larry's Big Day*. It won a first place award in 2010 from TATOA (Texas Association of Telecommunications Officers and Advisors) and received the 2011 NTRLS (North Texas Regional Library System) Margaret Irby Nichols Award. He also won the 2011 TLA (Texas Library Association) Branding Iron PR Award for Speechwriting. He has a forthcoming chapter in the book *Bringing the Arts into the Library* (ALA, 2012).

Jennifer L. **Hopwood** is the head of youth services at the Franklin T. DeGroodt Memorial Library, Palm Bay, Florida. She obtained her MLIS from Florida State University and is a member of the American Library Association, the Association for Library Service to Children, and the Young Adult Library Services Association. She served as a guest speaker for the 2011 Florida Library Youth Program regarding community donations and partnerships. Her written contributions have appeared in the industry blog "The Gatekeepers Post" and the Florida Library Youth Program's *FLYP Forward* and *Bookends*.

Joanne **King** is associate director of communications at Queens Library in Jamaica, New York, one of New York City's three public library systems. She has been with the library since 1996. Queens Library is one of the most highly-publicized public library systems, frequently the focus of high-profile national and international coverage and the recipient of many national awards and recognitions, including the 2009 Library Journal Library of the Year Award.

Ramona **Lucius** is the outreach coordinator for San Antonio Public Library where she manages the bookmobile and coordinates mascot appearances and staff participation in community events. She has served public and special libraries since 1997 and holds an MA in English from Kansas State and an MS in library science from the University of Texas–Austin. Her previous work includes the essay "Women in Film" in *The Guide to United States Popular Culture*. She is a member of the Association of Bookmobile and Outreach Services.

Melanie A. **Lyttle** is head of public services at Madison Public Library in Madison, Ohio. She received her MLS in 2003 from the University of Illinois at Urbana-Champaign. An ALSC sponsored 2010 ALA Emerging Leader, she also participated in Library Leadership Ohio in 2008. She serves on Ohio Library Council's Northeast Chapter Action Council and facilitates the Northeast Ohio Regional Library System Children's Network.

Michelle A. **McIntyre**, MSLS, directs the Roaring Spring Community Library in Roaring Spring, Pennsylvania. She obtained her master's degree in library science from Clarion University of Pennsylvania through their online graduate studies program. As a member of the Pennsylvania Library Association, she chairs the Public Relations and Marketing Committee, and is vice chair of the Small and Rural Libraries Roundtable. She published a paper titled "Public Library Services to Special Needs Children" for *Rural Libraries* and wrote an article for the spring 2011 edition of *American Libraries.*

Barry K. **Miller** is director of communications and external relations for the University Libraries at the University of North Carolina at Greensboro (UNCG). He holds an MSLS from the University of North Carolina at Chapel Hill and a BA from Wake Forest. He spent 30 years in libraries, mostly as a corporate librarian, before joining UNCG, where he describes his job as "telling the library's story." He has published articles about marketing special libraries, reinventing one's career to meet changing organizational and personal needs, and historical topics.

Kathleen **Monaghan**, information services librarian with LAC Group at the NASA Goddard Library, obtained her MLS from the Catholic University of America in Washington, D.C. An experienced researcher and librarian with expertise in science, technology, and business research, Kathleen came to the NASA Goddard Library to work with the acquisitions, collections, and outreach team lead on planning and implementing marketing and outreach initiatives. Her specialties include branding and identity, marketing and outreach, and library management. She is fluent in Spanish and French.

Elisabeth **Newbold** is a librarian and manager at the San Diego County Library, Alpine Branch, in Alpine, California. She earned her MLIS at San Jose State University in San Jose, California, and has been awarded several grants in support of her coursework: the LIBROS/SERRA Multicultural Library Scholarship, the Public Library Staff Education Program grant, and the Librarians for Diverse Communities grant. She co-authored *Mount Whitney: Mountain Lore from the Whitney Store* (Westwind, 2003) and wrote "Emerging Trends in Native American Tribal Libraries" for Volume 33 of *Advances in Librarianship* (Emerald, 2011).

Karen **Okamoto** is a reference, instruction, and interlibrary loan librarian at the Lloyd Sealy Library, John Jay College of Criminal Justice, at the City University of New York in New York City. Originally from Canada, she obtained her MLIS degree from the University of Western Ontario. Her research interests include innovative teaching strategies in library instruction, library promotion, resource sharing and interlibrary loans, and environmental and social justice issues.

Christine A. **Olson** is the principal of Chris Olson & Associates, a consulting firm established in 1984 to help information professionals implement marketing, communications, and branding strategies. She combines a BA (art history), MLS and MBA with her extensive, hands-on experience to successfully accomplish a wide variety of library marketing projects. For 13 years she wrote and published *Marketing Treasures*, a newsletter with marketing ideas for librarians. In 2009 she was the president of the SLA Maryland Chapter and was named a Fellow of the Special Libraries Association (SLA) in 2012.

Mark Aaron **Polger** is an instruction and reference librarian at the City University of New York, College of Staten Island, in New York City. He obtained his MLIS in 2000 from the University of Western Ontario in London, Ontario, Canada. Since graduating, he has been employed at public, academic, and medical libraries. Originally from Montreal, he moved to New York City in 2008. His research interests include library marketing, library jargon, and user experience studies.

Melissa **Purcell** is the media specialist at Glynn Academy in Brunswick, Georgia, and is an adjunct professor in the Instructional Technology Department at Georgia Southern University. Her media program has been recognized twice as being an Exceptional Media Program for the State of Georgia. She was selected as the Library Media Specialist of the Year for Georgia Southeast District. She is a teacher support specialist, National Board Certified in Library Media, Gifted Education endorsed, and has had more than 10 articles published in educational journals, books, and newspapers.

Rosalind M. **Ram** obtained her graduate degree in library and information studies from the University of Hawaii–Manoa in 1993 and the following year joined the faculty at Brigham Young University–Hawaii in Laie, Hawaii. She is a co-editor of the award-winning book *Narratives and Images of Pacific Island Women* (Mellen Press, 2005). In 2010, she received the exemplary faculty service award from the BYUH President's Council. Currently, she is working on two book projects, runs marketing and assessment programs, and teaches intercultural communication.

Emily **Scharf**, instruction and liaison librarian at Webster University, St. Louis, Missouri, obtained her MALS from the University of Wisconsin–Madison. She is the liaison to the School of Education. A reference and instruction librarian at Southeast Missouri State University, she presented on federated searching at the MOBIUS Annual Conference in Missouri. She and a co-worker presented a poster session at ACRL about Webster Library's partnership with University Marketing, and she and another co-worker presented at the LOEX Annual Conference as well as the Missouri Library Association Conference.

Anna Ercoli **Schnitzer**, disability issues and liaison librarian, Taubman Health Sciences Library, University of Michigan, obtained her AMLS from the University of Michigan. A member of the Medical Library Association, the Mid-West Medical Library Association, the Michigan Academy of Sciences, Literature and the Arts, and the Greater Ann Arbor Society for Human Resource Management, she has contributed to *CRL News*, *Journal of Consumer Health on the Internet*, and *Journal of the Medical Library Association*. She received the "Laurita Thomas Diversity Champion" award in 2008 for diversity and disability issues.

Carol **Smallwood** has an MLS from Western Michigan University, and an MA in history from Eastern Michigan University. *Writing and Publishing: The Librarian's Handbook*, and *Librarians as Community Partners: An Outreach Handbook* are 2010 ALA anthologies. *Lily's Odyssey* and *Contemporary American Women: Our Defining Passages* are new releases outside librarianship. *Pre- and Post-Retirement Tips for Librarians* is her 24th published book. Her magazine credits include *The Writer's Chronicle*, *English Journal*, *Michigan Feminist Studies*; her library experience includes school, public, academic, special, as well as administration and being a consultant.

Sheila **Smyth** is research librarian for German, religious studies, philosophy, and logic and philosophy of science at the University of California, Irvine. She received her MLS from Indiana University, Bloomington, and her BA from the University of Notre Dame in German and anthropology. An abstractor for German-language materials for *Reference Review Europe Annual* (Casalini) since 2007, she has a recent article "Currency Trends and Collection Building" in *College & Research Libraries News*, 71, no. 10 (2010).

Christina **Stoll**, a library services consultant most recently for the Metropolitan Library System, obtained her MLIS from Dominican University in River Forest, Illinois. She currently serves as the managing editor of ALA's www.ilovelibraries.org newsletter, co-chair of the 2011 Illinois Library Association Conference Committee, and board member of the Special Library Association Illinois Chapter. She has contributed to developing library marketing networking groups, implemented library re-branding and logo re-designs, and worked on several library communication plans. She was named one of *Library Journal*'s Movers and Shakers in 2006.

Terri Pedersen **Summey** is a professor and the head of access and children's services at Emporia State University (ESU) in Emporia, Kansas. She earned an MSLS from North Texas State University and has an MA in history from ESU and is pursuing a Ph.D. in the School of Library and Information Management at ESU. A frequent presenter at conferences, she has published articles on a variety of subjects. Her research interests include distance learning library services, marketing, technology, information seeking, reference and user services, library 2.0, social networking, and Web 2.0.

Melinda **Tanner** is the district consultant librarian at Citizens Library & District Center, Washington, Pennsylvania. She obtained her MLS from the University of Pittsburgh and is an active member of both the Pennsylvania Library Association and the Association for Rural & Small Libraries. She has appeared in *Public Libraries* (2004), and coordinated the establishment of the Rural & Small Roundtable for Pennsylvania. She also maintains a blog for her libraries (www.washdlc.blogspot.com) as well as two Facebook pages: one for the District Center and one for her favorite local quilt shop.

Kimberly **Vardeman**, the general reference librarian at the Texas Tech University Library, received her MS in library science from the University of North Texas in 2008. She is one of the instructors for the Introduction to Library Research course and is generally found at the service desk helping patrons. A member of the American Library Association and Texas Library Association, she has presented at the Texas Library Association Annual Conference. Outside of the library, she is a classical pianist who teaches piano lessons privately.

Shawn D. **Walsh** is the senior technology analyst for Northeast Ohio Regional Library System. Working with libraries since 1997, he has been in his current position since 2007. With a BS/AS in computer information systems from Youngstown State University, he is a past coordinator and also a long-standing member of Ohio Library Council's Information Technology Division. He regularly makes presentations and teaches continuing education programs around Northeast Ohio focusing on helping libraries expand their online presence and learning about emerging technologies.

Karen J. **Wanamaker** is the outreach librarian at Kutztown University of Pennsylvania's Rohrbach Library in Kutztown, Pennsylvania. She obtained her MLS from Clarion University of Pennsylvania and her MEd from Lock Haven University of Pennsylvania. A member of the American Library Association, Association of College and Research Libraries, and the Pennsylvania Library Association, she serves as a site supervisor to a public relations intern each semester and is the co-advisor to her university's library science fraternity. She also oversees her library's curriculum materials and children's literature collections.

Sara **Wedell** joined the Chelsea District Library as head of adult services in August 2009. Along with programming, community partnerships, collections and supervisory duties, her position involves projects such as the "Stories of Chelsea" documentary series, available at www.storiesofchelsea.org. A presenter at the 2010 Public Library Association conference and the 2008, 2010, and 2011 Michigan Library Association conferences, she previously served as the adult services librarian at the Delta Township District Library. She received her master's degree in the science of information from the University of Michigan's School of Information.

Michaela D. **Willi Hooper**, reference librarian at Prescott College, Prescott, Arizona, obtained her MSI from the University of Michigan. She has facilitated workshops about social media at the Center for Scholarship in Teaching and Learning at Southeast Missouri State University and co-presented a poster about satellite reference at the MOBIUS Annual Conference in Missouri. She has worked in a variety of academic and special libraries as a museum assistant, biological station librarian, information commons librarian, head of information services, and interim director. She serves adult low-residency students.

Index